Scanners For Dummies®

Cheat Sheet

Recommended Breeds of Scanners

Type	Common Applications	Suitable For
Hand scanner	Portable scanning with a laptop	Scavengers and laptop owners
Flatbed	Almost anything	Most computer owners
Sheet-fed	Home office and business	Office users
Photo	Photo prints	Amateur photographers
Negative	Photo slides and negatives	Professional photographers
Business card	Business cards	Office users and laptop owners

Recommended Optical Scanner Resolutions

"Common" DPI	True DPI	Common Applications	Suitable For
300 x 600	300	School projects	Kids
600 x 600	600	Line art, photographs	Most computer owners
600 x 1200	600	Almost anything	Business and power users
1200 x 2400 and higher	1200	Design and graphic art	Photographers, artists, designers

Recommended Scanner Bit Depth

Bit Depth	Common Applications	Suitable For
24-, 30-bit	Basic color scanning	Kids, scavengers
36-bit	Almost anything	Most computer owners
42-bit	Design and graphic art	Photographers, artists, designers

Scanners For Dummies®

Recommended Scanner Interfaces

Interface	Common Applications	Suitable For
Parallel port	Basic scanning	Scavengers
USB	Almost anything	Most computer owners
FireWire and SCSI	Design and graphic art	Photographers, artists, designers

Image Formats

Format	Compression	Color Depth	Grayscale	Web-Friendly
JPEG	Yes	16.7 million (24-bit)	Yes	Yes
GIF	Yes	256 colors (8-bit)	No	Yes
Bitmap	No	16.7 million (24-bit)	Yes	No
TIFF	Yes	16.7 million (24-bit)	Yes	No
PNG	Yes	16.7 million (24-bit)	Yes	Yes

Some Common Copyright Myths Dispelled

- A work doesn't have to carry a copyright mark to be copyrighted.
- Movement from document to digital does not "cancel" a copyright. Scanning a document doesn't make it your property.
- The source where you obtained the work is immaterial. Taking an image from a newsgroup or Web site doesn't make it legal.
- No such thing as a "blanket" copyright exists. Permissions must be individually obtained for each work.
- Changing an original doesn't change the copyright.

Cheat Sheet $2.95 value. Item 0783-4.
For more information about Hungry Minds, call 1-800-762-2974.

Scanners
FOR
DUMMIES®

by Mark L. Chambers

HUNGRY MINDS, INC.

New York, NY ◆ Cleveland, OH ◆ Indianapolis, IN

Scanners For Dummies®

Published by
Hungry Minds, Inc.
909 Third Avenue
New York, NY 10022
www.hungryminds.com
www.dummies.com

Library of Congress Control Number: 00-110794

ISBN: 0-7645-0783-4

Printed in the United States of America

10 9 8 7 6 5 4 3 2

1B/QS/QU/QR/IN

Distributed in the United States by Hungry Minds, Inc.

Distributed by CDG Books Canada Inc. for Canada; by Transworld Publishers Limited in the United Kingdom; by IDG Norge Books for Norway; by IDG Sweden Books for Sweden; by IDG Books Australia Publishing Corporation Pty. Ltd. for Australia and New Zealand; by TransQuest Publishers Pte Ltd. for Singapore, Malaysia, Thailand, Indonesia, and Hong Kong; by Gotop Information Inc. for Taiwan; by ICG Muse, Inc. for Japan; by Intersoft for South Africa; by Eyrolles for France; by International Thomson Publishing for Germany, Austria and Switzerland; by Distribuidora Cuspide for Argentina; by LR International for Brazil; by Galileo Libros for Chile; by Ediciones ZETA S.C.R. Ltda. for Peru; by WS Computer Publishing Corporation, Inc., for the Philippines; by Contemporanea de Ediciones for Venezuela; by Express Computer Distributors for the Caribbean and West Indies; by Micronesia Media Distributor, Inc. for Micronesia; by Chips Computadoras S.A. de C.V. for Mexico; by Editorial Norma de Panama S.A. for Panama; by American Bookshops for Finland.

For general information on Hungry Minds' products and services please contact our Customer Care Department within the U.S. at 800-762-2974, outside the U.S. at 317-572-3993 or fax 317-572-4002.

For sales inquiries and reseller information, including discounts, premium and bulk quantity sales, and foreign-language translations, please contact our Customer Care Department at 800-434-3422, fax 317-572-4002, or write to Hungry Minds, Inc., Attn: Customer Care Department, 10475 Crosspoint Boulevard, Indianapolis, IN 46256.

For information on licensing foreign or domestic rights, please contact our Sub-Rights Customer Care Department at 650-653-7098.

For information on using Hungry Minds' products and services in the classroom or for ordering examination copies, please contact our Educational Sales Department at 800-434-2086 or fax 317-572-4005.

Please contact our Public Relations Department at 212-884-5163 for press review copies or 212-884-5000 for author interviews and other publicity information or fax 212-884-5400.

For authorization to photocopy items for corporate, personal, or educational use, please contact Copyright Clearance Center, 222 Rosewood Drive, Danvers, MA 01923, or fax 978-750-4470.

About the Author

Mark L. Chambers has been an author, computer consultant, BBS sysop, programmer, and hardware technician for more than 15 years. His first love affair with a computer peripheral blossomed in 1984, when he bought his lightning-fast 300 bps modem. Now he spends entirely too much time on the Internet and drinks far too much caffeine-laden soda. His favorite pastimes include collecting gargoyles, following St. Louis Cardinals baseball, playing his three pinball machines and the latest computer games, fixing and upgrading computers, and rendering 3-D flights of fancy with TrueSpace. During all that, he listens to just about every type of music imaginable.

With a degree in journalism and creative writing from Louisiana State University, Mark took the logical career choice and started programming computers. However, after five years as a COBOL programmer for a hospital system, he decided that there must be a better way to earn a living, and he became the documentation manager for Datastorm Technologies, a well-known communications software developer. Somewhere in between organizing and writing software manuals, Mark began writing computer books; his first book, *Running a Perfect BBS,* was published in 1994. He now writes several books a year and edits whatever his publishers throw at him. You can reach him by visiting his book site on the Web at `http://home.mlcbooks.com`. He welcomes all comments and questions about his books.

Mark's rapidly expanding list of other books includes *Building a PC For Dummies, The Hewlett-Packard Official Printer Handbook, The Hewlett-Packard Official Recordable CD Handbook, The Hewlett-Packard Official Digital Photography Handbook, Computer Gamer's Bible, Recordable CD Bible,* and *Teach Yourself the iMac Visually* (all published by Hungry Minds, Inc.), as well as *Running a Perfect BBS, Official Netscape Guide to Web Animation,* and the *Win 98 Optimizing & Troubleshooting Little Black Book.*

Dedication

I'd like to dedicate this book to Tim Kilgore. Tim, for the past ten years, you've been a fellow hardware technowizard and computer game expert, a door programmer and BBS sysop before modems were "cool," and a great friend who has always been there for me. Sometimes I wonder if we're actually twins and don't know it.

Here's to the next ten years!

Author's Acknowledgments

Unlike other types of books an author can tackle, a *...For Dummies* book is a very personal project. Writing a book like this one simply involves distilling everything I know about a subject into words, so just about everyone that I need to appreciate, praise, and applaud works for my favorite publisher — Hungry Minds!

First, I owe a continuing debt of thanks to the Production team, this time led by Project Coordinators Leslie Alvarez and Bill Ramsey: You've all done it again! These folks take care of everything from producing new line art to designing the layout and proofreading the text before it heads to the printer, and the quality of this finished book is a tribute to their hard work.

Thanks are also due to my editorial manager, Constance Carlisle, and my technical editor, Jeff Wiedenfeld. Each of them reviewed either the grammar or technical accuracy of every page (and even the general coherency from time to time)! It's a demanding job, and I'm always grateful for the extra eyes checking my words.

And no, I will *never* forget the tireless efforts of the two editors who made this very project possible. My heartfelt appreciation goes to the dynamic duo of Stacee Ehman, my acquisitions editor, and my project editor, Rebecca Whitney (although I know her as Becky). Without their help, this book would literally not exist — and I wouldn't have been able to work with such a great group of people!

Publisher's Acknowledgments

We're proud of this book; please send us your comments through our Online Registration Form located at www.dummies.com.

Some of the people who helped bring this book to market include the following:

Acquisitions, Editorial, and Media Development

Project Editor: Rebecca Whitney

Acquisitions Editor: Stacee Ehman

Technical Editor: Jeff Wiedenfeld

Permissions Editor: Laura Moss

Media Development Specialist: Brock Bigard

Media Development Coordinator: Marisa Pearman

Editorial Manager: Constance Carlisle

Media Development Manager: Laura Carpenter

Media Development Supervisor: Richard Graves

Editorial Assistant: Amanda M. Foxworth

Production

Project Coordinators: Leslie Alvarez, Bill Ramsey

Layout and Graphics: Julie Trippetti, Jeremey Unger

Proofreaders: Laura Albert, York Production Services, Inc.

Indexer: York Production Services, Inc.

General and Administrative

Hungry Minds, Inc.: John Kilcullen, CEO; Bill Barry, President and COO; John Ball, Executive VP, Operations & Administration; John Harris, CFO

Hungry Minds Technology Publishing Group: Richard Swadley, Senior Vice President and Publisher; Mary Bednarek, Vice President and Publisher, Networking and Certification; Walter R. Bruce III, Vice President and Publisher, General User and Design Professional; Joseph Wikert, Vice President and Publisher, Programming; Mary C. Corder, Editorial Director, Branded Technology Editorial; Andy Cummings, Publishing Director, General User and Design Professional; Barry Pruett, Publishing Director, Visual

Hungry Minds Manufacturing: Ivor Parker, Vice President, Manufacturing

Hungry Minds Marketing: John Helmus, Assistant Vice President, Director of Marketing

Hungry Minds Online Management: Brenda McLaughlin, Executive Vice President, Chief Internet Officer

Hungry Minds Production for Branded Press: Debbie Stailey, Production Director

Hungry Minds Sales: Roland Elgey, Senior Vice President, Sales and Marketing; Michael Violano, Vice President, International Sales and Sub Rights

◆

The publisher would like to give special thanks to Patrick J. McGovern, without whom this book would not have been possible.

◆

Contents at a Glance

Cartoons at a Glance
By Rich Tennant
The 5th Wave
By Rich Tennant
©RICHTENNANT
"NO, THAT'S NOT A PIE CHART, IT'S JUST A CORN CHIP THAT GOT SCANNED INTO THE DOCUMENT."
page 7
The 5th Wave
By Rich Tennant
©RICHTENNANT
"Of course graphics are important to your project, Eddy, but I think it would've been better to scan a picture of your worm collection."
page 39
The 5th Wave
By Rich Tennant
©RICHTENNANT
"Hey- let's put scanned photos of ourselves through a ripple filter and see if we can make ourselves look weird."
page 71
The 5th Wave
By Rich Tennant
ATTEMPTING TO SAVE MONEY ON FAMILY PHOTOS, THE DILBRANTS SCAN THEIR NEWBORN INTO A PHOTO IMAGING PROGRAM WITH PLANS OF JUST DITHERING THE CHILD INTO ADOLESCENCE.
©RICHTENNANT
Nope! She must have moved again! Run the scanner down her once more.
page 277
The 5th Wave
By Rich Tennant
©RICHTENNANT
WELL, THERE'S YOUR DRAWING SCANNED INTO YOUR BOOK REPORT. I JUST CAN'T FIGURE OUT WHAT THAT GREY FUZZY THING IS ALONG THE EDGE.
page 149
The 5th Wave
By Rich Tennant
©RICHTENNANT
IMAGE editor
PHOTO MAKER
GRAPH Accent
CAMERA SOFT
PICTURE CLICK
"...and here's me with Cindy Crawford.. And this is me with Madonna and Celine Dion..."
page 221
Cartoon Information:
Fax: 978-546-7747
E-Mail: richtennant@the5thwave.com
World Wide Web: www.the5thwave.com

Table of Contents

Part V: The Part of Tens 221

Introduction

When you think of a computer system, what parts automatically come to mind? Of course, you have "the box" itself, a monitor, keyboard, and mouse. What additional pieces do most folks add to their computers? Until three or four years ago, you probably would have considered a printer, a set of speakers, and a joystick. Today, however, more and more prospective computer owners are considering a scanner as a "must-have." Scanners are less expensive than ever — you can easily find several models online (or at your local Maze O' Wires computer store) for less than $100 — but I think that that's only part of the reason. If you choose a Universal Serial Bus (USB) or parallel-port scanner, it's also among the easiest computer peripherals to install. Again, that counts for something, although I don't think that's the heart of the matter.

The *real* reason that scanners have enjoyed such a surge in popularity is that more computer owners now recognize just how useful a scanner can be! More applications than ever make use of your scanner, and the Internet makes it easy to share the documents and images you scan through e-mail or your Web site. Many computer owners are even turning to their scanners for handicrafts, like creating custom-printed items!

I wrote this book especially for scanner owners who want to find out all about what that marvelous piece of machinery can do. You can start from the basics and work your way to the tips, tricks, and technology used by scanner experts. As with any other *...For Dummies* title, I use the English language you studied in school, with no jargon and as few ridiculous computer acronyms as I can possibly manage! As you can tell already, I also include a little humor — at least, what my editors *agree* is humorous.

What's Really Required

"Do I need a degree in advanced thakamology to use this thing? Or will I end up spending more on software than I do on food?" Rest easy! Allow me to tell you first what's *not* required for this book:

- I make no assumptions about your previous knowledge of computers, graphic arts, software, or Italian cooking.
- Haven't bought your scanner yet? This is the book for you because I introduce you to each of the features you should look for and how to install and configure both your scanning hardware and software.
- Some unbelievers seem to think that creating great scanned images, editing them just the way you like them, and using them in your projects requires either a lifetime of graphic arts experience or a $1,000 program. I'm here to tell you that everything you do in this book, you can accomplish with no previous art training and the software that probably came with your scanner.

So what is required? A scanner, the software it needs to run (which you should have received with the scanner), and a desire to improve your scanning skills. (Oh, I almost forgot: A curious nature and an urge to experiment are good when working with special effects, too.)

About This Book

Each chapter in this book has been written as a reference on a specific topic relating to your scanner. Note that you can begin anywhere because each chapter is self-contained; unless you've already had some experience with installing and using a scanner, however, I think that you'll benefit the most from reading from front to back. (The linear order of the book makes a great deal of sense.) The book also includes a glossary of computer and scanner terms and an appendix with information about manufacturers of scanning hardware and software.

Conventions Used in This Book

I can decrease the technobabble to a minimum, but, unfortunately, there's no such thing as a computer book that doesn't have at least a few special keys you have to press or menu commands you have to choose.

Stuff you type

From time to time, I may ask you to type a command within Windows or Mac OS. That text often appears like this: **Type me.**

Press the Enter (or Return) key to process the command.

Menu commands

I list menu commands using this format:

Edit⇨Copy

To illustrate, this shorthand instruction indicates that you should click the Edit menu and then choose the Copy menu item.

Display messages

From time to time, I mention messages you should see displayed on-screen by an application or the operating system. Those messages look like this: `This is a message displayed by an application.`

For the technically curious

Few subjects in this book require me to talk technical — scanners are mild-mannered, cultured creatures — but from time to time, you may be curious about those technical details. Because you don't have to know it, the techy stuff is formatted as a sidebar. Read it only if you want to know what makes things tick.

How This Book Is Organized

After careful thought (read that "flipping a coin"), I've divided this book into six major parts, with an index so that you can locate all the nasty acronyms, part names, and relevant items in the index. If additional coverage of an important topic appears elsewhere, it's cross-referenced for your convenience.

Allow me to introduce you to the six parts:

Part I: The Scam on Scanners

This part introduces you to what a scanner does and how it's constructed, discusses the various types of scanners on the market, and establishes important concepts, like color depth and resolution. For those of you shopping for a new scanner, I discuss features in detail, and you find out how to evaluate your own scanning needs. Finally, I help you decide whether to buy your new toy online or from a local store.

Part II: Surviving the Installation

And you *will* survive unscathed! These chapters cover the installation of different types of scanners, including USB, FireWire, parallel port, and SCSI models. I also provide guidelines for installing your software and testing your new scanner and a number of side issues you should consider (including the addition of a printer, CD-RW drive, and hard drive to your system).

Part III: Bread-and-Butter Scanning

You can't build without a solid foundation, and these chapters provide a thorough tutorial in basic scanning techniques. I cover the scanning process, of course, and I include tips on scanning different types of materials, procedures for configuring your scanning software, and an introduction to my favorite image editor, Paint Shop Pro.

Part IV: The Lazy Expert's Guide to Advanced Scanning

That's me, all right! In this part, you discover the advanced stuff you'll be craving if you read the first three parts first: image formats, Internet and Web tips and tricks, advanced image editing, scanner maintenance and troubleshooting, and even a chapter devoted to projects like creating a custom T-shirt, creating a slide show CD-ROM of your images, using an OCR program, and sending a fax using a scanned image.

Part V: The Part of Tens

The four chapters that make up the famous "Part of Tens" section are a quick reference of tips and advice on several topics relating to your scanner. Each list has ten tips. I especially recommend Chapter 17, where I introduce you to my top ten favorite special effects. In fact, skim that chapter first so that you get an idea of the magic you can perform on your scanned photographs! A little inspiration never hurts when you're just getting started!

Part VI: Appendixes

The appendixes feature a scanner hardware and software manufacturer list, a glossary of computer terms and (mostly unnecessary) acronyms, and a description of the programs on the companion CD-ROM.

Icons Used in This Book

I like important notes to stand out on the page! To make sure that you see certain paragraphs, they're marked with one of these icons:

This icon points out information that saves you time and trouble (and perhaps even cash).

If you're considering buying a used scanner, or if someone has given you one, watch for this icon. It points out information and recommendations for using older hardware.

This stuff happens behind the curtain. If you used to take apart alarm clocks to see how they worked, you'll like this information. Remember that you can also ignore this stuff with impunity!

Something could be damaging to your scanner or your software, or even both. *Always* read the information for this icon first!

If you had a highlighter handy, you would mark this information. The way I see it, a reminder never hurts!

Where to Go from Here

My recommendations?

- If you're thinking about buying a scanner, the box is still unopened in the trunk of your car, or you're knee-deep in the installation, I would start with Part I.
- If you need help with operating an existing scanner, start with Part II.
- For all other concerns, use the index or jump straight to the chapter you need. (You can always return later, at your leisure.)

I hope that you find this book valuable. Take your time and remember that your scanner can do *much* more than just produce images of documents and photographs!

Part I

The Scam on Scanners

"NO, THAT'S NOT A PIE CHART, IT'S JUST A CORN CHIP THAT GOT SCANNED INTO THE DOCUMENT."

In this part . . .

Your journey begins with an introduction to the scanner itself: what it does, what it contains, and what happens during the digitizing process. You'll learn about resolution and color depth and why they're important to scanner owners. I'll discuss the features and limitations of each type of scanner, and I'll help you to evaluate your needs if you're thinking about buying a scanner. I'll round out this part by weighing the pros and cons of buying online versus buying from a local store.

Chapter 1

Let's Get Digitized!

In This Chapter

- Understanding what a scanner does
- Finding material to scan
- Recognizing the different breeds of scanners
- Identifying parts common to all scanners
- Explaining resolution
- Understanding bit depth

In medieval times, magicians known as alchemists used to weave tales of a wonderful box. In this box, they said, one could place an ordinary item (an egg, for example), close the lid, and — presto! — the egg would turn to pure gold or a flawless diamond. Many alchemists spent their lives trying to perfect this nifty little household appliance. In fact, some said that they actually did, and these people became the performers we know today as magicians. (A few politicians and used-car salesmen are probably in that group also.) Everyone knows that a machine like that is a fairy tale.

But, wait: What if I told you that such a box really *does* exist — one that can take ordinary paper and turn it into creative magic? Imagine a machine that can bring a smile to the faces of your friends and family or reshape opinions, safeguard your memories, and perhaps even help sell your '79 Pinto?

Computer scanners now can do all that and more, and you don't need a degree in the magical arts (in other words, a computer programming degree) to use one with your PC or Macintosh computer system. The facts get even better, too: The perfect scanner for most home and small business use costs you less than $150, and you can connect it and produce your first scanned image in less than five minutes. After all, the faster you get a picture of that '79 Pinto on your Web site, the better the chance you can finally unload it!

In this chapter, I introduce you to the computer equivalent of the alchemist's magic box: what you can do with a scanner, what types of scanners are available, what makes them tick (if you want to know), and the importance of resolution and color.

"Okay, I'll Bite — What's a Scanner?"

Although many different types of scanners are available — flatbed, sheet-fed, color, and black-and-white, just to name a few — they all perform the same function. Therefore, it's easy to define exactly what a scanner is:

Scanner. (n) A machine that reproduces an image from a source object, producing an identical digital image for display or processing.

There — that explains everything, at least for technotypes. In plain English, a scanner "reads" the image from an object (typically a piece of paper) and then creates a copy of that image as a picture file on your computer. (If you're curious about what goes on, I explain the process later in this chapter.)

Of course, my explanation also has exceptions. It figures, right?

- You don't necessarily have to scan something from a sheet of paper. For example, your source image can be printed on fabric or other material, or you can scan photographic negatives.
- A scanner doesn't necessarily have to create a picture file on your computer; if you've used a fax machine or a copy machine, you've been using a scanner. After the scanner read the image, it was simply sent somewhere else. The fax machine sent it as data over the telephone line, and the copy machine sent it to the built-in printer to create a duplicate.
- You may not be scanning that original to create an image file on your computer. Scanners can now also recognize the printed characters on a page and enter them into your word processor. I discuss this process, called *optical character recognition* (or OCR, for those who crave acronyms), in detail and show you how to use it later in this book.

Most of the work done with scanners these days, however, is done as I describe in my definition: You want an image from a magazine in a form you can use with a document you've created with Microsoft Word. Or, perhaps you want to send that picture of Aunt Martha through e-mail to your folks living a thousand miles away.

What Can I Scan, Mr. Spock?

No, you're not scanning the surface of an alien planet from the bridge of the starship Enterprise, so you don't hear me say "Fascinating!" Instead, we humans here on planet Earth scan these types of materials:

- Books
- Photographs

- Magazines
- Business cards
- Printed text
- Flat objccts
- Fabric
- Photograph negatives
- Sketches and original art
- Cereal and pizza boxes

You get the idea — if it's reasonably flat and it has any type of image on it, it's likely to be scanner material. Scanners can record surface detail, too; however, the results vary widely according to the material that makes up the object. (Naturally, the darker the material, the harder it is for your scanner to deliver a clear image.)

Different Breeds of Scanner

Over the past few years, different types of scanners have evolved for different jobs. Some types provide a better-quality scan, some take up less room, and some are designed especially for one type of original media. In Chapter 2, I get into the specifics of which type of scanner is perfect for you; for now, take a moment for a scenic overview of what's available. Sit back and enjoy the tour. (Have an hors d'oeuvre!)

- **Flatbed:** Imagine the top of a copy machine, and then cut off the rest of it — and you have a flatbed scanner, as shown in Figure 1-1. With a flatbed, you're likely to get the best resolution with the least distortion, and you can easily scan pages from a magazine or book.

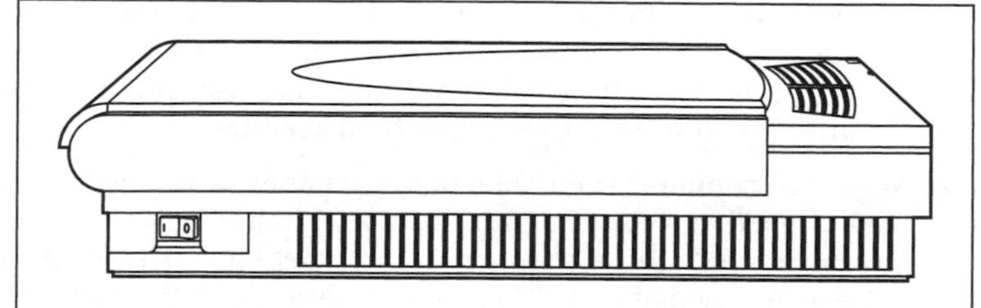

Figure 1-1: The flatbed scanner — have you ever seen anything so beautiful?

- **Sheet-fed:** Limited space on your desk? A sheet-fed scanner may be the answer. The shortest models are about the size of a roll of aluminum foil, and other models look suspiciously like a fax machine. (As a matter of fact, a fax machine has a built-in scanner that it uses to create an image of the page.) Figure 1-2 illustrates a typical sheet-fed scanner.

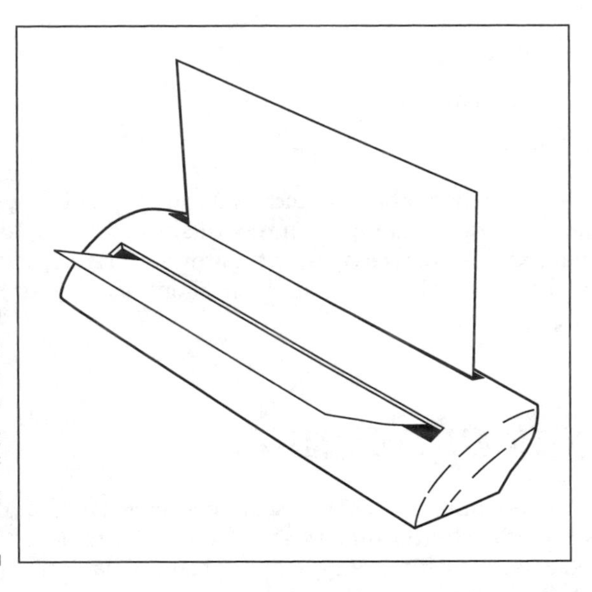

Figure 1-2: A sheet-fed scanner does a great imitation of a fax machine.

- **Photo scanner:** Most photo scanners are internal computer components, which means that they fit inside your computer's case, as shown in Figure 1-3. Photo scanners are specially designed to read individual pictures taken with a film camera (or even small printed items, like business cards or a driver's license).
- **Handheld or pen scanners:** Handheld scanners come in many different shapes and sizes, ranging from a handheld model that can scan three or four inches at a time to a pen scanner that reads a single line of text. Naturally, handheld scanners don't offer the picture quality and convenience of a flatbed scanner. They can fit in a laptop case (or even a pocket), though, so they still have their place for the road warriors among us. Figure 1-4 shows a handheld scanner.
- **Negative scanners:** The snobs of the scanner world, negative scanners are designed for only one purpose: to scan photographic slides and negatives. Although these scanners are usually hideously expensive, if the images you need are on slides or you want the best possible scan of a photograph negative, a negative scanner is really the only way to produce a high-quality image. Figure 1-5 provides glimpse of a negative scanner.

Quite a lineup, eh? Darwin himself would have been proud of the way that scanners have adapted to their environment.

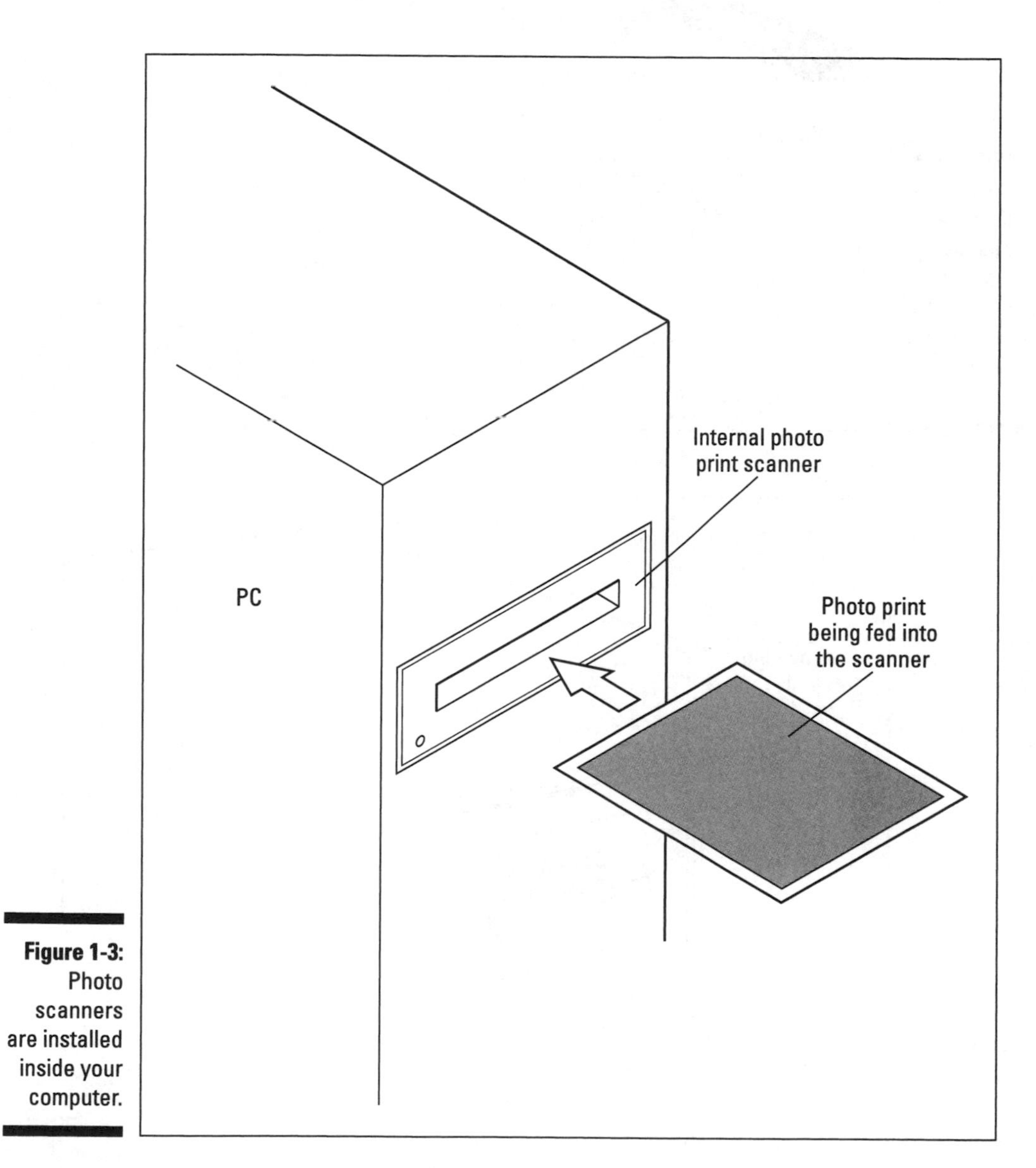

Figure 1-3: Photo scanners are installed inside your computer.

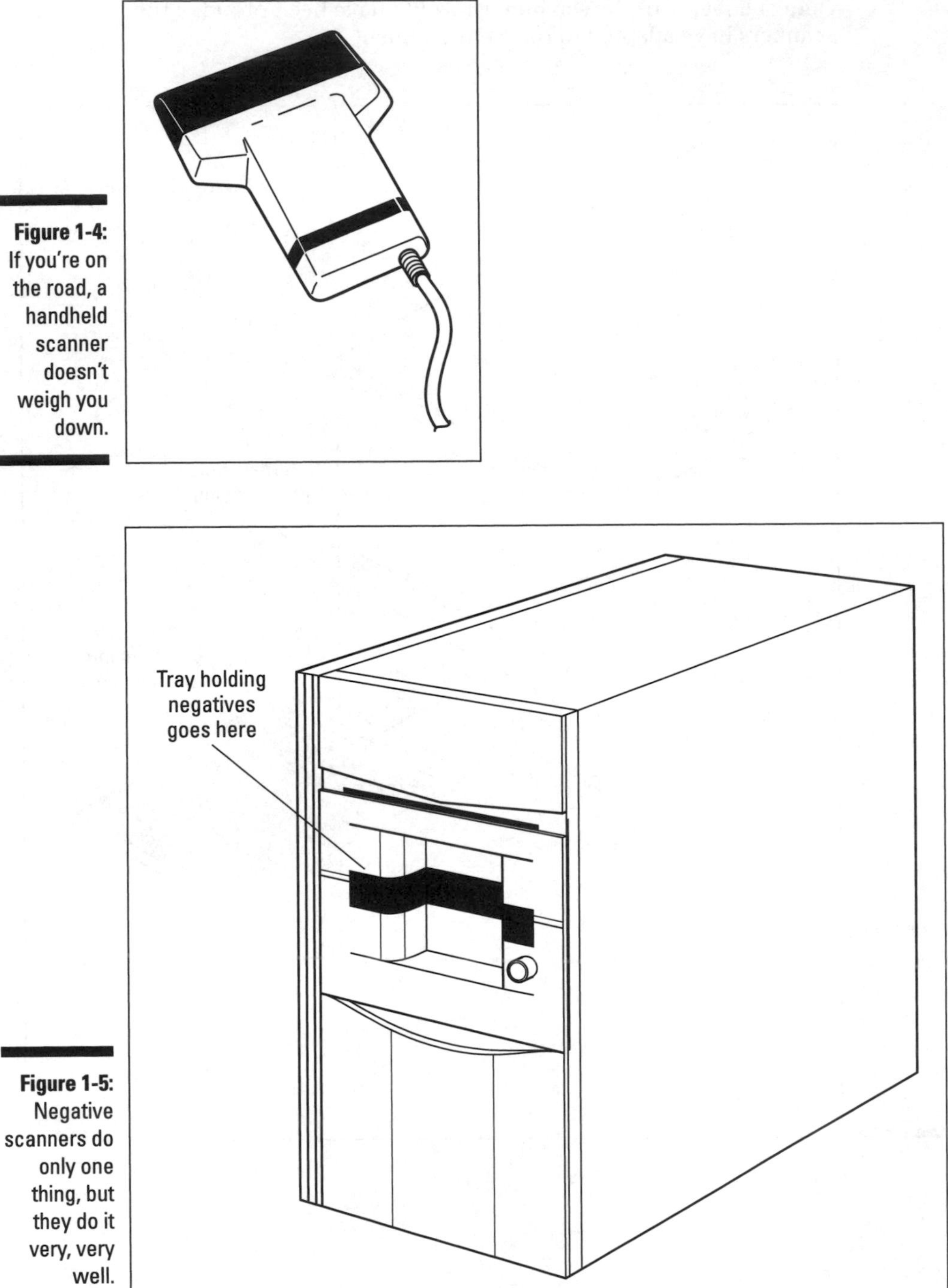

Figure 1-4: If you're on the road, a handheld scanner doesn't weigh you down.

Figure 1-5: Negative scanners do only one thing, but they do it very, very well.

Examining the Innards

Okay, I know what you're thinking. (Didn't know that little tidbit about computer book authors, did you?) You're wondering, "Do I *really* have to read this stuff?" Ladies and gentlemen, the answer is a big "No!" None of the material in this section has any cosmic meaning, so if the closest you want to get to your scanner's mechanical side is plugging in the power cord to the wall outlet, feel free to jump ahead!

(Pause.) Hey, if you're still reading, you're curious about mechanical mysteries, like I am. Did you disassemble alarm clocks when you were a kid, too? (Dad eventually had to lock his up in the garage.) Read on — I explain the common parts shared by every scanner.

The sensor

The sensor is the star of the show. The scanner sensor is composed of an array of individual photosensitive cells. Wait — don't drift off yet — it gets better! Each of these cells returns a certain amount of electrical current to the scanner's brain; how much current is determined by the amount of reflected light the cell receives as it passes by the original image. Figure 1-6 illustrates how this process works.

If you're knowledgeable about your human anatomy (or, like me, you were able to stay awake in high school biology class long enough to pass), you can see the parallels between this process and how the human eye works. In the eye, the photosensitive nerves perform the same function: They send impulses to your brain that depend on the amount of light they receive.

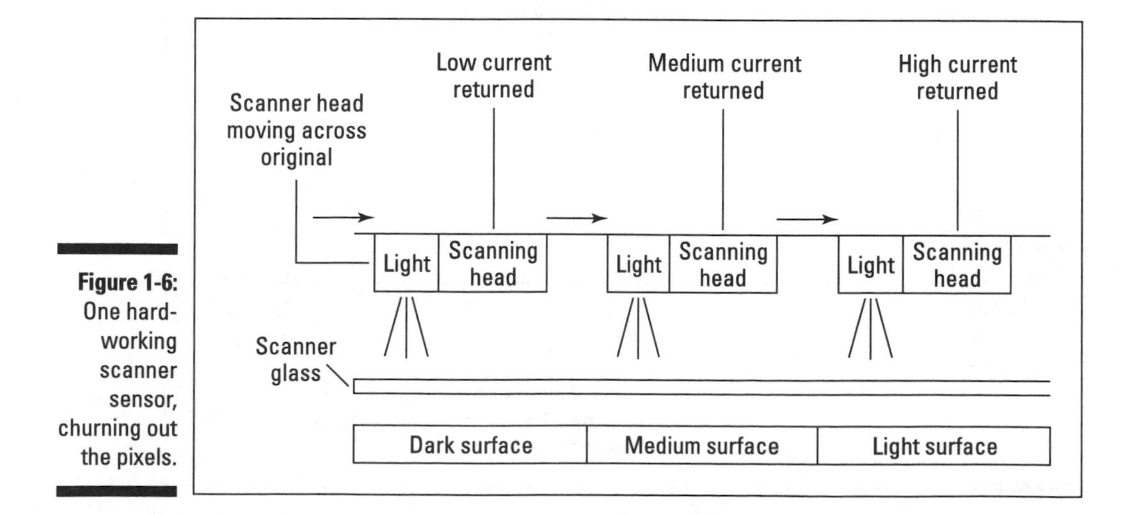

Figure 1-6: One hard-working scanner sensor, churning out the pixels.

Each of the cells in the scanner's sensor reads a single dot of the image — and that basic building block, the *pixel,* is a unit of measure I return to time and time again. Your computer monitor is also measured in pixels, as are digital cameras. All digital images are made up of individual pixels. Your eye and brain work together to combine them into the image you see.

The motor

Of course, the sensor doesn't do you a tremendous amount of good if it just sits in one place on the image. You would get a single line of pixels from the original! (That makes for a very bad scan, as you can imagine.) The designers of the first scanners knew that they needed to move the sensor across the surface of the original so that they could scan the entire thing, so they added the motor.

Figure 1-7 illustrates the two types of motors in today's scanners: In effect, one design moves the scanner head past the original, and the other moves the original past the scanner head (which is fixed in one spot). In later chapters, I explain which is better for you — both types of motor drives have their advantages.

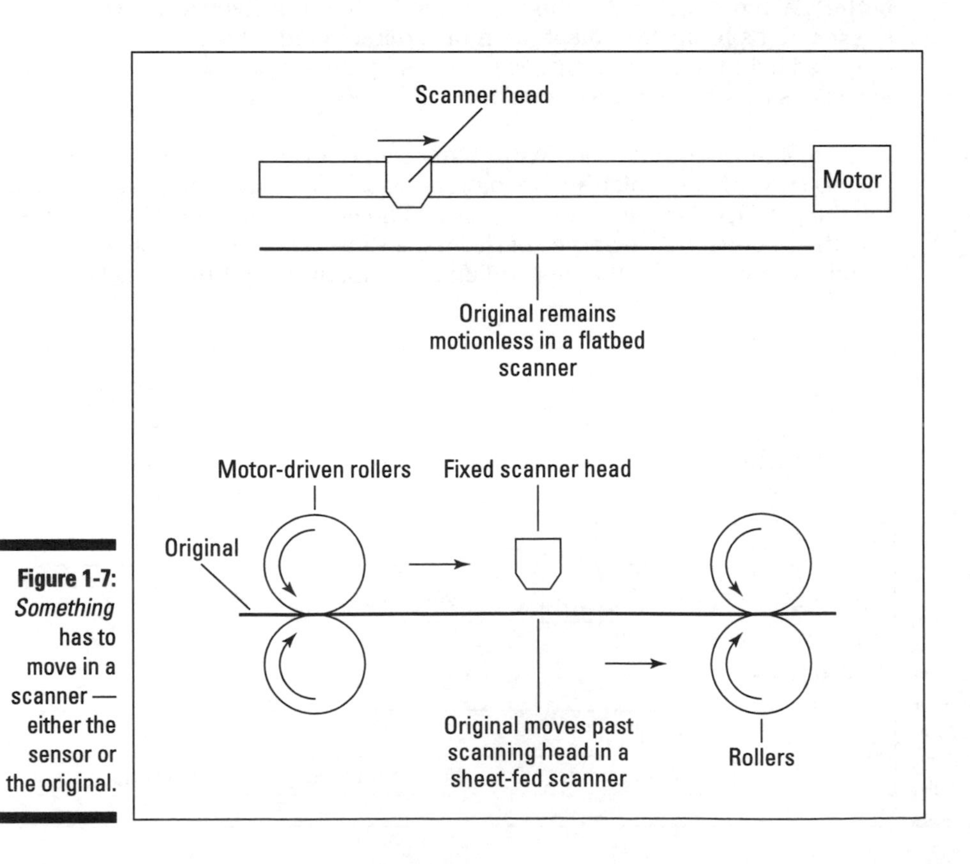

Figure 1-7: *Something* has to move in a scanner — either the sensor or the original.

The light

Naturally, a sensor that's sensitive to light needs illumination, and your scanner carries its own built-in "reading lamp" — the light that's reflected from the original is picked up by the sensor. Most scanners have this light mounted right next to the scanner head.

The brain

Like just about everything in the world of computers, your scanner has an electronic brain for processing image data. The brain isn't sophisticated compared to your computer's central processing unit (CPU), which has a master's degree in several subjects; a scanner's brain has at least passed the fourth grade, though. I talk more about this processing in the next section.

The interface

Every scanner needs a connection of some sort to your computer. In all their wisdom (and their surprisingly intermittent common sense), computer hardware designers have to have a separate word for this connection. For some reason, the word *connection* didn't hack it. Therefore, they call the type of connection your scanner uses an *interface.* Although most scanners made these days use the *Universal Serial Bus* (USB, for normal human beings), I introduce you to all the connections (whoops — there I go again) — the interfaces — found on scanners. I help you determine which is best for you.

Scanning Explained (for Normal Folks)

Here I go, trying to explain the alchemist's magic box. If you don't care how the box works and you would rather jump right to the next section, I can meet you there. This stuff is *absolutely* not necessary. If you're like me, however, and you stick your head into everything electronic from sheer curiosity, keep reading!

Here's the process your scanner uses to produce that spiffy digital image (use Figure 1-8 to follow along, if you like):

1. The scanner light is turned on.
2. The sensor head moves slowly past the original — or the original is moved slowly past the sensor head. (Anyway, movement and a motor are involved, as I mention in the preceding section.)

3. The sensor reads the amount of light reflected by the original in each pixel of the current scan line and sends those signals to the scanner's brain.
4. The signals are converted to binary data and sent to your computer through the interface.
5. The sensor head moves to the next line of pixels, and the process begins again with Step 3.

This process is repeated until the scanner has read each line of pixels in the original image. Depending on the type of scanner, the sensor head my make as many as three passes across the original to capture a complete, full-color image. I tell you more about this process later in this book.

Although this operation sounds lengthy, things are moving at computer speeds. For example, most scanners can read an entire page of text in fewer than 15 seconds and can read an entire full-page image in fewer than 30 seconds.

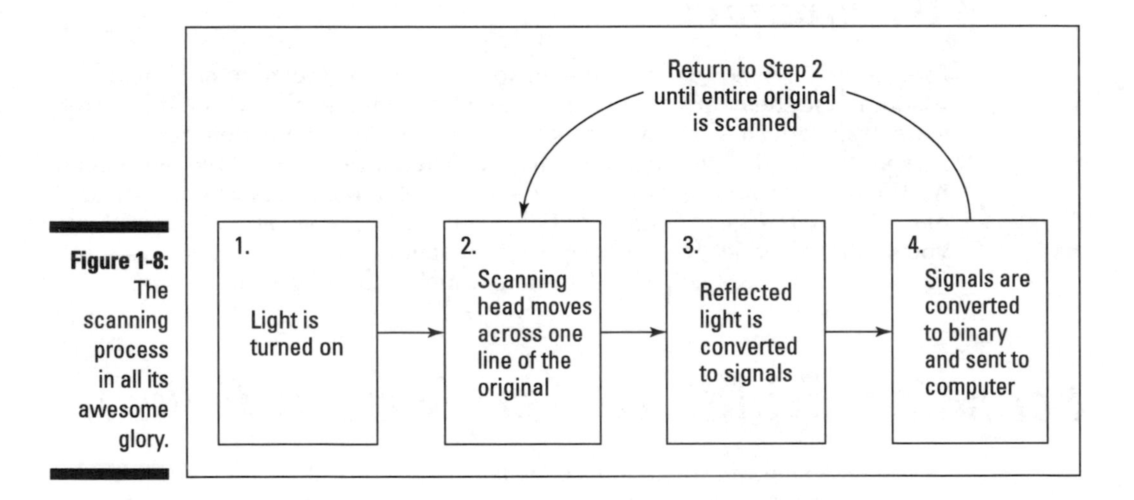

Figure 1-8: The scanning process in all its awesome glory.

Resolving Resolution

If you've read the section "Examining the Innards," earlier in this chapter, you remember the array of photosensitive sensors I mention. (If not, don't worry about it — I don't give you a test on that stuff.) The sensor array in a typical scanner is composed of hundreds of individual sensors. The density of these individual sensors leads to what's likely the most important single specification you should consider in a scanner: *resolution*.

Scanner resolution is commonly measured in *dots per inch* — the number of individual dots scanned per inch of the original image. The dpi measurement is usually expressed as horizontal (the number of individual sensors in the array) by vertical (the distance the sensor head moves between individual lines), as in 600 x 1200. I call this measurement the "common" dpi because most scanner manufacturers use it in their specifications.

Other scanner manufacturers may give you only one dpi figure. That's what I call the "true" dpi because it measures only the number of pixels horizontally. It's the resolution measurement used by professional graphic artists, service bureaus, and publishers, so high-end scanners often provide only a single dpi figure.

TIP

If you're comparing a scanner that's listed with two figures, as in "600 x 1200 dpi," with a scanner listed with just one figure, as in "600 dpi," don't panic! Just compare the first figure, which is the horizontal dpi measurement. In fact, because both scanners offer 600 dpi, they have the same horizontal resolution.

TECHNICAL STUFF

If you want to be a stickler, however, using a dpi rating to describe a scanner's resolution is technically incorrect. I tell you more about this subject in the nearby sidebar, "Positive peer pressure!"

A picture is worth a thousand words. Somebody famous said that, I'm sure — and the next two figures are good examples. In Figure 1-9, you see the same photograph of an apple printed at 300 x 300 and at 600 x 600 dpi. Figure 1-10 shows a close-up of one edge of the same two images (illustrating why a higher resolution results in sharper edges in your digital image).

Figure 1-9: Tell the truth: Which apple would you rather eat?

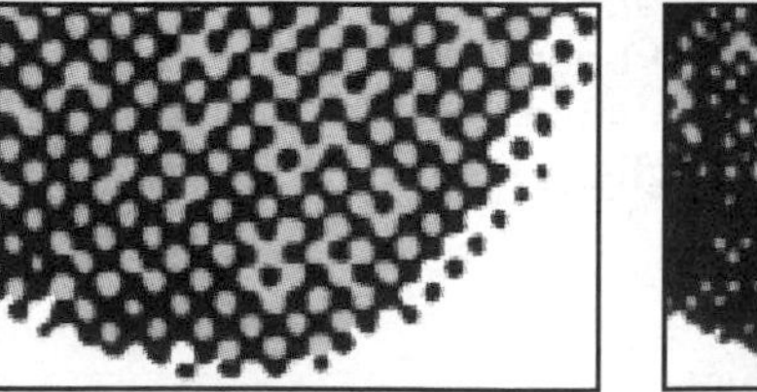

300 x 600 dpi

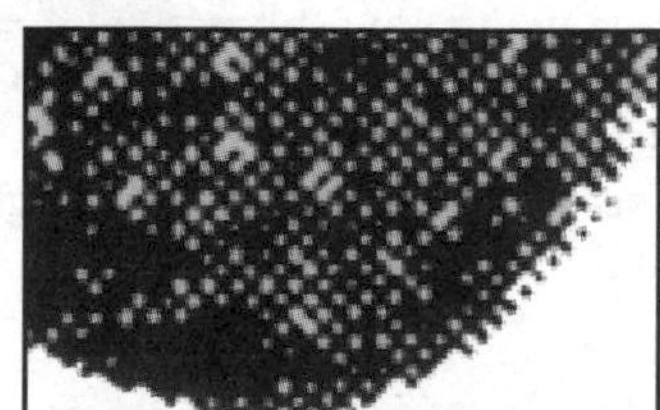

600 x 600 dpi

Figure 1-10: Those extra dots really make a difference.

Positive peer pressure!

If I'm going to be completely accurate here, I should use a different measure of resolution, called *samples per inch* (spi) rather than dots per inch. Samples per inch refers to the number of individual sensors in the array. A scanning purist would say that dpi is a term that belongs with computer printers, which print — rather than scan — dots.

You may be saying, "Now, wait a second. Isn't samples per inch *effectively* the same method of measuring as dots per inch?" You bet! That's why virtually every manufacturer of scanners on the face of this planet uses dpi in referring to resolution in their advertisements and specifications. It may not be strictly accurate, but everyone (and I mean *everyone*) uses it. In this book, I've caved in to peer pressure and elected to use dpi rather than spi.

Scanning purists can complain all they like. As long as I'm writing this book, I think that it's more valuable for you to know what people really use, not a technical term that you'll probably never see in an online store or on the side of a scanner box. (Besides, this way, you can discuss scanners with the "in" crowd at your next cocktail party while the technonerds sulk in the corner and grumble about spi.)

As you may expect, the *general* rule calls for a higher dpi: The higher the resolution, the better the quality and the higher the detail of your digital image. However, a higher resolution also results in much larger image files, and not every original really benefits from an astronomically high resolution. Therefore, you probably don't need to spend the extra $500 to buy a 1200 x 2400 dpi model when a 600 x 1200 dpi scanner will satisfy just about any PC owner or office worker. I discuss this subject in more detail in Chapter 2.

Before I leave the subject of resolution, however, I want to familiarize you with the difference between raw and interpolated resolution. Here are the definitions:

- The *raw resolution* value (also called the *optical resolution*) is the optical resolution at which the scanner reads an image — in other words, the actual number of dots the scanner reads from the image.
- The *interpolated resolution* (also called the *enhanced resolution*) is an inflated figure delivered by the software provided with the scanner. The interpolated value adds a large number of extra dots to the scanned image using a mathematical formula, *without* reading them from the original material. Interpolation is supposed to improve the quality of the image, which is why the interpolated resolution advertised for a particular scanner model is always higher than the raw resolution. (Those additional dots are ghosts!)

Here's the payoff: I *strongly* recommend that you judge scanners by their optical resolution while shopping! Forget about the interpolated value. It's nothing more than a guess made by a program, and in my experience it doesn't visibly improve the image. If an advertisement doesn't list the raw or optical resolution, find it on the manufacturer's Web site or the specifications on the box. This factor is important for comparing two different scanners.

How Deep Is Your Color?

I have one other massively important scanner topic to introduce here: color depth. The whole concept of color depth probably hasn't been a featured topic of conversation around your table (I know that it has *never* been mentioned around mine), although it can dramatically affect the appearance of your final scanned images and is the other criteria that will probably help you decide between those two or three different scanners on your shopping list.

Will that be Web color or print color?

So much for general rules. When it comes to color depth, "higher is better" is not the rule of thumb used on the Web! If you're experienced at building Web pages that feature full-color images — especially large ones — you've probably decided to use a color depth of 256 colors, or 8 bits. Why? The answer is simple: The lower the color depth, the less time it takes a 56 Kbps modem to download the image to your visitor's Web browser. (Downloading a huge, 16-million color image over a telephone modem connection brings new meaning to the name "World Wide Wait.") Also, many computer owners set their display color depth to 256 colors, so a 16-million color (24-bit) image is mostly wasted data. Until more people have high-speed Internet connections, like cable modems and DSL, 256 colors is probably the best choice.

On the other hand, if you're printing your images, anything less than 24-bit color is simply unacceptable. The fewer colors in your image (and the fewer colors your printer can deliver), the more your beautiful high-resolution digital photograph looks like a Sunday comic strip printed on cheap newspaper.

Which is best? That depends on two things: your output device (like your monitor or your printer) and your own eyes. Only you can determine whether the quality of the finished image is acceptable, so experiment while creating Web pages with scanned images or printing your scanned photos!

In the computer world, *color depth* refers to the number of colors in an image (whether that image is on a computer monitor, captured by a digital camera, or captured by a scanner). Color depth is referred to in two different ways:

- The maximum number of discrete colors (as in 256 colors or 16 million colors).
- The number of bits of information required to store color information for a single pixel (as in 8-bit or 24-bit color). This form of measuring color depth is also called *bit depth*.

Most scanner manufacturers use the second method to describe the color depth of their products. Again, the general rule is the higher the bit depth, the better the color because your scanner is better able to capture subtle differences in color and shading from the original.

The scanner you select *must* capture a minimum of 24-bit color, although most models sold these days can reach 30-, 32-, 34-, 36-, or 42-bit color. (The higher bit depths allow a more accurate color capture, even if the final image is only printed at 24-bit color.) That's all there is to color depth — no confusing acronyms, no exceptions, and no gimmicks. Refreshing, isn't it?

In Chapter 2, I describe other features and specifications you should look for while shopping for your scanner.

Chapter 2

The Joys of Buying a Scanner

In This Chapter

- Evaluating your needs
- Selecting an interface
- Understanding TWAIN support
- Choosing additional features
- Judging bundled software
- Buying a scanner online
- Buying a scanner locally

All right, as my dad used to say, "Let's get this show on the road!" You can buy a scanner in one of two ways:

Method One: Jump in your car, head directly to the Lots o' Wires superstore near you, ask a salesperson to point at his or her favorite scanner, and buy it.

Method Two: Research the scanner models with the features you want (either through the Web or through computer magazines), compare them, and buy your choice through an online or mail-order store.

Which technique is easier? Oh, I agree — Method One is as simple as it gets. On the other hand, which approach is practically *guaranteed* to save you money and identifies a scanner with more features that closely match your needs and your computer system? Definitely Method Two!

I know that you've already guessed which procedure I use — and which one I discuss in this chapter. (After all, if I preferred Method One, you wouldn't need this chapter.) I cover everything you need to know to decide for yourself which scanner is right for you and tell you how to buy that scanner for the lowest price possible! Keep a notepad and pencil handy to jot down what you need as you read.

In this chapter, I introduce you to the computer equivalent of the alchemist's magic box: what you can do with a scanner, what types of scanners are available, what makes them tick (if you want to know), and the importance of resolution and color.

A Game of Five Questions (Actually, Just Three)

Buying a scanner isn't as difficult as buying an entire computer system (which requires an entire ...*For Dummies* book all to itself), nor is it as simple as buying a new hard drive (which boils down to capacity and price for everyone other than technotypes). Although a scanner falls somewhere between the two extremes, you *absolutely* need to ask yourself only three questions before you continue reading about the other features and luxuries you should understand.

King size or hideaway?

Before you start shopping, you have to decide how big is too big: Can you dedicate the desk space for a flatbed scanner (which can actually take up more room than a typical computer)? Or will you stay lean and mean with a sheet-fed scanner? Although I briefly mention this dilemma in Chapter 1, you need to settle on a design before you go any further. To help you determine which to choose, I cover the advantages of both!

Reasons to pick a flatbed scanner

To be honest, I'm about as biased as I can be: *I want you to buy a flatbed scanner!* (So much for my neutral point of view.) Why the enthusiasm? Here are my reasons:

- **A flatbed scanner is far more versatile.** With a flatbed model, you can scan materials and three-dimensional objects *other* than paper, like a piece of fabric or a TV remote control (or even that new tattoo on your arm). Basically, if you've ever made copies of something on a copy machine, you can scan it with a flatbed.
- **A flatbed scanner doesn't cannibalize your material.** With a sheet-fed scanner, you can't scan pages from books or magazines unless you tear them out, and don't even think about scanning the surface of your arm. Plus, you don't have to worry about material that's too stiff (like your driver's license) or too small (like your driver's license). With a flatbed, like the Hewlett Packard 5300C scanner shown in Figure 2-1, material of reasonable thickness and just about any size can be scanned without fear of jamming the mechanism or losing something in the bowels of the machine.
- **A flatbed scanner produces a better scan.** With a flatbed scanner, the scanning head moves past the material, a process that is inherently more stable than having the material move past the scanning head (as in a sheet-fed model). This is the reason that just about any flatbed scanner features higher resolution (and often better color depth) than a sheet-fed scanner.

Figure 2-1: A modern flatbed scanner: the HP 5300C.

The reason to pick a sheet-fed scanner

"Now, wait a second, Mark. There must be *some* reason that I can buy a sheet-fed scanner!" You're right — and here it is:

> **It takes up less space.** A sheet-fed scanner takes only a fraction of the area used by a flatbed scanner on your desktop. In fact, some models are portable enough to be used on the road with your laptop computer. Most all-in-one printer/scanner/copier/fax devices on the market use sheet-fed scanning engines for this reason, like the Hewlett Packard LaserJet 3150 multifunction printer shown in Figure 2-2.

Unless size is a primary concern (and you're not seduced by the advantages I just mentioned), choose a flatbed — and be happy.

Note: If you're interested in a specialized film print, slide/negative scanner, or a business card scanner, remember that these rather exotic varieties are designed especially for these media. You can't scan *anything* else on them.

How many dots are enough?

As I explain in Chapter 1, the higher the dpi, the better. How high does an average person *really* need, though? Table 2-1 shows the breakdown I use in recommending resolution. Remember that the "common" dpi is expressed as two numbers (horizontal x vertical). Remember also that I'm talking about optical resolution, not resolution that has been "enhanced" or "interpolated" through software.

Table 2-1 Selecting the Right dpi: A Walk in the Park

"Common" DPI	*True DPI*	*Common Applications*	*Suitable For*
300 x 600	300	School projects	Kids, scavengers
600 x 600	600	Line art, photographs	Most computer owners
600 x 1200	600	Almost anything	Business and power users
1200 x 2400 and higher	1200	Design and graphic art	Photographers, artists, designers

Note: By the way, if you're wondering what a *scavenger* is, don't be offended! That's a term I coined in my other Dummies book, *Building a PC For Dummies* (published by Hungry Minds, Inc.). The term refers to someone (like me!) who acquires older hardware. For example, if your Uncle Milton gives you his old 300 x 600 scanner because he has just bought a new model, you're a scavenger. This concept also applies to hardware bought at a garage sale or on eBay. In Table 2-1, it means that you're not likely to find a new scanner now with a resolution of less than 600 x 600 on the market.

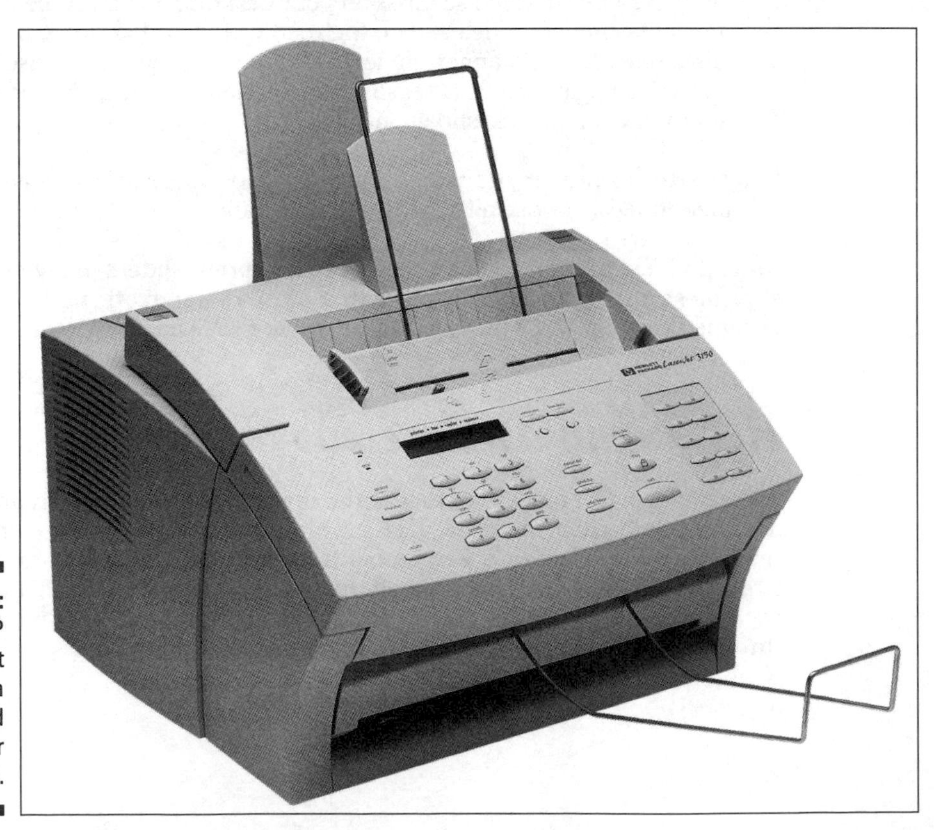

Figure 2-2: The HP LaserJet 3150 hides a sheet-fed scanner within.

Naturally, a model with a higher resolution can do everything a lower-resolution scanner can do. Also, these figures are the minimum: If you find two scanners with the right features and one delivers 1200 x 2400 resolution for only $50 more, I can see why you would want to spend a little extra.

A bit more about bit depth

Again, the higher the bit rate, the better the scanner. Should you spend extra cash, though, for a 42-bit scanner? Look out: Here's another of my patented, high-tech tables to help you decide this issue, too (see Table 2-2).

Table 2-2 Bit-Depth Choices

Bit Depth	*Common Applications*	*Suitable For*
24-, 30-bit	Basic color scanning	Kids, scavengers
36-bit	Almost anything	Most computer owners
42-bit	Design and graphic art	Photographers, artists, designers

Although 24-bit scanners technically produce more than 16 million colors, you won't find one in a store. If you're buying a new scanner these days, stick with a scanner that offers at least 36-bit color. Anything more than 36-bit is usually overkill for a typical home computer owner. But, then again, I wouldn't turn down a 48-bit model if someone gave it to me!

Have I Got an Interface for You!

For technowizards, discussing the pros and cons of hardware interfaces often results in passionate arguments that last for hours. In fact, I've dodged several floppy disks and a mouse pad or two thrown in the heat of the moment. Enough variety exists in the number of cables, ports, and different connectors to fill several catalogs. What's worse, many computer salespeople suffer from CECSAUB (short for Confusing Everything with a Collection of Silly Acronyms Used as Buzzwords).

Here's a promise: I reduce the interface confusion to a minimum! (You can thank me with an e-mail, if you like.) I present the four common connections you can use to add a scanner to your system and help you determine which is right for your system. I even try to keep the acronyms down to four letters or fewer.

Moving in parallel

Even the oldest computers are virtually guaranteed to have a *parallel port* (often called a *printer port*). Although the parallel port was originally used only to provide a connection for your printer, the port is now used almost as often to provide a connection for external devices, like scanners. Figure 2-3 illustrates a parallel port in all its 25-pin glory.

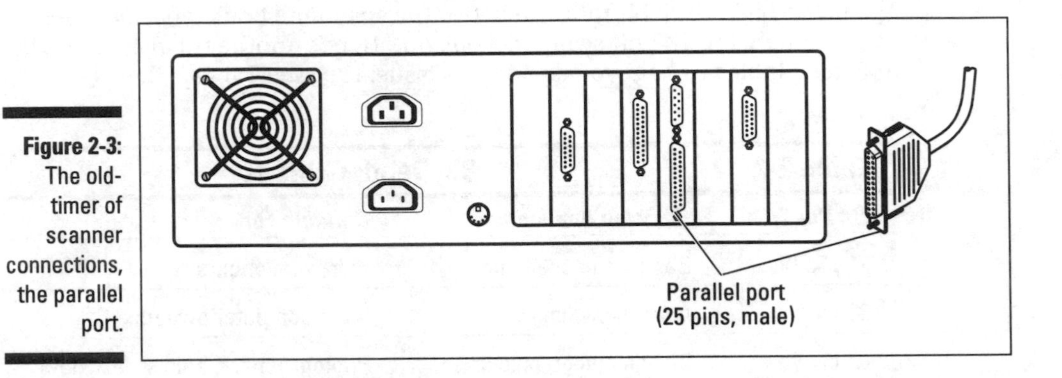

Figure 2-3: The old-timer of scanner connections, the parallel port.

If your computer was built within the past four years or so, you can probably use a parallel port scanner. If your machine is older, check the manual to determine whether the parallel port is bidirectional (or offers ECP and EPP modes). If so, it should work with a scanner.

- **Pros:** The universal nature of the parallel port means that you can use your parallel port scanner on just about any computer, including laptops. Parallel port scanners are usually the least expensive models you can buy.
- **Cons:** Parallel scanners are very slow compared to the other connection options I cover in this chapter. Also, if you're already using a Zip drive or other external device on your computer's parallel port, you may experience problems if you try to "daisy-chain" a scanner by hooking it up at the end of a connected series of parallel devices (for example, a scanner connected to a Zip drive, which is in turn connected to the computer's parallel port).

If your computer doesn't have one of the other connections or you have a laptop, a parallel port scanner may be your only choice. If you can use a USB model, however, you should pass on a parallel port connection.

The ultimate in usefulness

Here's an acronym I can appreciate: USB is short for *Universal Serial Bus.* (Personally, I think that the *U* stands for useful, or perhaps ultimate.) The USB port is the Holy Grail of computer owners everywhere: It's a high-speed, easy-to-use connection for attaching all sorts of peripherals to your computer, and it has proven as popular a piece of technology as the wheel. A USB port can support as many as 127 devices. Tell the truth here: Have you ever seen a computer with 127 different external devices connected *at one time?* (I couldn't even fit a system like that into my basement!) The latest version of USB can transfer data from a scanner to your computer at speeds as fast as 480 megabits per second. "Holy connection, Batman!" But, wait! You get more: A USB device is automatically recognized and installed by Windows 98, Windows Me, Windows 2000, Mac OS 9, and Mac OS X. You can even connect and disconnect that USB scanner without rebooting your computer, as shown in Figure 2-4.

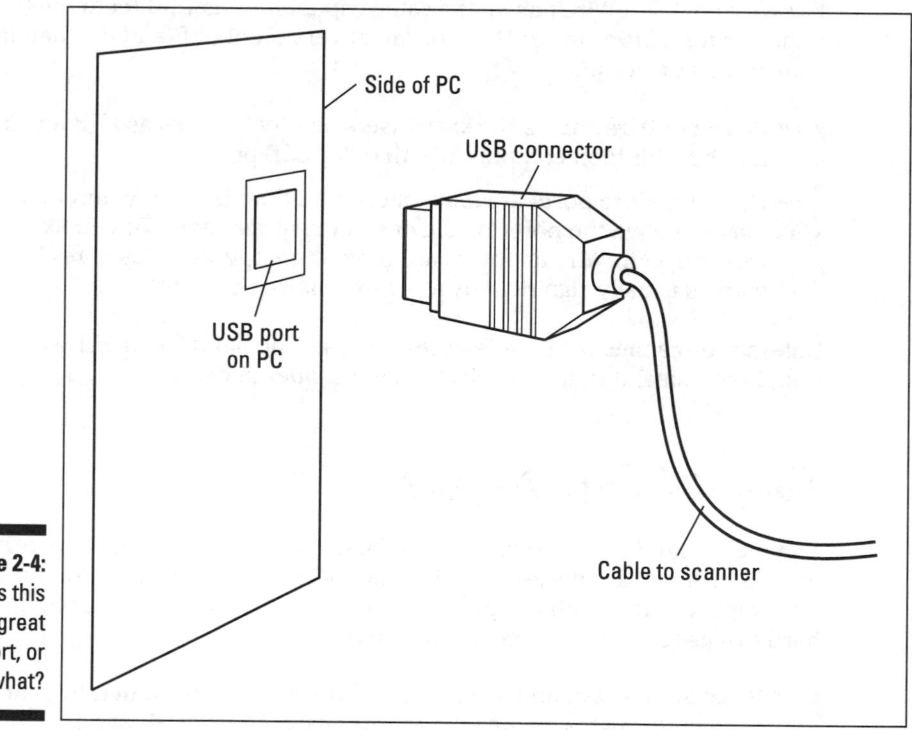

Figure 2-4: Man, is this USB a great port, or what?

- **Pros:** USB scanners are almost as inexpensive as their parallel port brethren, and they're much faster. A USB scanner is so simple to use that even a politician can connect one to a computer. That's what I call user friendly.
- **Cons:** If I had to list a disadvantage of USB scanners, I would have to mention that it's not available on PCs and Macintosh computers that are more than three years old.

Cheap, simple, and powerful — you can see why USB is the connection choice for most scanner shoppers, and I heartily recommend it!

For those in the fast lane

If you've invested in a more expensive scanner that delivers 36-bit color or higher, you may want to consider the speedy IEEE-1394 High Performance Serial Bus or, as power users and computer types would rather call it, a FireWire port. FireWire has all the same capabilities as USB technology, although it's a little slower than the latest version of USB and can handle only a measly 63 devices.

- **Pros:** FireWire shares the same user-friendly features as USB and is much faster than computers with older USB ports.
- **Cons:** FireWire ports are much more rare than USB, so your computer may not have the ports to use one of these scanners. (If you like, you can add a FireWire adapter card to your computer.) Plus, FireWire hardware is usually significantly more expensive than USB.

Unless the scanner with the features you want demands a FireWire connection, I recommend that you select a USB scanner instead.

Forget SCSI? Never!

The final candidate in the connection beauty pageant has been a favorite of computer hardware hackers for decades: *SCSI* (short for Small Computer Systems Interface) technology is used in computers now for everything from hard drives to CD recorders and scanners.

- **Pros:** SCSI is fast, and as many as 15 devices can be added to your system through a single SCSI adapter card. Unlike USB and FireWire, SCSI supports both internal and external devices.
- **Cons:** SCSI is harder to install and configure than any other connection types I cover, and SCSI scanners are typically more expensive than their USB counterparts.

If your computer already has SCSI onboard, you may want to consider a SCSI scanner. For complete details on SCSI, turn to Chapter 4.

TWAIN (Not the Tom Sawyer Guy)

Hey, don't get me wrong — Samuel Clemens (also known as Mark Twain) is my favorite author! In this case, though, TWAIN is another computer acronym you should remember. Yes, I know that it's more than four letters long, but TWAIN actually stands for *absolutely nothing!* In fact, the acronym means *t*echnology *w*ithout *a*n *i*nteresting *n*ame. (It's obviously the only acronym in this book coined by folks who understood what normal people think of computer technobabble.)

The TWAIN standard was conceived and developed to ensure that your scanning hardware, image capture, and editing software all talk the same language, no matter who made what. As long as everything is TWAIN compatible, you know that everything you use to scan recognizes everything else — and TWAIN is supported by both Windows and Mac OS.

Check any scanning hardware or software you're buying to make sure that it's TWAIN compatible and save yourself a headache.

Scanner Features to Covet

Let's talk about the other features that can separate a good scanner buy from a great one. Although none of these extras is a requirement, each of them is nice to have.

One pass, one scanner, one king

In scanning terminology, a *pass* is a single sweep of the scanning head across the material. Therefore, a *single-pass* scanner takes only one trip across your photograph or document, digitizing the entire image at one time. Although a *triple-pass* scanner may be cheaper, it has to make three complete passes to capture the same data. These extra passes can result in distortion within the image because even a slight bump can shift the source material between passes (especially if you're trying to scan a three-dimensional object, like a book cover or a canned ham).

That's not all. Naturally, a triple-pass scanner also requires three times the scanning time, which means that you have more time to spend wishing that you had a single-pass scanner! I heartily recommend that you save yourself those minutes and concentrate your comparison shopping on single-pass models.

Let your finger do the scanning

Most scanners are controlled entirely from the computer. In other words, you have to run the capture software that comes with your scanner before you can do anything. On the other hand, if your scanner features *one-button* scanning, you don't have to load any program. By pressing the button on the scanner, it automatically turns on, runs the capture software, and starts scanning! As you can imagine, this feature is quite a time-saver; in fact, one-button scanning has become such a popular feature that many higher-priced scanners also throw in one-button copying and faxing features.

Feed me!

Can you imagine a printer without a paper tray? You would end up loading sheets of paper into your printer by hand! Some people feel the same way about scanners. Personally, I don't scan that many documents in one day, although if you're working in an office environment or your work involves heavy-duty scanning of dozens of documents, a document feeder is a good idea. Your scanner may come with a document feeder already installed, but this feature is typically offered as optional equipment. Check a scanner's specifications on the manufacturer's Web site to see whether it can accept a feeder.

Adapt to transparency

As I mention earlier in this chapter, you can buy a scanner that's specially designed for slides and negatives — and many high-end flatbed scanners can do a fine job of digitizing transparent material. Just look for a scanner that includes its own light source; these models can "backlight" a transparent original, allowing the scanning head to correctly interpret the colors. With a *transparency light* (sometimes also called a *transparency adapter*), you can scan 35mm slides, photographic negatives, and the transparencies used in overhead projectors.

Your warranty is your shield

Most scanners now on the market have a one-year warranty, although it never hurts to check for extras (that you hope you won't need). For example, does the manufacturer offer free technical support over the phone, or will you end up paying? Is the company's Web site up-to-date, with software patches and driver updates posted regularly? Some companies also provide e-mail technical support from their Web sites.

While you're visiting any hardware manufacturer's Web site, look for *FAQ* files (that's short for Frequently Asked Questions) that you can download about the product you're considering (or a scanner you've bought). These files are usually chock-full of information, tips, and solutions to customer complaints.

Software You've Just Gotta Have

Okay, you may be familiar with the hardware, but the software you receive "bundled" with your scanner is just as important. If you have the wrong software, even the most expensive scanner model turns out a poor-quality image. Also, many scanner applications depend on software, like OCR, faxing, or copying. Without the right software, your scanner can't perform these tasks.

In this section, I discuss the software you need to keep your scanner healthy and happy.

Note: Your scanner may combine several different programs into a software suite that can perform some or all of the applications in this section. If so, that's a powerful advantage to consider when you're comparing one scanner with another.

The image editor

For most scanner owners, the image editor is the primary program used every day. Not only can it control the scanner during the actual image acquisition, but you can also edit and improve the scan after it has been saved to your hard drive. (Plus, you can go totally wacky in an artistic sort of way.) The image editor is to digital photographs what a word processor is to written documents.

I can't think of a better example of an image editor than Paint Shop Pro, from Jasc, Inc. (`www.jasc.com`), which I use extensively in examples throughout this book. I first started using this great program in its shareware days, back in the hoary late 1980s and early '90s. (I know that makes me a microprocessing Methusela, but no cracks about my age, please.) The latest version of this program packs the same power as Adobe Photoshop, but for hundreds of dollars less. Naturally, Paint Shop Pro is TWAIN compatible, so it's a good match for just about any scanner. Figure 2-5 illustrates an image I'm editing.

What can you do with an image editor? I discuss this subject in-depth over in Chapters 9 and 11, but let me run through the top 10 quickly:

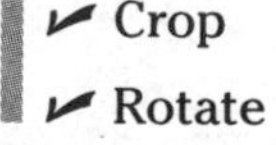

- Crop
- Rotate

- Change colors
- Add special effects
- Add text
- Resize
- Change contrast and brightness
- Fix individual pixels
- Convert to other image formats
- Convert color to black-and-white

As I said, you can do a great deal with a good image editor!

The OCR program

Next in our cavalcade of scanning software is the *OCR (optical character recognition)* program, which can "read" the text from a scanned document and insert it into a word processor, just as though you had retyped the text yourself. Many OCR software packages can also handle photographs and line art as well as simple text, creating a virtual copy of the original within Microsoft Word or Corel WordPerfect.

Figure 2-5: Paint Shop Pro, the all-in-one Swiss Army knife of image editors.

This feature sounds cosmically neat, and it can be. However, I think that it's important to remember that *no OCR software is perfect.* The accuracy of the recognition depends not only on the program you use but also on a host of other conditions, including

- The font used in the original material.
- The quality of the original. (Naturally, a pristine sheet of paper scans better than a crumpled sheet you've rescued from your trash can.)
- The dpi resolution you selected during the scan.
- The color of the text on the page and the page itself.

For this reason, the page you scan from a library book may produce only one or two errors in the final Word document, and a color brochure from your company may be practically incomprehensible to your OCR program. You can fix these errors by individually correcting words the software couldn't recognize, although I don't want you to think that the process is foolproof.

The faxing program

As Frank Gorshin may have asked Adam West in my favorite classic TV series, "Riddle me this, Batman: Why is a fax-modem not like a fax machine?" Allow me to answer that, Caped Crusader: A fax-modem can send only documents you create electronically, like a resume or a digital photograph. If you want to send Aunt Harriet a copy of a recipe from the newspaper, however, you're out of luck. You have no way to fax from a physical original (called a *hard copy* by technotypes and media types alike).

But, wait! With a scanner, a program like WinFax PRO (as shown in Figure 2-6) can turn your computer system into a true fax machine that's as good as the expensive model you have at work.

The copying program

Need a full-featured copier for your home or office? To be honest, you can't find the answer in this book. Although the addition of a scanner can turn your computer system into a basic copy machine, the scanner still can't deliver the versatility and features of the real thing.

If all you need, however, is the occasional copy of a document, your scanner fits the bill perfectly. You can even do basic resizing. This feature usually isn't built-in to the software, though, so you probably have to zoom in or zoom out manually with your image editor.

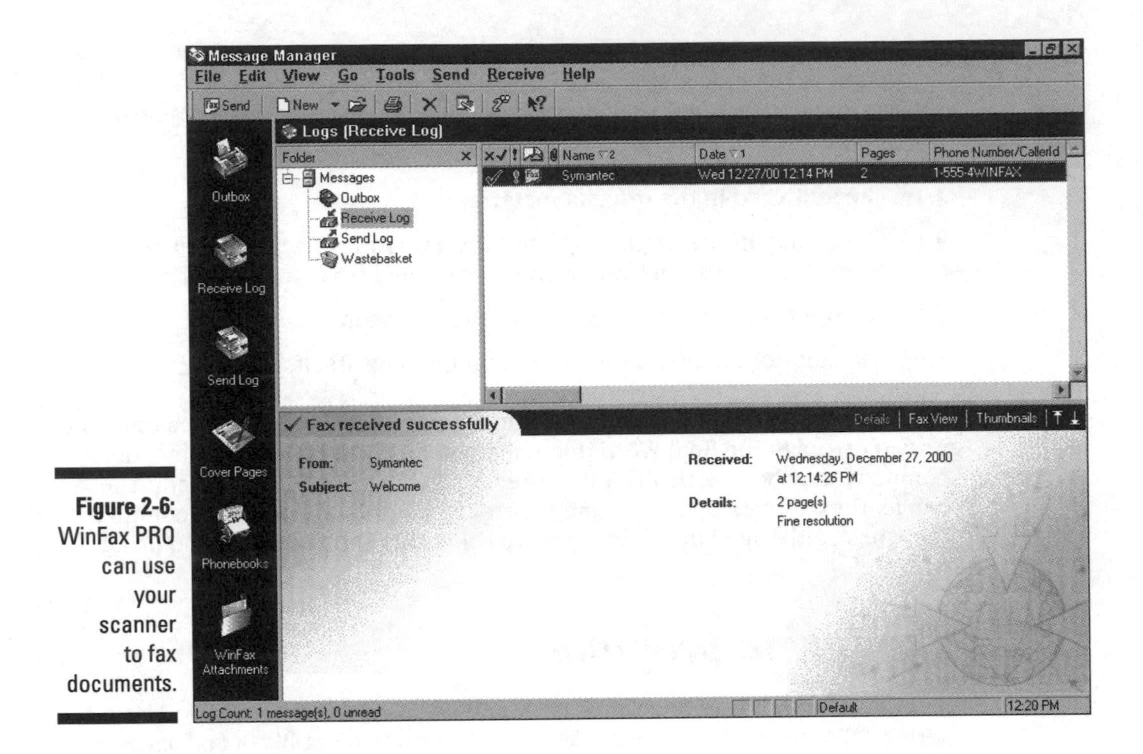

Figure 2-6: WinFax PRO can use your scanner to fax documents.

And the Winner Is. . . .

It's totally up to you! Look over any notes you may have made if you've read this chapter, and you have the complete picture of the scanner you need. For example, suppose that you've written down the following:

Flatbed, 600 x 1200, 36-bit, USB, TWAIN, one-pass, one-button scanning, image editor, OCR

With those specifications, you can go comparison shopping — either on the Web or in a real, live brick-and-mortar store — confident that you know exactly what you need.

Note: Are you wondering "Where can I compare?" If you have an Internet connection, I recommend browsing through the electronic versions of the major computer magazines. Finding reviews is easy, and the awards that a particular scanner wins in a magazine comparison indicate that it's a good buy. I also like `www.pricewatch.com` and `www.computershopper.com` — two sites that offer online comparisons and help guide you to the lowest price online.

"Should I Buy on the Web?"

Speaking of online shopping, have you ever bought anything on the Web? If not, you may be a little nervous about providing your credit card number, and you may be wondering why so many people are shopping with their computers these days. Let me take a moment to fill you in on the advantages of buying your scanner online:

- **Prices are lower.** Of course, this is probably Reason Number One that most folks shop online. You can't beat the prices.
- **Shopping online is a timesaver.** After you're familiar with your favorite online stores, you can compare models, find the lowest price on the model you choose, and buy it, all within an hour or two. (You save gas as well.)
- **You may save on sales tax.** Depending on your location, you may not have to pay sales tax on your online purchase.
- **It's in stock!** You can not only find any scanner on the market online, but also always find a store with one in stock.

When you're using your credit card online, follow the golden rule of Web shopping:

> *Never entrust your credit card to any Web site that doesn't use a secure connection!*

Reputable online stores use this encryption to safeguard your credit card data as well as your sensitive personal information.

Both Netscape Navigator and Microsoft Internet Explorer (the two big guns in Web browsing) support secure sessions. If you're not using at least version 3.*x* of either browser, you should update it before you order. When you see a "locked" padlock icon appear on the status line at the bottom of the browser window, you know that the session is secure.

Also, check on the amount the store charges for shipping. Many stores use second-day shipment as a default option, which is much more expensive than regular ground shipment. If you can afford to wait a few days for your new toy, you can save a significant amount of spending money by choosing the slowest shipping method.

Supporting Your Local Hardware Hut

I should mention the advantages of the dull, boring, oh-so-'90s trip to your local Mess 'O Wires computer store. Yes, you still have reasons to buy from a salesperson! They include

- **Hands-on shopping:** Although the selection may not be the same as an online store, you can try out the scanner you're considering and check out the software before you buy.
- **Returns are easy:** If you buy online and you end up with the famous Lemon Scanner, it's a quick trip back to the store for a replacement. If you order online, however, you're stuck with the hassle of obtaining an RMA and sending the scanner back. You end up waiting for the replacement, too.
- **Personal help:** With luck, you can talk to a knowledgeable salesperson who can answer your questions. (Without luck, you're stuck with a blank stare.)

Okay, that's the bright side. Here are the possible scams you may encounter at your local store:

- **The Hidden Surprise:** Your local store may charge a restocking fee if you return your scanner, even if it's unopened. This trick is a particularly insidious one that I despise. In effect, the store is charging you 15 or 20 percent just to put a box back on the warehouse shelf. If the store does charge this fee, make very sure that you're buying the right scanner. And don't forget to give the manager a piece of your mind before you leave the premises.
- **Whatever *you* call it, *I* call it used:** I also recommend that you avoid a *refurbished* scanner; stores call them by different names — the important thing is that they're *used.* Although you may save a few bucks, is it worth buying a used scanner to save $20? A refurbished piece of hardware has already malfunctioned once, and you have no way of determining how the previous owner treated it. Plus, you're likely to receive either a very short warranty or no warranty.
- **What's wrong with the free warranty?** I should warn you about the so-called "extended" warranty that most stores like to sell you — generally at an inflated price. If you're buying an expensive laptop or an entire computer system, an extended warranty may make sense. A scanner has very few moving parts, though, and they're not prone to failure. Besides, your new scanner is already covered by the manufacturer's warranty (usually a year). Why spend $20 to $40 extra when the cost of a brand-new scanner is only $200?

Now that you've bought your scanner, you're ready to Plug and Play. In Chapter 3, I cover how to install a scanner.

Part II

Surviving the Installation

"Of course graphics are important to your project, Eddy, but I think it would've been better to scan a picture of your worm collection."

In this part . . .

In this part, I'll demonstrate how to connect several types of scanners (including complete coverage of SCSI technology), and I'll help you test your scanner. You'll find information on installing your software and additional hardware you may want to consider buying that will make your scanning much easier.

Chapter 3

"Will That Be Parallel, USB, or FireWire?"

In This Chapter

- Understanding Plug and Play
- Unpacking in style
- Connecting a parallel port scanner
- Connecting a USB or FireWire scanner
- Installing drivers

What do you find scarier: leaping off a bridge with a flimsy-looking rubber hose attached to your ankle or connecting a new peripheral to your computer?

If you chose the latter, don't head for Bungee Village yet. Besides, I've heard that they use refurbished cords. (Sorry — I couldn't resist.) Scanners are somewhat unique in the computer world: They belong to that elite group of external computer hardware that can boast a truly *easy* installation process! (Other members of this club include the external modem and all breeds of printers.)

As you can see from the relatively short length of this chapter, installing a scanner with a USB, parallel, or FireWire interface is so simple that you should be done in five minutes flat.

Just in case your chosen path takes you in a different direction (namely, SCSI), I had better provide a signpost. SCSI scanners are a different animal entirely — in fact, the installation of a SCSI device takes an entire chapter to cover completely! If you picked a SCSI scanner, do *not* panic. Instead, take heart and turn to Chapter 4. Although SCSI may be a little more complex than the connections in this chapter, I make sure that you're well-prepared.

The Plug and the Play

USB and FireWire are Plug and Play connections, which means that you simply connect them to your PC or Macintosh, and the computer automatically recognizes them. No hassles! If you're running out of USB ports, you can disconnect your USB scanner after you're finished with it and plug in another USB peripheral. (Note that a parallel port connection isn't Plug and Play, so if you've just connected your parallel scanner, you have to reboot your PC before you can use it.)

If you have only two USB ports and four USB devices you want to keep connected all the time, you need a *USB hub*. A hub functions just like a multiple-outlet AC adapter for your wall socket — most hubs split a single USB port into four ports so that you can connect all four of your USB toys at one time.

Luckily, most of us can just connect and go, but if your system has a problem recognizing your USB or FireWire scanner, you may have to consider these three requirements for proper Plug and Play operation:

- **Your computer must support a Plug and Play operating system.** Most PCs built within the past five to six years support Plug and Play, so this issue probably isn't a problem. However, if your machine is older, check your manual to see whether your machine can handle Plug and Play. Older Macintosh computers built before the days of USB need, unfortunately, an expensive SCSI-to-USB converter to add USB support. It's probably a better idea to buy a SCSI scanner if you have an older Macintosh.
- **Plug and Play must be turned on in your BIOS.** Your BIOS holds a number of important settings that control your PC, and one of those settings usually controls whether your PC uses Plug and Play. This setting is almost always enabled by default, although not every computer is a winner. To check this setting and change it (if necessary), you must press the correct key when you first turn on your computer — usually Delete or F1. When you press this magical key, your computer displays its BIOS configuration menu. The key to press should be listed in your manual and is probably also displayed on your monitor when you first turn on your PC. If you have to turn Plug and Play on, don't forget to save your changes!
- **You must be running Windows 95.** Windows 3.1 (and System 7 on the Macintosh) just don't cut it. They were designed long before the days of USB, FireWire, and Plug and Play, so if you're still running an older operating system it's time to upgrade. Also, USB support was not provided on the first versions of Windows 95, so if your Windows CD-ROM doesn't say that it has USB support built-in, you should upgrade to Windows 98 before trying to install your scanner. Mac folks should be running Mac OS 8.

Before You Begin. . . .

If you're sitting next to your computer desk, ready to rip open the box and scan up a storm, *stop!* — at least for a second — and let me remind you of three important steps you should take while unpacking any piece of computer hardware!

Your box is your castle!

Why a castle? For a start, the original box can protect your scanner if you need to move it, but there's much more:

- If you sell your scanner later, it's generally worth more if it's in the original box.
- If your scanner is a lemon, it should be in the original box when you take it back to the store (or send it back through the mail) for a replacement.
- If you need to send your scanner back for servicing, the original box is worth its weight in gold.

How long should you keep your original box? I recommend that you hang on to it for at least a year (and toss it then only if you need the room)!

Register, register, register!

Believe me — I know that nothing is worse than filling out a registration card, besides being abducted by aliens, that is. However, I still fill out those cards and send them off, and you should too. No, I really do register my stuff — you've got to believe me!

Without registering, you may not be eligible for technical support, and you may have problems obtaining warranty or service on your scanner. You can avoid all that with a few minutes' worth of effort, so resist that strong temptation to install until you've registered.

Check for packing materials!

Don't forget to read your scanner manual to determine whether you need to remove any packing materials from the unit before you turn it on. For example, many manufacturers have a locking mechanism that holds the scanning head motionless during shipment, and you can *seriously* screw up your new hardware if you turn it on before unlocking the scanning head. Better safe than sorry later!

Docking at the Parallel Port

Did you decide on a parallel port interface for your new scanner? If so, follow these instructions to connect your scanner to your PC:

1. **Find the 25-pin parallel port on the back of your computer case. It may also be labeled Printer Port.**
2. **If your computer printer is already connected to the parallel port, disconnect the printer cable and set it aside for a moment.**
3. **Align the connector on the end of your scanner's cable with the parallel port and push it in firmly.**

   Note that the connector has angled edges to ensure that it goes on the correct way.
4. **Turn the knobs (or screws) on the connector clockwise to tighten it.**

   You may be tempted to leave the cable hanging if it's firmly connected, but it's always a good idea to take a few extra seconds to tighten things down; if you move your computer, you also risk moving the cable enough to cause an incomplete connection. (This problem is often the cause of this classic PC owner's comment: "I swear — this thing works half the time, and the other half it sits there like it's disconnected!" That's because it is.)
5. **If you also have a printer for your system, connect the parallel cable from the printer to the Printer port on your scanner — this is the daisy-chaining process I speak about in Chapter 2.**
6. **Connect the power cord from your scanner to the wall socket and turn your scanner on.**
7. **Restart your PC.**

USB or Bust (and FireWire, too)

USB and FireWire scanners are installed in exactly the same fashion, so I give my keyboard a break and just show you how to connect a USB model. Refreshingly enough, both Windows and Macintosh use the same steps, too. Eerie, isn't it?

Follow these steps to install a USB scanner under Windows or Mac OS:

1. **Some USB scanners have their own cables permanently attached, and others accept standard USB cables. If your scanner fits in the latter category, connect the USB cable to the device.**

   If your scanner uses a separate cable, that cable should be included in the box.

2. **Plug in your scanner and turn it on.**
3. **Allow Windows or Mac OS to boot normally.**
4. **Plug the USB connector on the cable into a USB port (or your USB hub) on your computer.**

   Your computer suddenly notices that you've added a USB scanner and decides to add the new kid on the block.

5. **The first time you connect your scanner, you're prompted to load the manufacturer's CD-ROM so that it can install the correct drivers. If you're installing under Windows, you may also be prompted to load your Windows CD-ROM. If you run a software installation program from the manufacturer before you connect your scanner, the program may load these drivers beforehand.**

Don't Forget Your Driver!

I wonder whether Tiger Woods owns a scanner? Anyway, golf fans, I'm not talking about a club here. I mean a *software driver* — a program, written by the manufacturer, that allows your operating system to use your new scanner.

As I say in the preceding section, the manufacturer of your scanner should send you a driver for use during installation — either by itself or as part of a complete software installation program. You should use this driver whenever you're prompted by Windows, as I show you in the preceding section. For most PC owners, that's it. They immediately forget about the driver and put the CD-ROM away.

That's not the end of the tale, though. If you want to become a scanning powerhouse, *update your drivers!* Most scanner manufacturers periodically release new versions of their drivers, which may include one or more of the following:

- Bug fixes
- Improved performance
- New features
- Compatibility with new versions of the operating system

To keep an eye on your drivers, visit the manufacturer's Web site. If you have scavenged an older scanner and can no longer find support on the Web from a scanner manufacturer, I can heartily recommend a trip to these great sites:

- www.driverzone.com
- www.windrivers.com
- www.drivershq.com

These sites are great for all your hardware. You should check on video card drivers at least once a month, for example.

All right, troops, if you've had your fun with the three types of connections described in this chapter, you may want to check out Chapter 4, where I show you how to attack SCSI and win!

Chapter 4

And Then There's SCSI

In This Chapter

- Introducing SCSI connections
- Determining the right termination
- Selecting a SCSI ID
- Installing a SCSI adapter
- Connecting your scanner
- Troubleshooting SCSI problems

I'll be honest with you — back in the days of DOS and Windows 3.1, adding SCSI to a PC used to be somewhat akin to building Hoover Dam with a toothbrush (and a broken one, at that). If you were a novice PC owner, nothing about a first-time SCSI installation went easily, and even a veteran hardware technician, like yours truly, often encountered problems. (I woke up screaming after more than one SCSI installation, back in those DOS years.) After you did get things working, though, you couldn't help but appreciate the performance and versatility of a SCSI system — and yes, you do pronounce it "skuzzy."

With the introduction of Windows 95 and Windows NT, however, everything changed for the better. Support for SCSI is now built-in to Windows, and things are *practically* automatic. Why the one-word disclaimer? Because you still have to make decisions and perform configuration tasks correctly, or else your SCSI scanner still won't work. Unlike with USB and FireWire, things are definitely not Plug and Play in the SCSI world.

Now, nothing is wrong with simply hauling your computer, your new SCSI card, and your scanner to your local computer store and having a hardware technician do the work I describe in this chapter — or working that old family magic on a technosavvy relative and asking her to help. If you decide that you're ready to install SCSI yourself, however, I'm here for you.

Note: Here's an ironic side to this quest for Macintosh owners: Until about three years ago, all Macs used SCSI hard drives and offered SCSI external ports as standard equipment! With the introduction of the iMac and "blue and white" G4 machines, however, Apple has turned away from SCSI and embraced USB and FireWire (which the company developed). Therefore, if you own a newer Macintosh computer and you're reading this chapter, you have to follow the same guidelines. Sorry about that.

In this chapter, you and I face the task of a SCSI scanner installation together, without the need for weapons or armor! King George would be proud — and probably a little surprised to boot.

The Way Things Should Work

Okay, before I tell you how to configure your SCSI scanner, I want to give you a quick overview of how things are supposed to operate in the SCSI scheme of things. In other words, if your SCSI device chain isn't working to begin with, configuring your scanner is entirely moot.

If you're installing a SCSI adapter card just for your scanner, the scanner connects to the external SCSI port on the card. If you're also adding a SCSI hard drive or internal CD recorder, it's connected to the adapter card by a separate cable inside the computer. So far, so good.

Here's where you turn up the heat: Your SCSI scanner and adapter card (and any other SCSI devices you have) must meet two important requirements before everything hums:

- Each device on your SCSI cable (or cables) has to be "named" so that it doesn't argue with the other SCSI devices. You must therefore assign a *unique SCSI ID number* to each of your SCSI devices (including the adapter card itself). If you assign the same ID number to your scanner and your SCSI adapter card, they argue about who's who and your entire system freezes up.
- The combination of a SCSI adapter card and your SCSI devices — both internal and external — is called a *chain.* Your SCSI adapter, however, doesn't know how long the chain is, so the two ends of the chain need to be *terminated;* think of a terminator as a stop sign for your SCSI adapter card. In effect, the terminator is telling your SCSI adapter card, "Hey, no other devices are connected to the chain past this point." If your SCSI devices (including the SCSI adapter itself) aren't properly terminated, your SCSI adapter card continues to search for new devices forever, and your computer again freezes up — or your computer steadfastly refuses to recognize your new scanner.

You probably noticed that the words *freeze up* just occurred twice there — and that's one reason that SCSI can be so frustrating to install if you don't watch your hardware settings. If you've chosen your ID numbers carefully, however, and you've set termination correctly, the process should go smoothly.

Look Out, It's the Terminator!

Although this particular terminator is much less dangerous than the film variety, it can still wreak havoc on your system if you don't handle it correctly on both your SCSI adapter card and your scanner.

It's an end thing, man

If you're adding just a SCSI card and a SCSI scanner, you're in luck: This SCSI chain arrangement is the simplest because you need to indicate only one external device through termination. Because your adapter card and scanner are both at an end of the SCSI chain, both need to be terminated, as shown in Figure 4-1.

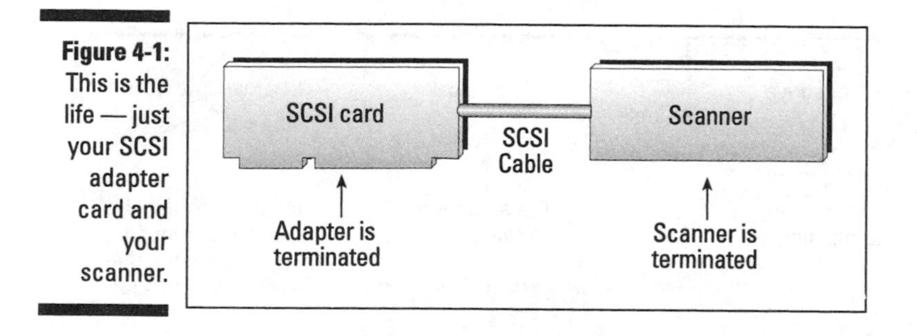

Figure 4-1: This is the life — just your SCSI adapter card and your scanner.

But what if you have a second SCSI device, like a hard drive? I was afraid that you'd ask that. No, I'm kidding — it's really no big deal! Figure 4-2 shows a properly terminated chain. Notice that the hard drive is internal, which puts the adapter in the "middle" of the new chain.

Now suppose that you forget to disable the termination on the SCSI adapter. Do not try this at home! Figure 4-3 illustrates the problem: Because the SCSI adapter card is improperly terminated, it thinks that the chain ends with itself and never even attempts to find the scanner. Your computer simply ignores the scanner until you change the termination on the SCSI adapter card.

So, what have you found out? If your computer doesn't recognize your SCSI scanner after you connect it, termination is probably the culprit, and it needs to be set correctly.

On a truly huge SCSI chain with five devices or more, it may help to map things out on a piece of paper so that you can keep track of what device is at the end of both the internal and external portions of the chain. (Of course, if you've already installed a chain that large, you could write this chapter too, but this trick works for any chain, no matter what size, so I stick by my Tip!)

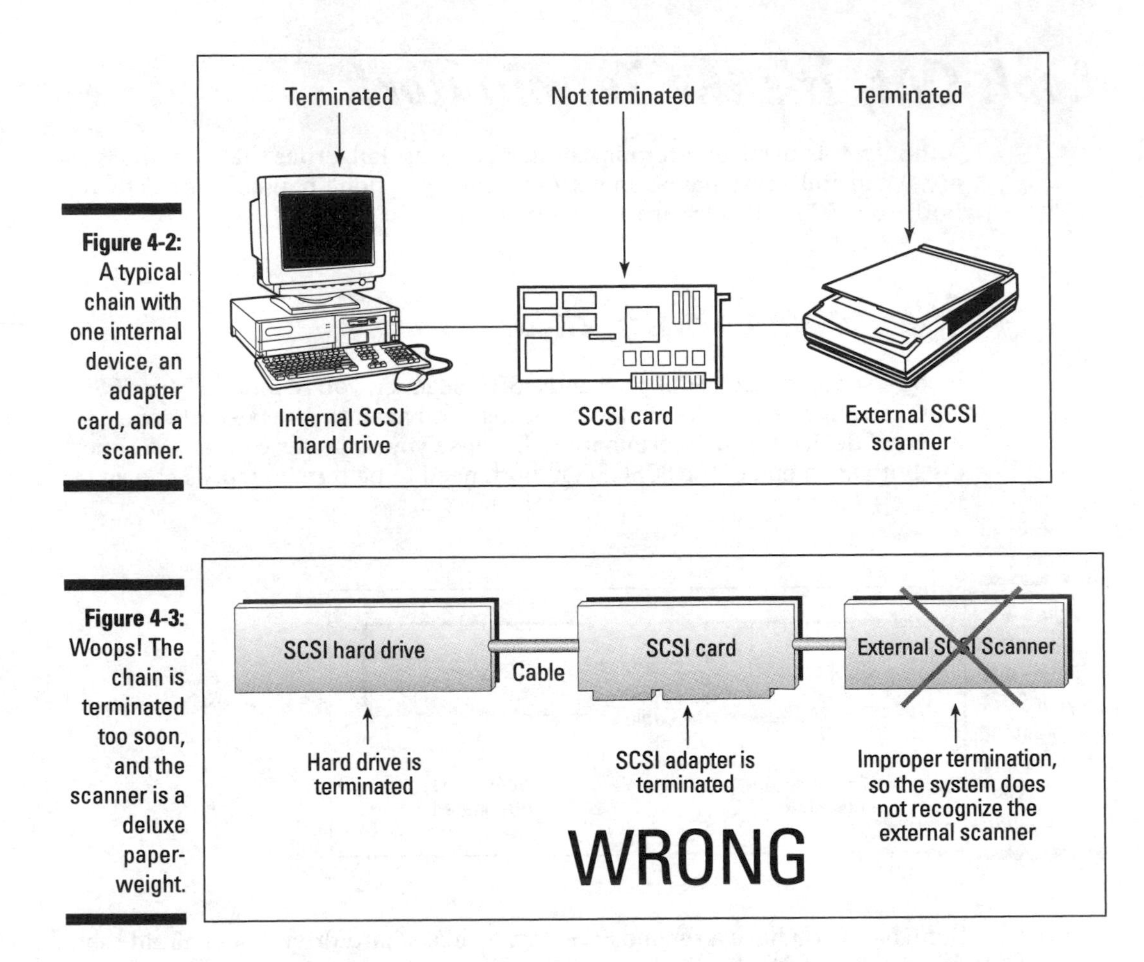

Figure 4-2: A typical chain with one internal device, an adapter card, and a scanner.

Figure 4-3: Woops! The chain is terminated too soon, and the scanner is a deluxe paperweight.

Setting termination can be fun (almost)

Three methods are typically used on SCSI hardware to set termination:

- **Change the DIP switch.** Using the tip of a pencil, slide or press the switches to the right combination listed in the manual to enable or disable termination. The On direction for the switch should be marked to make things easier, as shown in Figure 4-4.

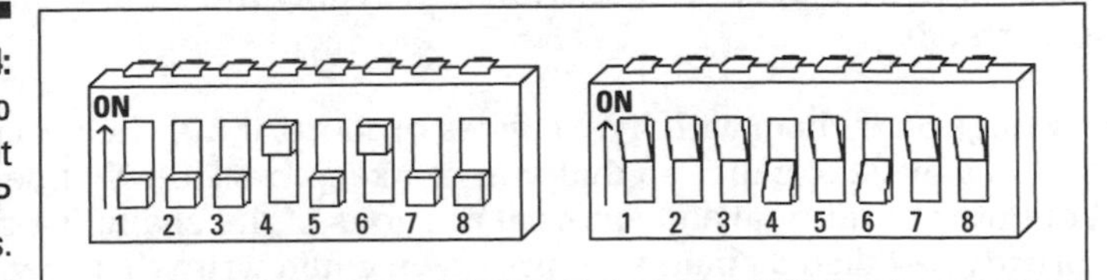

Figure 4-4: Two different types of DIP switches.

- **Use the resistor pack.** Older SCSI devices usually use a resistor pack like the one shown in Figure 4-5, which is simply a plain, electronic resistor you either plug in (to enable termination) or remove (to disable termination). For directions on locating the socket, refer to the device's manual. And, for goodness' sake, if you remove a resistor pack from an older SCSI device, hang on to it like it's made of pure gold! (They're practically impossible to find — take it from someone who knows.)

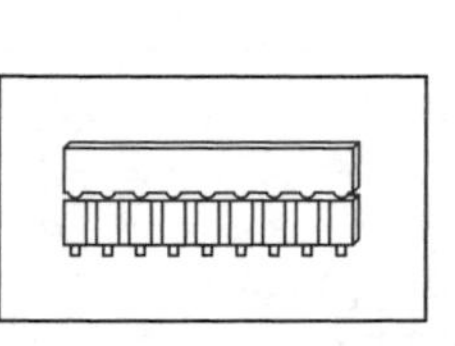

Figure 4-5: Man, that is one boring looking resistor pack. Goes with the territory, I guess.

- **Change the jumper.** To change the ID number on a device that uses a plastic *jumper,* like the one shown in Figure 4-6, use a pair of tweezers to pull the jumper off the original set of pins and press it on the correct sequence of pins. For example, you may move a jumper connecting pins 4 and 5 to pins 5 and 6 instead.

Figure 4-6: Use a pair of tweezers on a jumper.

Can I See Some ID, Please?

How do you set a unique SCSI ID for your scanner, adapter, and other SCSI devices connected to your computer? Most SCSI cards use a range of numbers from either 0 to 7 or 0 to 14, depending on the variety of SCSI you're using. The ID numbers 7 and 14 (respectively) are usually assigned by default to the adapter card itself. You can use all the other ID numbers for other devices, including your scanner. Your card's manual tells you which number has been reserved for your card, your scanner, and any other devices you're installing.

Figure 4-7 illustrates a typical SCSI device chain with the SCSI ID numbers set — three unique values, no problem.

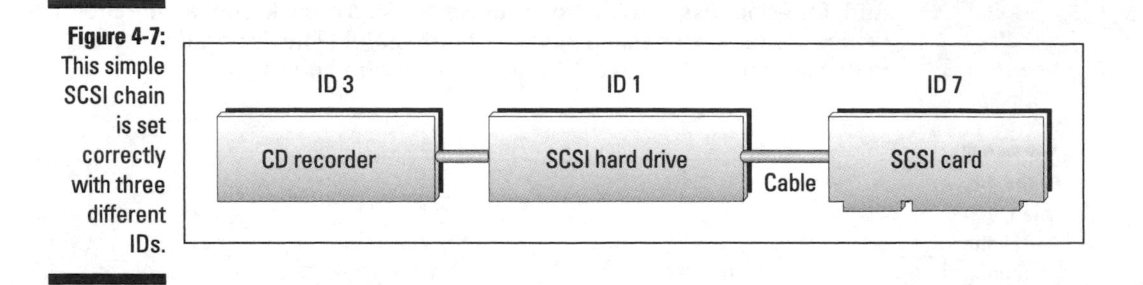

Figure 4-7: This simple SCSI chain is set correctly with three different IDs.

If all the defaults in this cozy arrangement are unique already, you can rejoice and count your blessings. If not, you have to change the SCSI ID numbers that match until all the ID numbers are unique. Your SCSI adapter card should stay at the default, if possible. (If not, you probably have to run the manufacturer's software to change it.)

I should mention that many SCSI adapter cards can set their own SCSI device IDs automatically. If you have one of these and your scanner supports this feature, let the hardware do the work! Your SCSI adapter card and all your devices must support SCAM (a nasty-sounding acronym, but it really stands for SCSI Configured Automatically).

If you have to do things manually (sigh), you use one of two methods to set the number on a device:

- **Spin the wheel or throw the switch.** To change the ID number using a thumbwheel, as shown in Figure 4-8, turn the wheel until the unique number you want appears. Your scanner may also have a simple sliding switch you can set.

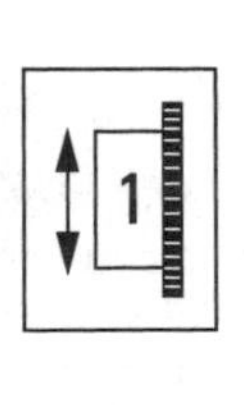

Figure 4-8: The thumbwheel looks innocuous, but don't forget to set it!

- **Move the jumper.** As with termination, your SCSI device may use a jumper to select an ID number. Move the jumper to the correct set of pins, as instructed in the manual for the device.

Installing Your SCSI Card

All right! If you've been following along in this chapter, you undoubtedly have come through it unscathed, and now you're ready to grab your magnetic screwdriver and install your SCSI adapter card. Again, *make sure that you've set the termination correctly before you install the card.* Setting a jumper or adding a resistor pack is much easier now than after you've installed the card. As I mention earlier in this chapter, you should leave the SCSI ID number for your card set to the default, if possible.

Here we go! Follow these steps:

1. **Turn your computer off and unplug the power cable.**
2. **Remove the cover from your case.**

   Don't be ashamed to refer to your computer's manual to determine how to do this step. All cases used to be fastened from the back with screws, although these days cases are held on with connectors of many types.
3. **Select an open adapter card slot for your SCSI card.**

   These slots are located at the back of the case. Most motherboards have a selection of PCI and ISA slots, which are quite different in layout. Any open slot of the right size works with your card.
4. **Touch the metal surface of your computer's chassis before you touch your card.**

   This step dissipates static electricity from your body, which can destroy computer components like Darth Vader destroys X-wing fighters.
5. **Remove the screw and the metal slot cover adjacent to the selected slot, as shown in Figure 4-9.**
6. **Align the card's connector with the slot on the motherboard, as shown in Figure 4-10.**

   The external connector should be visible from the back of the computer, as shown in Figure 4-11.
7. **Apply even pressure to the top of the card and push it into the slot.**

   With a snug fit, the bracket should be resting tightly against the back of your computer's chassis.

8. **Add the screw you removed in Step 5 and tighten the bracket.**
9. **If you have internal SCSI devices, attach the cable from the internal portion of the device chain to the proper connector on the card. Check the manual for the location of the connector.**
10. **Replace the cover on your computer.**
11. **Plug the power cord back into your computer and turn it on.**
12. **Check your card's manual for specific steps you need to follow to load the SCSI driver software for your card.**

A testing procedure should be outlined in your card's manual to help you determine whether the adapter is working properly.

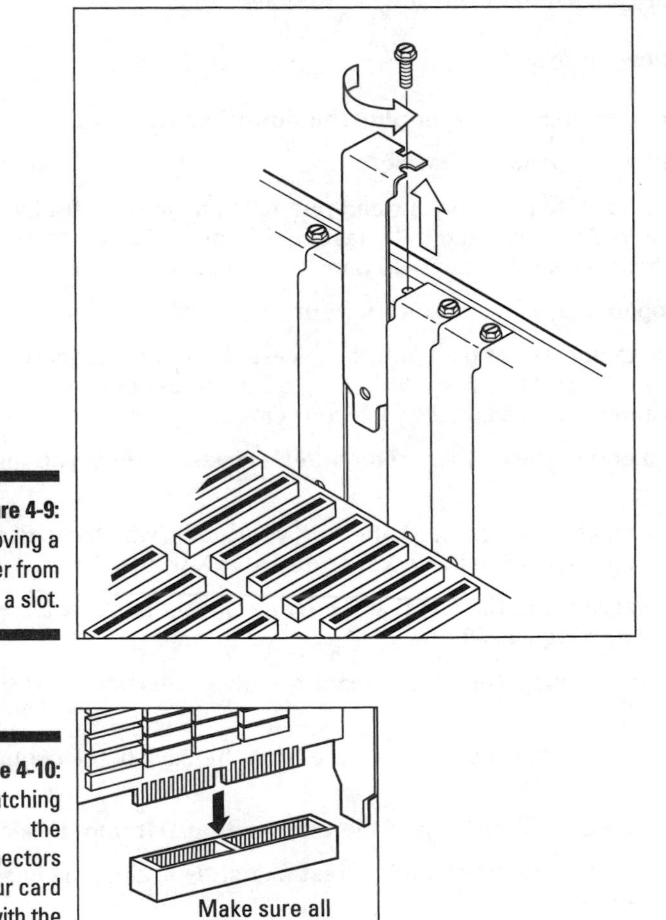

Figure 4-9: Removing a cover from a slot.

Figure 4-10: Matching the connectors on your card with the slot.

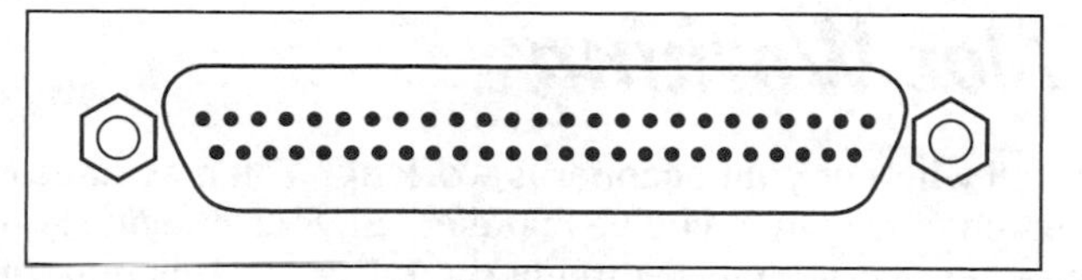

Figure 4-11: Hello, I'm an external SCSI port.

Connecting Your SCSI Scanner

After your SCSI adapter has been installed and is working properly, you're ready to connect your SCSI scanner to your system. Make sure that someone is standing by with a camera to capture the moment! Here we go:

1. ***Make sure that your termination and SCSI ID number have been correctly set for your scanner!***
2. **Locate the external SCSI port on the back of your case.**

   Are you adding your scanner to an existing external chain? If so, connect the cable from the scanner into the secondary SCSI port on the external device that used to be last on the chain. (Don't forget to disable termination on that device too because it's no longer at the end!)
3. **Check the alignment of the connector and the port (notice that the connector can only go on one way) and push the connector on firmly.**
4. **"Lock" the connector in place by snapping the wire clips toward the center of the cable, as illustrated in Figure 4-12.**

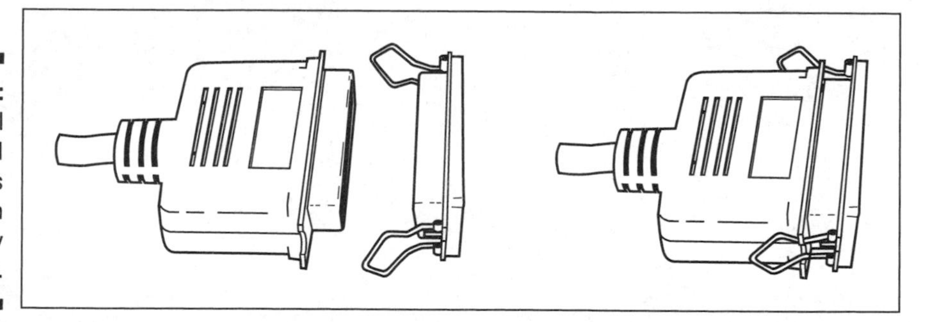

Figure 4-12: An external SCSI connector is held in place by clips.

5. **Connect the scanner's power cord to the wall socket and fire that puppy up.**

Uh . . . It's Not Working

How can you tell whether your scanner is working? You may have to visit the end of the next chapter (when you've installed all your imaging software) to determine whether everything is working right. Even at this point, though, your scanner should at least be recognized and listed as a SCSI device by your card during the boot sequence (or from the SCSI testing software I mention in the preceding section).

If you continue to experience problems with your SCSI installation, however, here's a list of troubleshooting tips that may help you track down the cause:

- **The *T* word.** Yes, I know — you may be sick to death of my harping about termination, but, still — check to make sure that the last devices on both the internal and external portions of the SCSI chain have been terminated. Nothing between them should be terminated!
- **Is your scanner plugged in and turned on?** Hey, it happens.
- **Are all SCSI IDs unique?** Keep your scanner from participating in petty arguments over ID numbers with other SCSI devices.
- **Have all drivers and support programs been installed?** If not, don't panic. Loading the software your SCSI adapter card and scanner need may do the trick.

If you're still having problems after reviewing this checklist, I recommend a call to the manufacturer of your SCSI card and the scanner itself for technical support.

Chapter 5

Installing the Extra Stuff

In This Chapter

- Installing software for your scanner
- Installing an image editor
- Adding storage
- Adding a printer
- Testing your scanner

The title to this chapter says it perfectly: Although you've installed your scanner and added the necessary drivers to the computer's operating system, you have more to do:

- Without the right software, you can't capture an image or edit it for use in other applications.
- I also need to discuss additional storage requirements and extra hardware you may need to consider.
- I need to help you run through a quick test of your entire installation to make sure that everything's working.

In this chapter, I lead you through the steps you need to take to finish your scanner's installation (after you've followed the instructions in Chapter 3 or Chapter 4, whichever one you may have used). I also describe some extras you may want to add that can improve your system — after which, I'm happy to say, you will *indeed* be a lean, mean scanning machine!

Installing Your Scanner Software

Because some scanner manufacturers combine their hardware drivers and scanner software in one installation, you may have already taken care of this step in Chapter 4. If you can already run a program that operates your scanner (it probably looks something like Figure 5-1), you can probably skip this section and move on.

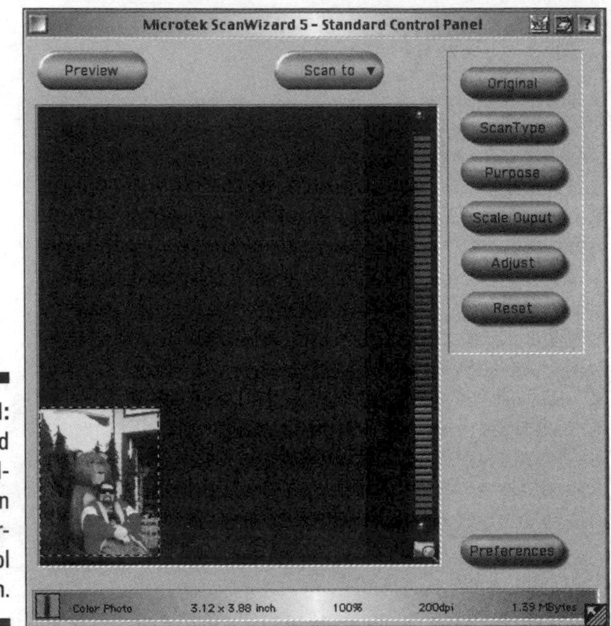

Figure 5-1: ScanWizard is a well-known scanner-control program.

Just in case, though, let me walk you through the installation of a popular scanning-control software package — in this case, Microtek ScanWizard.

Note: Remember that software that runs like a dream under Windows 95, Windows 98, and Windows Me may not work at all under Linux, Windows NT, and Windows 2000! If you discover that your scanner software is incompatible with your operating system, contact the manufacturer's Web site to determine whether you can download the correct version, or contact Technical Support.

Make sure that your scanner is turned on and follow these steps:

1. **Load the ScanWizard CD-ROM into your drive.**

   If you're running Windows 95 or a later version, Setup should start automatically. Under Mac OS, click the ScanWizard installer icon.

2. **Select the appropriate language.**

   Choose English from the drop-down list box, click OK, and click Next on the Setup Welcome screen to continue.

3. **Choose an interface.**

   On the screen shown in Figure 5-2, enable the check box for the connection you'll be using and click Next.

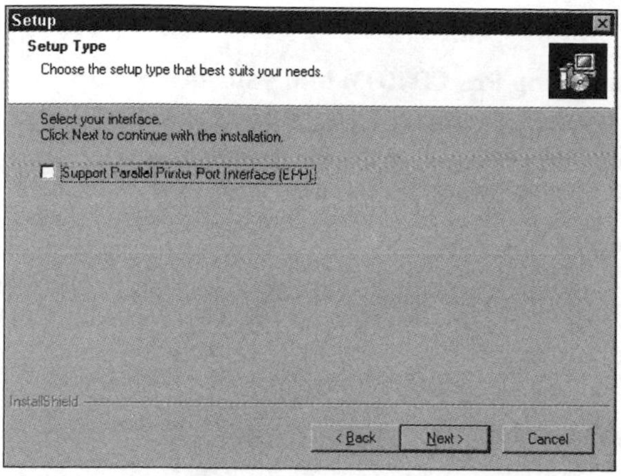

Figure 5-2: It's time to play Choose Your Interface! Is that your final answer?

4. **Specify a program folder.**

   The ScanWizard default is usually a good choice here, although you can click an existing program folder if you would rather have the program icons appear within another folder. Click Next to begin copying the files.

5. **Scan for, well, you know — your scanner.**

   Click Yes to see whether your computer system recognizes your scanner — or click No if you want to follow my simple step-by-step test, later in this chapter.

6. **That's it!**

   You've installed all the basics you need to control your scanner. Click Finish to return to Windows.

Pile On an Image Editor

Okay, turn your attention to installing an image editor — and I can't think of a better example than my old friend Paint Shop Pro, which I use later to illustrate the fun you can have with your images.

Note: The following step-by-step instructions apply to the commercial Windows release of Paint Shop Pro Version 7. If you're installing the trial version from this book's CD-ROM, follow the instructions displayed by the CD-ROM menu program instead.

Follow these steps to install Paint Shop Pro:

1. **Load the Paint Shop Pro CD-ROM into your drive.**

   Under Windows 95 and later versions, the Setup program starts automatically and displays the screen shown in Figure 5-3. Click Install to continue and click Next on the opening Setup screen.

2. **Agree to the software license.**

   If you do not agree to the terms of the Jasc, Inc., software license, the installation ends. Read the terms carefully — you can scroll the window to read the entire text of the license. if you like what you've read, click I accept. Click Next to continue.

3. **Select a configuration.**

   Setup displays the screen shown in Figure 5-4. There, you can choose whether you want the complete install (where everything is copied) or a custom install (where you can choose the "pieces" of the program you want to copy). Personally, I use Complete install. Although it takes additional space, it includes sample files and much more functionality than attempting a bare-bones custom installation. (You may need that stuff someday.)

4. **Select a location.**

   On this same screen, you can specify the location where the software will be installed. I recommend that you use the default location. It helps when you upgrade or patch your copy of Paint Shop Pro — although you can click the Browse button and select a new location on your hard drive, if necessary. Click Next to continue.

5. **Let's do it.**

   Click Install to begin copying files, or click Back if you need to change something.

6. **You're done!**

   Setup displays a completion dialog box. If you like, you can enable the check box that displays the program's README file (always a good idea) or the check box that creates an icon on your desktop for Paint Shop Pro. Click Finish to return to the pretty CD-ROM menu, and then click Exit to return to Windows.

Now you're ready to use Paint Shop Pro later in this book for all sorts of cool stuff. But don't skip to the back — you still have work to do.

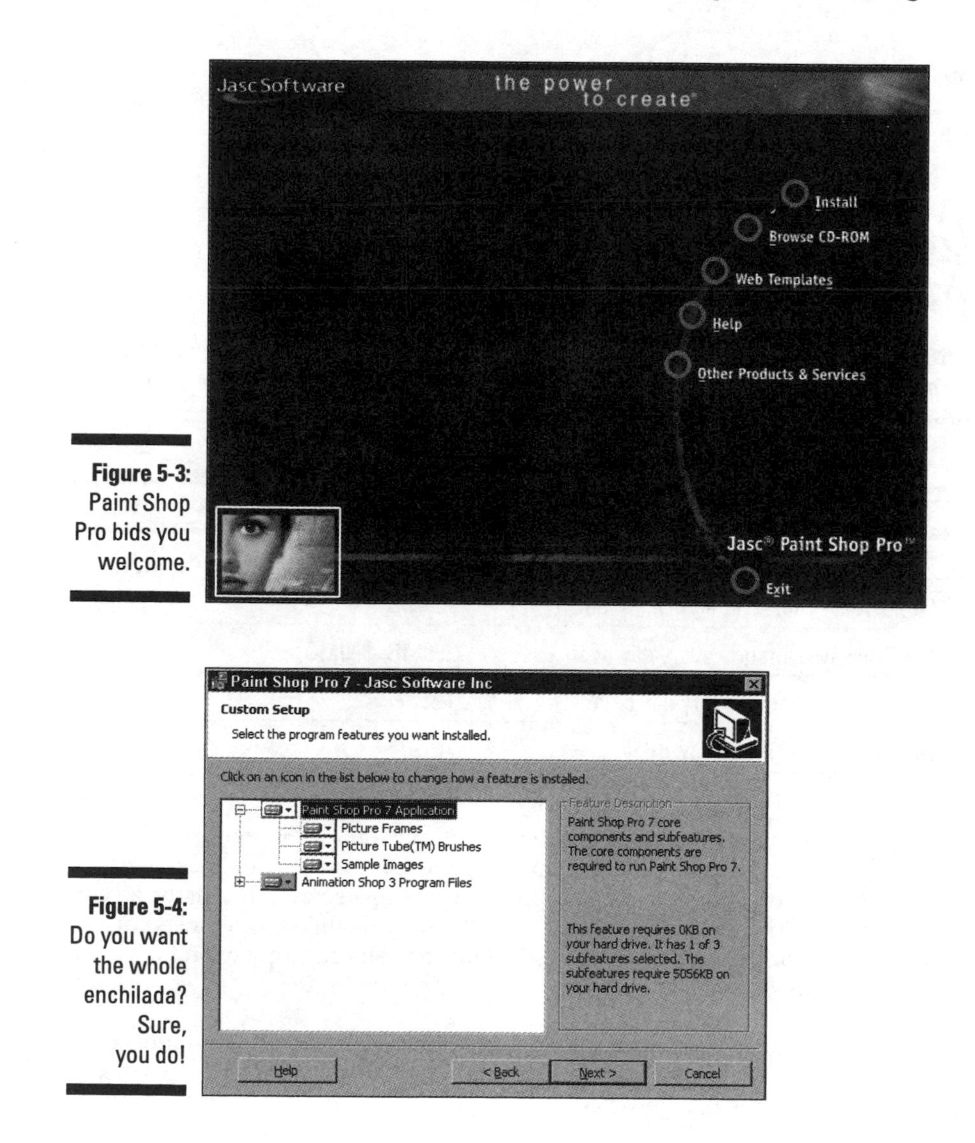

Figure 5-3: Paint Shop Pro bids you welcome.

Figure 5-4: Do you want the whole enchilada? Sure, you do!

"Do I Need More Storage?"

Most technotypes are always ready with the maxim "There's no such thing as too much storage!" Of course, that's only if you have no monetary constraints, and you can easily afford a 500GB RAID storage array. (Forget that I even said that.) Personally, I can't — and you don't need 500 gigabytes to use your scanner, no matter what Bill Gates tells you.

So how much is really enough? In this section, I'm here to help you answer the two questions that determine how much storage (and what type of storage) you may need to add to your computer system.

Query One: What's your free-space situation?

Within a certain range of free space, your system doesn't need any additional storage to use your scanner. Table 5-1 is another spectacular member of my arsenal.

Table 5-1 How Much Free Space Is Enough?

Scanner Usage	*Desirable Free Space*
Light: Two or three images per week	100MB
Medium: Two images every day or so	250MB–500MB
Heavy: Five images every day or so	1GB
Bodacious: Ten images per day	2GB

If you're thinking that I'm padding those amounts somewhat, you're right. From experience, I'm also adding in extra space for conversion, image editing, and the room you need for multiple or truly huge scans. (Honestly, a scan at a very high dpi level can easily top 100MB all by itself!) Plus, I tacked on additional megabytes for those who store more than one copy of an image for different purposes.

To check how much free space a drive has under Windows 98 or Windows Me, click My Computer and right-click on the drive to display its Properties page, as you can see in Figure 5-5.

Under Mac OS 9, click the drive on the desktop and press ⌘-I to display the General Information Pane, as shown in Figure 5-6.

If your system has enough free space to provide the amount of room you need without feeling pinched, you really have no need to add more storage at this time. However, remember that you have to back up those images, and you have to maintain that much space to ensure that you don't run out. Plus, you can't send that hard drive to someone else halfway across the country in a Priority Mail envelope.

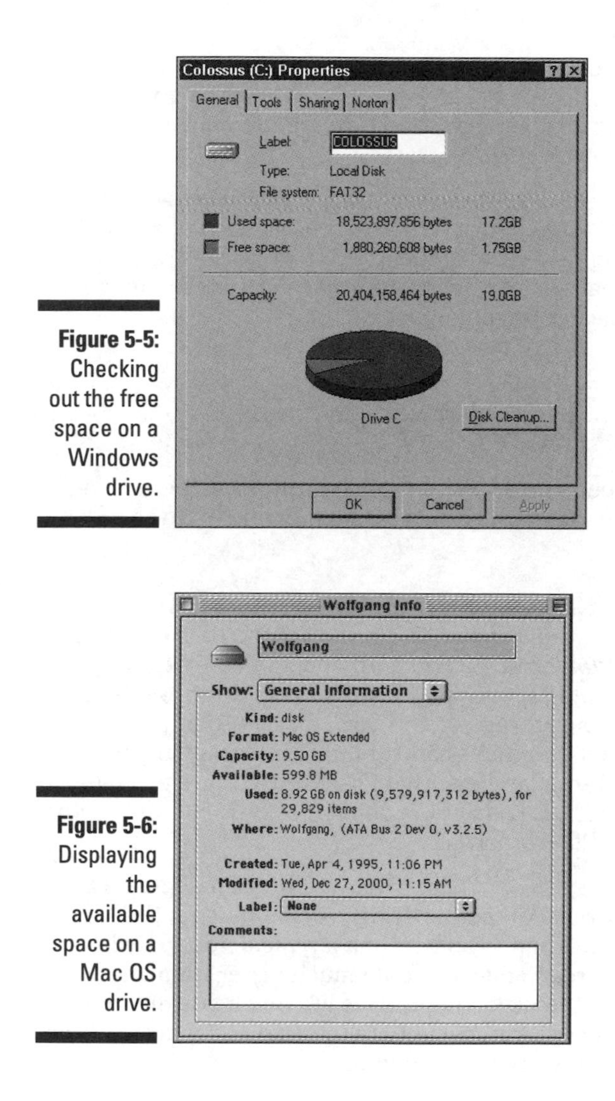

Figure 5-5: Checking out the free space on a Windows drive.

Figure 5-6: Displaying the available space on a Mac OS drive.

Query Two: Are you a road warrior?

Are you on the road with a laptop, or do you need to carry your images with you? If so, you find that an external storage solution like a portable Zip drive, CD-RW drive or hard drive is more of a necessity than a luxury — and here are the reasons:

- **Teeny-tiny drives.** Laptop computers are notorious for their smaller-capacity hard drives (especially older models). If you've stuffed Microsoft Windows 98, Microsoft Office, and all sorts of business applications on your laptop system, you may find that you don't have enough elbow room still available for your scanning software and several high-resolution images.

- **Removable is good.** A portable drive that uses removable media — for example, a Zip drive or a CD-RW drive — is perfect for storing your images in a form you can easily carry, send through the mail, or hand to a customer.
- **To serve and protect.** Storing your images using a CD-RW drive is a great method of protecting them from the stress and strain of a long trip (and clearing 700MB from your cramped laptop drive). As long as you protect CD-RWs from heat and scratches, they can easily resist magnetism and your average baggage-handling robot.

Three easy ways to add space

If you've decided that you need more space — or you just want the convenience and security of removable storage — you can buy one of three great solutions. To wit:

- **CD-RW:** I'll be honest: A $250 CD-RW drive is my personal-favorite pick for a data repository. After all, I'm also the author of the *Hewlett-Packard Official Recordable CD Handbook,* conveniently published by Hungry Minds, Inc. (Gee, what a plug!) Anyway, a CD-RW drive can provide as much as 700MB of reusable storage — and you can record both CD-ROMs for use on other computers and audio CDs to play in your car or home stereo. Both internal and external CD-RW drives are available in USB, FireWire, parallel port, IDE, and SCSI configurations. Figure 5-7 illustrates a typical external CD-RW drive.
- **Zip:** The Iomega (`www.iomega.com`) Zip drive, as shown in Figure 5-8, can hold either 100MB or 250MB per cartridge (depending on the model), and the disks aren't much bigger than a typical floppy disk. However, a Zip drive can read and write data much faster than an archaic floppy drive, and the disks themselves are much sturdier and more reliable. Zip drives are available in both internal and external form, using USB, parallel port, IDE, and SCSI interfaces.
- **Hard drive:** Of course, nothing can stop you from adding an additional hard drive (either internal or external) or replacing your existing drive with a larger-capacity model. Hard drives are inexpensive these days, and they're available with USB, FireWire, IDE, and SCSI connections.

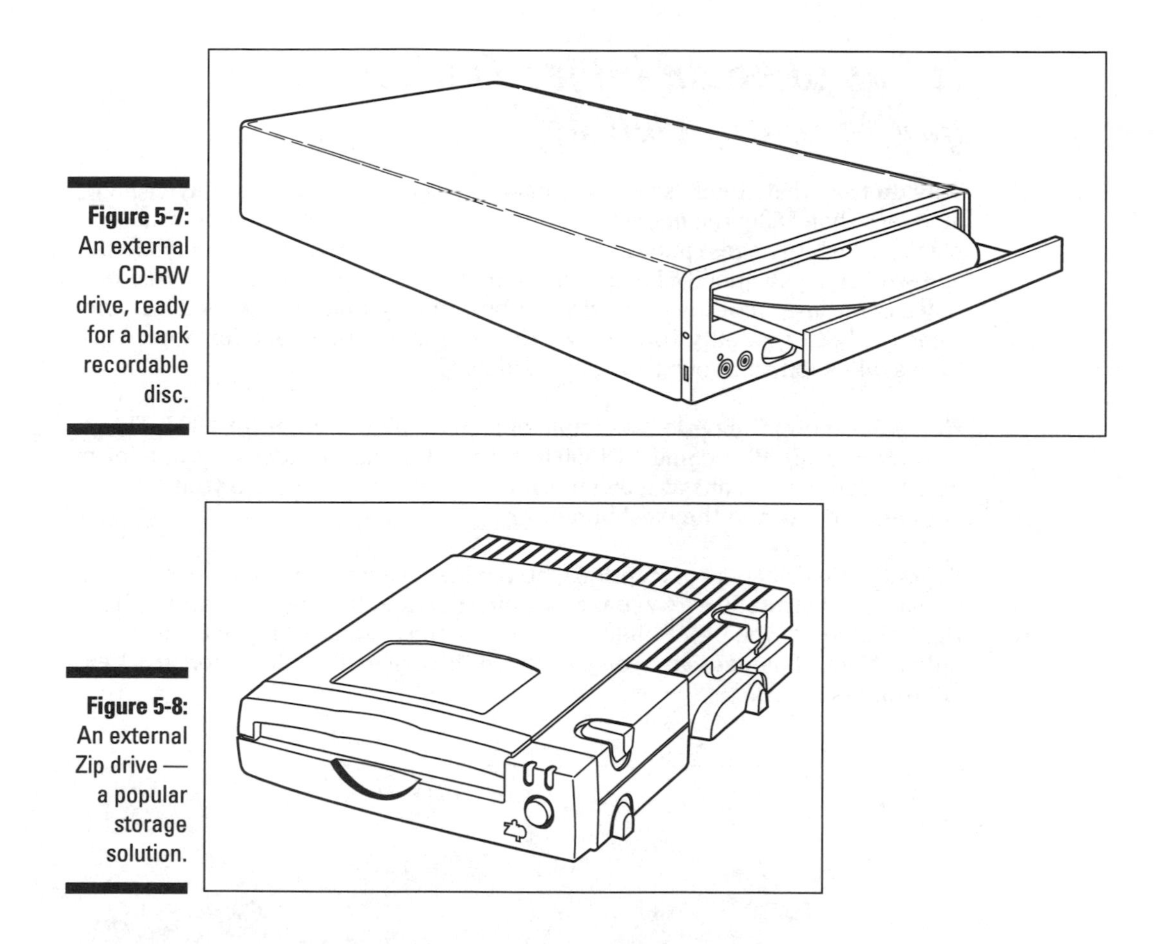

Figure 5-7: An external CD-RW drive, ready for a blank recordable disc.

Figure 5-8: An external Zip drive — a popular storage solution.

Printers, Printers, Printers

Granted, a printer really isn't necessary to operate your scanner — but then, a helmet really isn't necessary for skateboarding, either. The point is, if you don't already have a printer on your system, you're going to want one sooner or later. Why not use your scanner as an excuse?

In this section, I outline the features you should look for in a printer that delivers photo-quality hardcopy from your scanned images. (If you want all the details and a complete discussion of the world of computer printers, pick up a copy of my book *The Hewlett-Packard Printer Handbook,* published by Hungry Minds, Inc. Yes, another shameless plug!)

It has to be an inkjet (unless you're really well off)

Why do I say that? Because two common types of printers these days weigh in at less than $500: the *inkjet* printer (which can produce both color and black-and-white pages) and the *laser* printer (which can produce only black-and-white). If you spend $1,500 or more on a laser printer, you can indeed buy a color laser model — but why not buy an inkjet model that delivers the same (or better) quality and save $1,100 or $1,200 of that cash for other things, like food and your mortgage payment?

Figure 5-9 shows the perfect example of a great inkjet printer for $300: The Hewlett-Packard PhotoSmart P1000 inkjet printer can produce the same print quality from your scans as a 35mm camera, but can also handle your business documents and the kids' homework.

For once, that's it — no exceptions, no confusing acronyms, and no decisions to make! For virtually every home computer owner, the inkjet is simply the right choice. On the other hand, if you're buying a printer for your home office or your business and you can afford the price of a color laser, you benefit from its speed.

Figure 5-9: One sweet piece of printing hardware: an HP PhotoSmart P1000 inkjet.

It has to have these features

Here's a quick rundown of the features a scanner owner should look for in an inkjet printer:

- **Resolution:** There's that word again! Like your scanner, the higher the resolution figures on your printer, the better your scanned images look on paper. I recommend a printer model with a minimum resolution of 720 x 720 (which should cost you less than $200), although you can pick up a 2400 x 1200 model by spending $300 instead.
- **Speed:** Everyone loves a sports car, and a printer that delivers eight pages or more per minute in color has the pickup you need.
- **Interface:** Because I go into detail about USB and parallel port connections earlier in this tome, I don't discuss the details here. Either method works, but I've been using a USB printer for a couple of years now (there's a broad hint for you). Also, be sure to check out what I say in Chapter 2 about troubles you may encounter in daisy-chaining a parallel port printer and a parallel port scanner. If you have USB, save yourself the potential headache.
- **Cartridges:** If you want quality results, invest in a printer that has at least two ink cartridges onboard at all times (that's one with black ink and at least one other cartridge for color). A single-cartridge system forces you to swap the cartridges when you want to print color — that is not a good thing.

Better printers now have several cartridges, allowing you to change just the ink colors you need. For example, if your business logo is printed in purple on every document, you run out of magenta before any other color.

Testing the Whole Doggone Thing

If you installed ScanWizard earlier in this chapter, you may have already successfully tested your scanner. Another scanner controller program may test your hardware as part of the installation, however, so in this section I lead you through a general checkup you can follow using Paint Shop Pro. If you're using the controller software that accompanied your scanner, don't worry — you should be able to follow along.

Follow these steps:

1. **Turn on your scanner.** Remember that if you're using a parallel port scanner and it wasn't powered on when you booted, you should reboot after turning on your scanner so that Windows can recognize it.

2. **Place an original document in your scanner.** If you have a flatbed model, lift the cover and place the original face-down on the glass at the corner indicated, and then lower the cover. If you have a sheet-fed scanner, load the original into the scanner. It should be pulled slightly into the machine by the scanner's motor.

3. **Run your scanner control program.** In this case, you run Paint Shop Pro by clicking the Start button and choosing Programs⇨Jasc Software⇨ Paint Shop Pro.

4. **Choose your TWAIN source.** In Paint Shop Pro, click the File menu and choose Import⇨TWAIN⇨Select source. The program displays the dialog box shown in Figure 5-10. In the example, pick ScanWizard and click Select.

5. **Choose the Acquire command.** Within Paint Shop Pro, click File and choose Import⇨TWAIN⇨Acquire. Your scanner should make a noise somewhat reminiscent of a hive of angry bees being poked by a stick. Don't panic: You're not in danger of being stung; your scanner is simply resetting itself and moving the scanning head to preview the material. After the bees have escaped (woops — sorry about that — I mean after the *preview* is finished), you should see a screen somewhat like the one shown in Figure 5-11. This screen should have some sort of Preview window and a toolbox full of controls and buttons. (You may have to click Preview or something similar, however, before your scanner actually digitizes an image of the original material.)

6. **Close the scanning program.** Okay! If you've received similar results and a smaller version of the original document appears in the Preview window, the test is complete, and your scanner is working fine. Click File and choose Exit to leave the program and return to Windows.

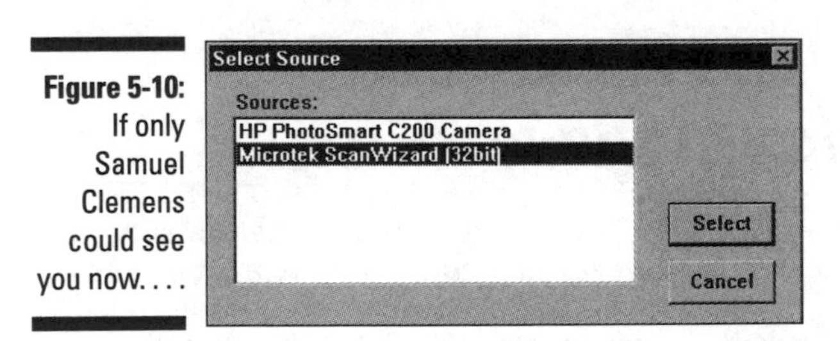

Figure 5-10: If only Samuel Clemens could see you now. . . .

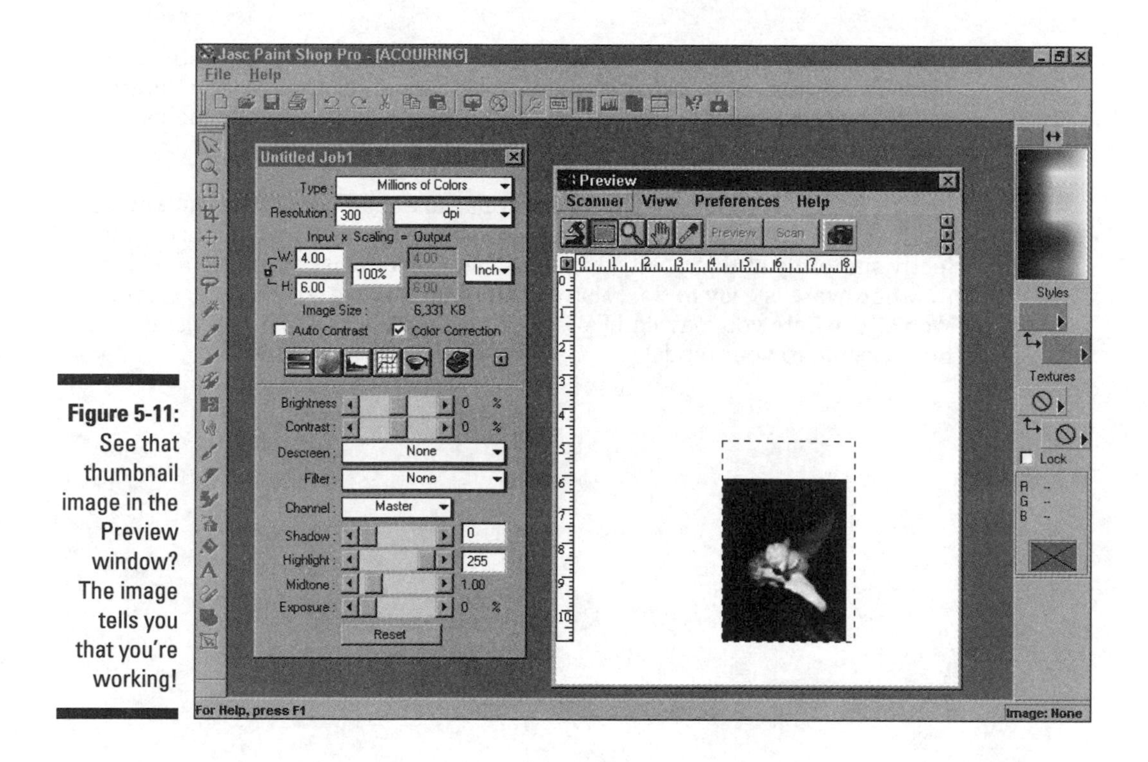

Figure 5-11: See that thumbnail image in the Preview window? The image tells you that you're working!

If, on the other hand, things *don't* go as planned, here's a checklist of possible troublemakers:

- **Are the cables connected?** Check the cabling between your scanner and your computer.
- **Did you reboot?** You shouldn't have to reboot for a USB scanner, but a parallel port model likely needs to be restarted under Windows.
- **Did you unlock the scanning head?** If your scanner has a lock that can hold the scanning head in place, check to make sure that you've disabled it.
- **Did you pick a TWAIN source?** Your scanning software needs to know the source of the incoming image before it recognizes your scanner.
- **Did your scanner activate when you clicked Preview?** If so, the driver itself is probably working, so it may be the scanning software. You may try removing the scanning software and reinstalling it.

If your answer is "Yes" to these questions, try running any diagnostics software that accompanied your scanner. The program may be able to determine where the problem lies. The scanner's manual also may provide the information you need.

Remember that technical support for your particular scanner should be no further than a telephone call away, so don't despair if things don't run perfectly smoothly at this point. Overlooking something when you're installing new hardware is easy to do. I also recommend visiting the manufacturer's Web site, where you may find FAQ information and troubleshooting information specific to your model.

Part III
Bread-and-Butter Scanning

"Hey- let's put scanned photos of ourselves through a ripple filter and see if we can make ourselves look weird."

In this part . . .

Find out all about the basic scanning techniques you'll use each time you fire up your scanner. In addition to giving you a tutorial of the scanning process, I'll discuss how to scan different types of original material and how to configure your scanning software. I'll also give you the basics of Paint Shop Pro.

Chapter 6

Just Plain, Basic Scanning

In This Chapter

- Preparing your scanner
- Aligning the original
- Configuring the settings
- Previewing the scan
- Selecting a scan area
- Using a one-button scanner

At this point in your quest for scanning excellence, you may have successfully chosen a scanner, paid for it (I hope), and installed both the necessary hardware and software. Life is good — take a break, refill your cup or glass, and pat yourself on the back for a job well done.

Wait! I know that I'm forgetting something. Leave it to me to get all caught up in the hardware and software side, and — wait, I've got it! You probably haven't *scanned* anything yet!

Let's fix that right now; this chapter covers all the basics you need to know to operate your new scanner. Remember that you use the default settings and configuration in this chapter, so don't worry about "optimizing" this or "fine-tuning" that. I wade into those deeper waters in Chapter 7, when you find out how to scan different materials for different purposes.

Note: I have another reason for covering basic scanning in a separate section: The default settings used by your software are probably correct for a wide range of jobs, so what you discover here may well be all you need to know for a typical scanning session!

Before You Scan

You should take four important steps before leaping into a scan; call them the Four *C*s, if you will. Skipping one or more of these steps saves you time — but it's possible that you may also significantly reduce the quality of your finished image! Even if you don't take care of each one of these preparations each time you use your scanner, at least consider whether they're needed.

Clean that glass

First and foremost: *Grime, dust, and fingerprints do not add flavor or artistic touches to your scans!* This situation isn't a problem with a sheet-fed scanner, of course, although a layer of accumulated crud can really cause a problem with a flatbed scanner, often resulting in visible smudges and specks that even the best image editor would find challenging to fix. The higher the resolution, the more a dirty glass affects the final image.

Therefore, I recommend that you wipe your flatbed scanner's glass at least once every five or so scans. Keep these guidelines in mind:

- **Never touch the glass.** If you're scanning a periodical, document, or page from a book, lifting the original off the glass without touching it after you're done scanning is usually pretty easy — although a photograph or card-size original is a different matter. (Don't even think about scanning a body part.) Of course, you end up with a fingerprint or two from time to time, but a good wipe takes care of such problems.
- **Keep your flatbed's cover closed.** The best way to maintain your flatbed scanner's glass is to keep the cover closed whenever possible; virtually all scanners have a padded underside that locks out dust and protects the glass from fingerprints.
- **Never use abrasive or household cleaners.** I can tell you about this one from experience. As a consultant, I have seen what happens when someone wipes his scanner down — *inside and out* — with a famous-name, all-purpose household cleaner. A close examination of the glass revealed dozens of tiny scratches, some as thick as a human hair. With the scanner set to average resolution, you could even see many of them in the final image. My advice to the person was to buy a new scanner. I'm also talking about typical household glass cleaners here. They may work on your kitchen window, but they can leave behind deposits that affect your scan.
- **Use antistatic lens or monitor wipes.** "Okay, Mark, what should I use to wipe my scanner's glass?" I'm glad you asked! I recommend one of two choices: a photographer's lens wipe or a computer monitor wipe. Whichever you choose, make sure that the product is antistatic, which helps repel dust from the surface of the glass.
- **Never wipe the glass in circles.** Wipe your scanner's glass directly from side to side in a straight motion, as shown in Figure 6-1. This motion helps to prevent scratches that could be caused by repeated circular buffing (or, as scanner jockeys like to call it, RCB).

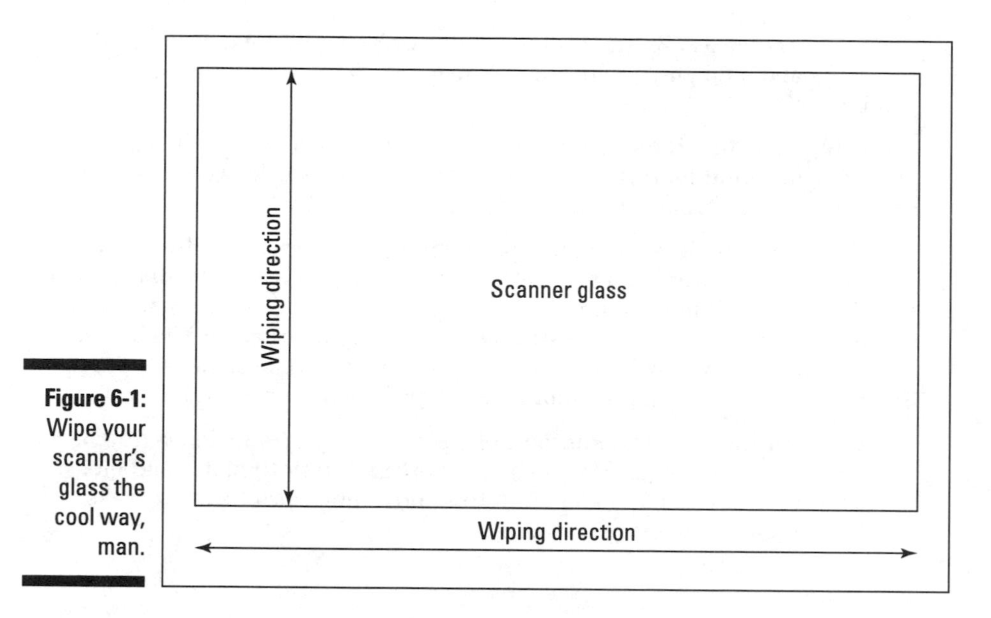

Figure 6-1: Wipe your scanner's glass the cool way, man.

Today's computer hardware is well built, although your scanner was not manufactured to be a weightlifter. Use common sense! While you're cleaning your scanner, *never apply more pressure to your scanner's glass than you would to a typical window in your home* — and never try to scan an object that weighs more than a pound or two. If the glass shatters, it's dumpster time — and perhaps time for a trip to the hospital.

Check your original

You often need to prepare your original beforehand to improve the quality of your scanned image. At higher resolutions, the most minor surface imperfection is magnified, and you don't notice the problem until you've loaded the image (which usually results in having to repeat the entire scanning process, usually accompanied by a few choice epithets). Why not save yourself that trouble?

Here are a number of tips you can follow to prepare an original document:

- **Remove staples.** Three reasons apply here: First, staples can potentially scratch your scanner's glass. If you're using a sheet-fed scanner, staples can come loose inside or cause a paper jam. Finally, if the staple appears in the body of the document (like that Britney Spears jumbo poster in the center of your latest fan magazine), touching up the scanned image can be harder. (As you see in Chapter 11, fixing two holes that remain when the staple is removed is easier than fixing the staple itself.)

- **Smooth creases.** By smoothing down a crease or wrinkled area in the original document, you preserve the image with as little distortion as possible.
- **Add a backing, if needed.** Is your original printed on translucent paper or transparent film? If so, a white sheet of paper works wonders as a backing that brings out the details in the document.
- **Remove "invisible" tape, plastic wrap, or glue.** Because clear tape is nearly transparent, many scanner owners make the mistake of thinking that it doesn't need to be removed. However, your scanner is sensitive enough to record both the surface covered by the tape and its boundary, so remove it whenever possible before you scan. The same is true for plastic wrap and glue — your scanner picks them up as well.
- **Wipe off fingerprints.** Photographs pick up fingerprints like a dog picks up a bone, and fingerprints can show up against both matte and gloss finishes. You can use a soft cloth to remove fingerprints and streaks from an original before scanning it.

Consider a sleeve

Will you be using a sheet-fed scanner? If so, you probably need a transparent plastic sleeve for original items that are smaller than a sheet of paper; for example, a business card or a school photo. The sleeve looks something like a resealable plastic bag, although it's stiff enough to hold its shape while moving through the rollers of a sheet-fed scanner (as shown in Figure 6-2). Every sheet-fed scanner I've ever used has come with at least one sleeve.

Unless the manufacturer of your scanner specifically states otherwise in the manual, *never attempt to scan a small original item without a sleeve;* otherwise, you risk a paper jam (or even worse).

Clear the space

Another *C* in the list of things to do before you scan stands for "clearing" — as in freeing up the necessary disk space on your hard drive to hold the images you're about to scan. Check your target drive (whether it's your main hard drive or a removable media unit, like a CD-RW or Zip drive) and verify that you have enough room to handle the workload.

As I mention earlier in this book, leaving enough space for Windows to use as virtual memory while you're editing your image is a good idea also. It's not uncommon for an image-editing program to lock up or close with an error when you're trying to resize a 70MB high-resolution image with only 100MB of free space on your hard drive!

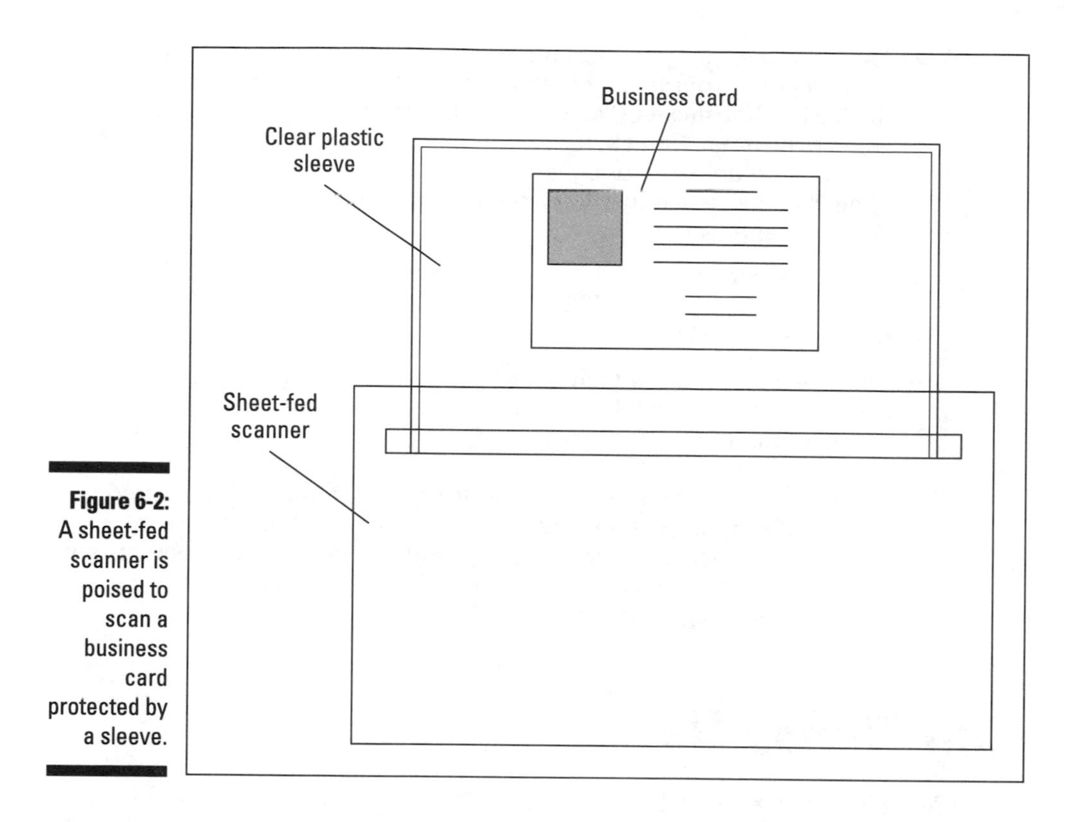

Figure 6-2: A sheet-fed scanner is poised to scan a business card protected by a sleeve.

How much space does an image take? Although your scanner's capture software may be able to guess-timate the final size, you really have no way to tell for sure. However, you can control five settings you make in your scanning-capture software to help keep file sizes to less than 200MB:

- **The dpi:** At 75 dpi, an entire page of a document may take only 10MB; at 300 dpi, that figure jumps to 45MB. (That's why I've never scanned at the maximum "interpolated" mode with my scanner. I've never needed such a level of detail, and you can imagine how big a 9600 dpi image may be!)
- **The area you select:** Later in this chapter, in the section "Choosing a Chunk," I show you how to specify exactly how much of your original document you want to scan. Scan only what you need, to save yourself both time and hard drive space!

By the way, a common misconception exists that scanning a blank piece of paper produces a very small file. After all, nothing is on it, right? Ah, but don't forget: Unless you're using an OCR program, your faithful scanner doesn't care about "what's on the paper" and doggedly spends many, many megabytes of space and lots of wasted time digitizing that blank page! You'll probably end up with an artistic (and realistic) 20MB image — of a blank piece of paper.

- **The color depth:** If your scanning software allows you to choose the color depth of your final image (and most do), you can reduce the size of the file by choosing 8-bit or 16-bit color rather than 24-bit (or higher) color. Remember, though, that anything less than 24-bit color doesn't look as good on paper or on your screen, so you may not use this trick often. It comes in handy when you're scanning material for the Web or your OCR application.
- **The file format:** I cover file formats in depth in Chapter 10. Suffice it to say at this point that the JPEG (or JPG) image format is always the best pick when space is at a premium.
- **The scale:** The scale of your image determines the size of the finished scan. I give you more info on this topic in the section "Make with the Settings," later in this chapter.

If you do need to clear off space on your drive, it's a good time to remove things like applications you no longer need, accumulated Internet temporary files, and the like. Some programs can help you free up room on your system: Windows folks can use CleanSweep, from Symantec, and Mac owners can turn to Spring Cleaning, from Aladdin.

Lining Things Up

All right, it's time to ready your scanner! Go ahead and turn it on, and load your scanner-capture software on your computer. After everything is on and idling nicely, I show you how to align your original for the best scan.

If you have a flatbed

Aligning an original on a flatbed scanner is much like using a copy machine: One corner of the glass is designated what I call "home corner," and one of the edges of your document or object should always meet this corner as closely as possible (as shown in Figure 6-3). Lift the cover of your scanner and look for markings on the area surrounding the glass that help you locate the home corner on your particular model.

If your document overlaps the glass, it's decision time:

- If the area you want to scan still fits completely within your model's scanning range, you have to adjust the original so that the material you want to scan is positioned over the glass.

- If you need to scan the entire area of the original and it's larger than your scanner can accommodate (usually the case with older hand scanners), try the next best thing: Scan the original in "pieces" (using multiple scanning sessions) to produce a number of images and then use your image editor to "stitch" them together. I have to warn you up front that it doesn't always work perfectly!

Make sure that you close the cover carefully to avoid moving the original. Many scanners feature an adjustable cover that can be "raised" for thick items, like books and three-dimensional objects.

Ever wondered whether you really need to lower the cover on your scanner before you use it? The answer is definitely "Yes!" Leaving the cover up can result in washed-out colors or a contrast and brightness problem. Close the cover, even for originals that completely cover the glass.

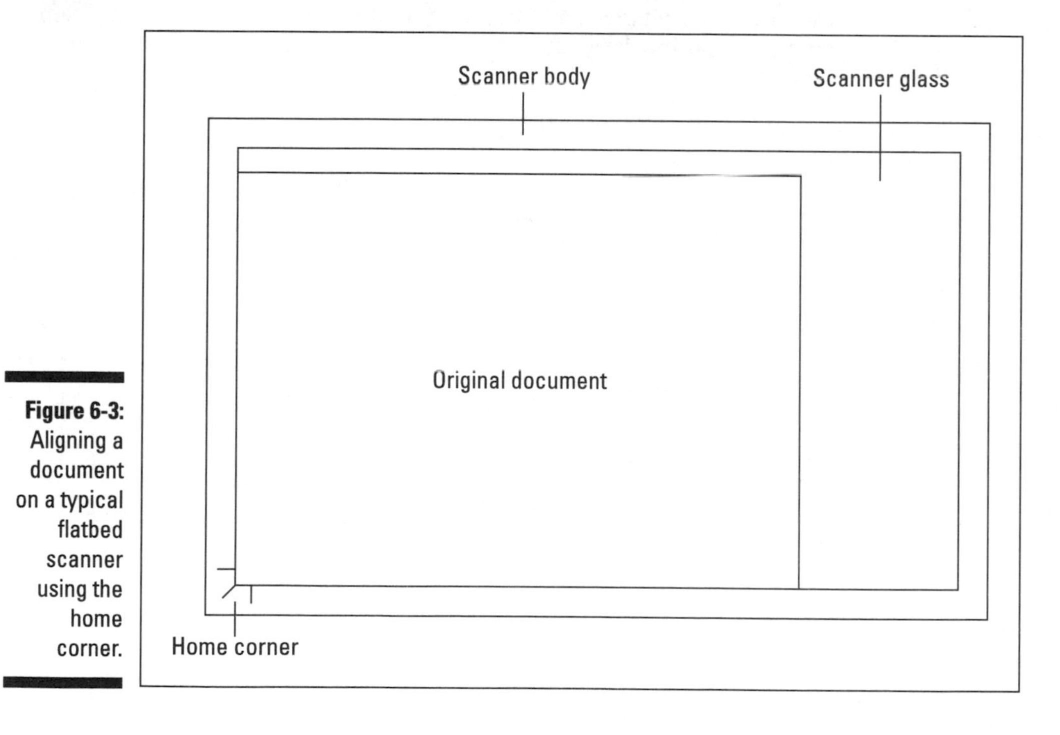

Figure 6-3: Aligning a document on a typical flatbed scanner using the home corner.

If you have a sheet-fed

Aligning an original on a sheet-fed scanner is very different from doing so on a flatbed scanner. Naturally, you're not going to "overlap" the scanning surface, although it's still possible to feed the original incorrectly. Keep these alignment tidbits in mind:

- **Face the document in the right direction.** Your scanner's manual provides more information about which direction the original should be facing when you feed it.
- **Don't feed an original askew!** Avoid tilting your document when you're feeding it into the scanner. Loading an original as shown in Figure 6-4 is bound to cause problems (ranging from a bad scan to an outright paper jam, which is harder to solve and potentially more damaging to the unit than a similar paper jam in a printer). As shown in Figure 6-5, the orientation of the original should be as straight as possible, even if the item being scanned has irregular edges.

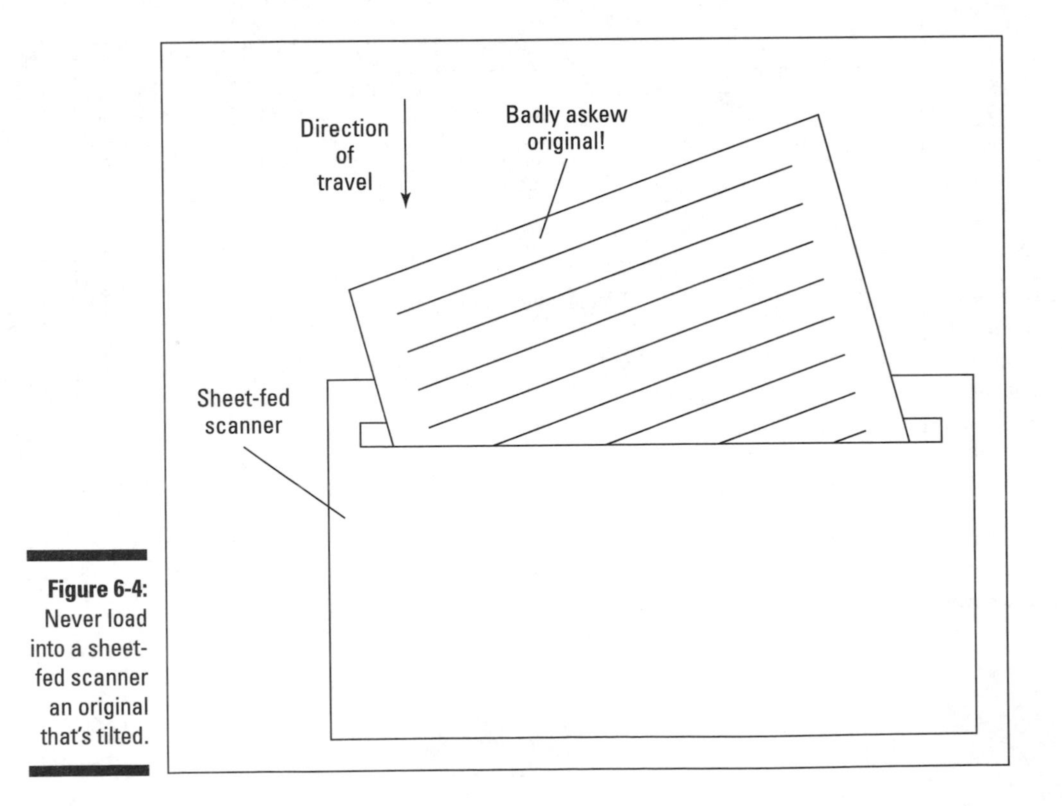

Figure 6-4: Never load into a sheet-fed scanner an original that's tilted.

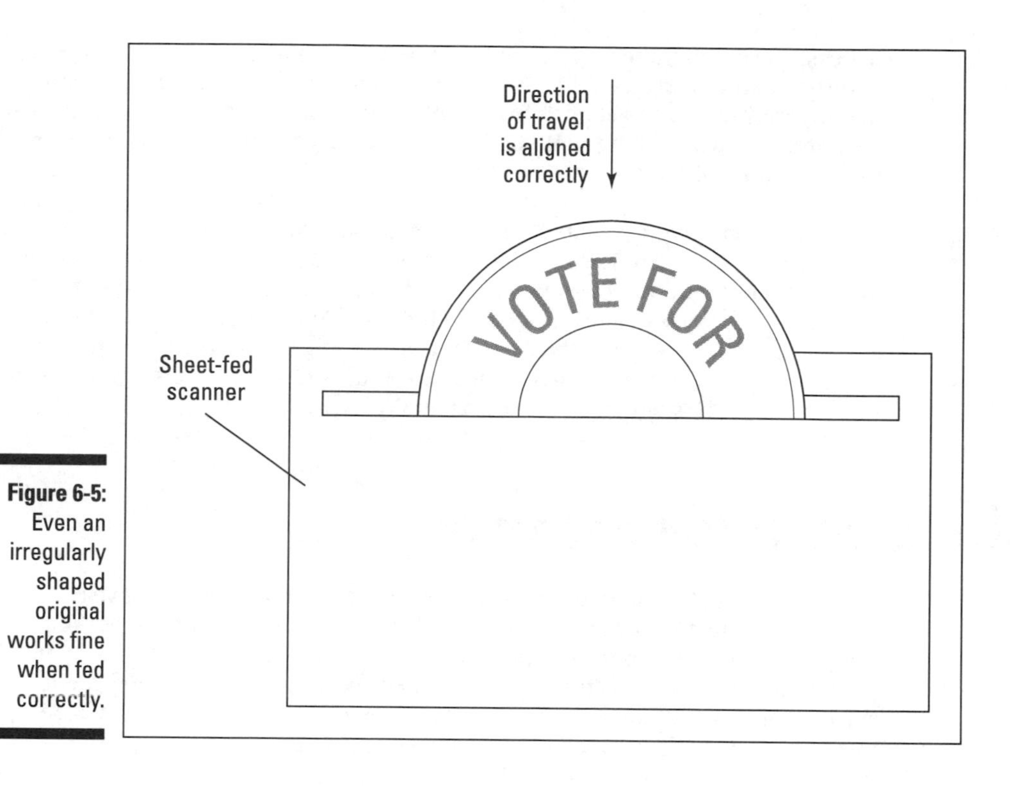

Figure 6-5: Even an irregularly shaped original works fine when fed correctly.

Remember that you may have to press a button to feed the original on a sheet-fed scanner, especially if you're the proud owner of a multifunction (or "all-in-one") unit that can print, scan, copy, and fax. The manual explains what you need to do when you're loading your document.

If you have something else

Using a negative scanner? These scanners are generally very easy to load because slides and photograph negatives are always uniform in size and shape; you typically mount the original in a sliding tray, or you may slide it into a slot on the front of the machine. If your scanner loads originals through a slot, remember the same rule that applies to sheet-fed scanners: Don't feed an original askew!

On the other side of the coin, you have no need to align a handheld or pen scanner. You move the scanner itself across the surface of the original (usually matching the edge of the region you want to scan with a pointer or marker of some kind on the body of the unit). With one of these scanners, it's necessary to remember only the edge of your last image if you're "stitching" together multiple scans. As I say earlier in this chapter, lining up and connecting multiple scans is both tiresome and less precise than using a flatbed scanner, so I'm assuming that you're a road warrior and you're using your hand scanner with a laptop.

If someone has given you an older hand scanner from the misty dawn of time (that is, the early 1990s), I *implore* you to toss it and invest in a flatbed model (unless, of course, you need it while traveling). Join the rest of us in Convenience City and leave the hassle behind! That garage sale hand scanner can't deliver the color depth or resolution of a modern flatbed scanner, and scanning an original any larger than about four inches across is likely to drive you nuts, which is why they're now virtually extinct.

Make with the Settings

With the original aligned and your cover closed — that is, if you have a cover — it's time to turn your attention to the software end of things. Your first task at the keyboard is to properly tune a handful of settings that control your scanner-capture software. As I mention earlier in this chapter, the default settings may work fine, although I want to cover the bare necessities here — just in case. (That's the kind of guy I am. I'm the type who has an eyeglass screwdriver handy when he needs it.)

In this section, I use the Macintosh version of the Microtek ScanWizard. Believe it or not, the Mac version of this great scanner-control program is almost identical to the Windows version; this makes it especially valuable to us rogues of the computer world who give both platforms equal time. Therefore, you should be able to follow along easily if you use this program, no matter which breed of computer you favor.

If, on the other hand, you don't use this program, this discussion is still valuable, so don't go away! Your program's buttons, levers, dials, and associated sliding things may be called something slightly different, although they should be there somewhere, and they have the same effects on your scanned image. If you need help in locating a particular sliding thing, use the program's online help or check the software's manual.

Note: If you have a one-button scanner, you could conceivably skip forward to the section "Look, Ma — One Button!" After all, most one-button models try to automate things as much as possible, so you may not have to change any settings or select a region to scan. I prefer that you go ahead and read through this section, however, because you have to use these procedures if you switch to your scanner's more advanced modes (where everything automatic suddenly becomes manually controlled, and you separate the tourists from the locals).

For my first scanning demonstration, I pick a common original: a color print from my collection. This print is a great photo of the last drive-in movie theater in my hometown of Columbia, Missouri. It's gone now, replaced by a parking lot. (Sigh.) Anyway, I show you how to scan this photograph in preparation for sending it across the Internet through e-mail to a friend. Follow these steps to choose your settings:

1. **Click the ScanWizard icon on your desktop to run the program.**

   After making that curious noise, your scanner makes a quick pass over the original and the Standard Control Panel, shown in Figure 6-6, appears; notice that the program has already selected the area of the original it thinks you want to scan. (Don't worry if the selected region surrounded by the animated dotted rectangle is incorrect. Later in this chapter, in the section "Choosing a Chunk," I show you how to select what you want.)

   Note the lower right corner of the panel. You see a square symbol that looks like an arrow pointing to the upper left. You can click and drag this corner of the panel to resize the entire window. Do this now if you want the panel a little larger or smaller.

2. **Click the Original button to check your first setting.**

   This step specifies what type of original material you're scanning and helps the program determine a default for the other settings. In this case, choose Photo.

3. **Click ScanType to choose the color depth.**

   The program allows you to choose True Color (16 million colors or 24-bit), Web Color (256 colors or 8-bit), Gray (grayscale or halftone), or Black & White (text documents). ***Remember:*** The more colors, the larger the image file; if you want your digital image to look its best, however, choose True Color.

4. **Click the Purpose button to set the dpi range for your image.**

   You can select from a wide range of applications or choose Custom to set your own dpi. Because this image is destined for display on the screen, pick Onscreen viewing, which sets the dpi to 72.

5. **The Scale Output button determines the relative size of the scanned image relative to the original. Leave this button set to 100% unless you're scanning something particularly small, like a business card.**

That's all you need to set — at least for a quick scan using the basic settings. At the bottom of the window, you see a summary line that presents the following settings information:

- The type of original you chose
- The actual size of the selected region
- The scale output setting you chose

- The dpi you chose
- The approximate size (just an estimate) of the image file to be created with these settings

You may have noticed that you didn't mess with the Adjust button. That's because it displays a number of advanced settings that I describe in detail in Chapters 8 and 9. Usually, you don't even need to adjust them anyway, as long as your original is sharp and the colors are bright.

Let me mention one more button in this section: The Reset button resets to their defaults all the values the program uses, so if you need to start over, give this button a click.

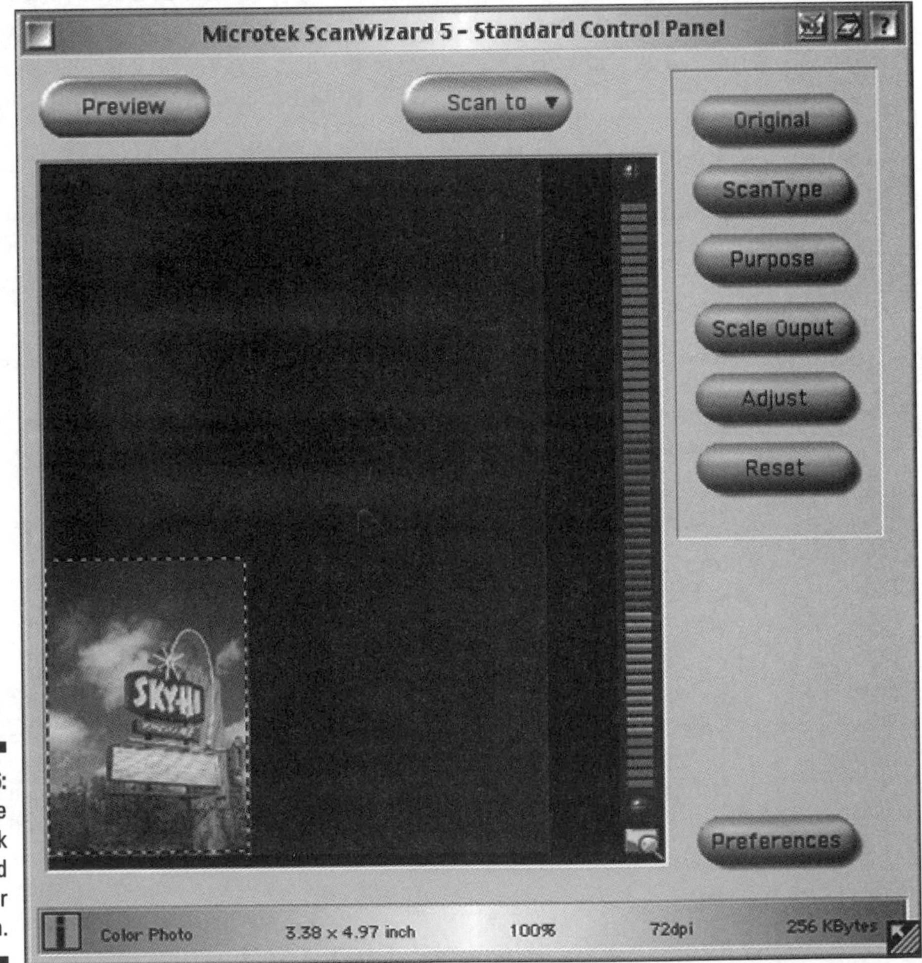

Figure 6-6: The Microtek ScanWizard is ready for action.

Previewing on Parade

That small thumbnail image of your original is called a *preview*. You use it to select the region of the original you want to scan. However, it doesn't have to stay thumbnail-sized — ScanWizard allows you to zoom in on the original for a closer look, which also gives you finer control over the region you select. For example, you may want to scan a single piece of clip art from an entire sheet. Why scan that entire page when you can simply zoom in on the one drawing you want and select it?

At the right side of the Preview window, you see a segmented control that looks something like a bar graph. At the top of this bar is a plus sign, and a minus sign is at the bottom. To zoom in on your original, you can either click directly on the bar — the higher you go up the bar, the more you zoom — or you can click on the plus button at the top to move to the next highest level of magnification. To zoom out, click a lower setting on the bar or click the minus button to move to the next lowest level of magnification.

Under the minus button, a panning button allows you to move the Preview window around at the higher magnifications. This button looks like a triangle with a magnifying glass. If you zoom in and your Preview window is no longer over the area where it should be, click the panning button, move the window wherever you want, and click again to center the window on that portion of the original.

Compare Figure 6-7 with Figure 6-6, which uses the default preview. In Figure 6-7, I've clicked the plus key twice and used the panning button to center the preview on the words *Sky-Hi* so that I can scan just that area of the original photograph.

If you decide that you need to switch originals, you don't have to restart ScanWizard to preview the new material. Just click the Preview button, and your scanner makes another pass and displays the new original.

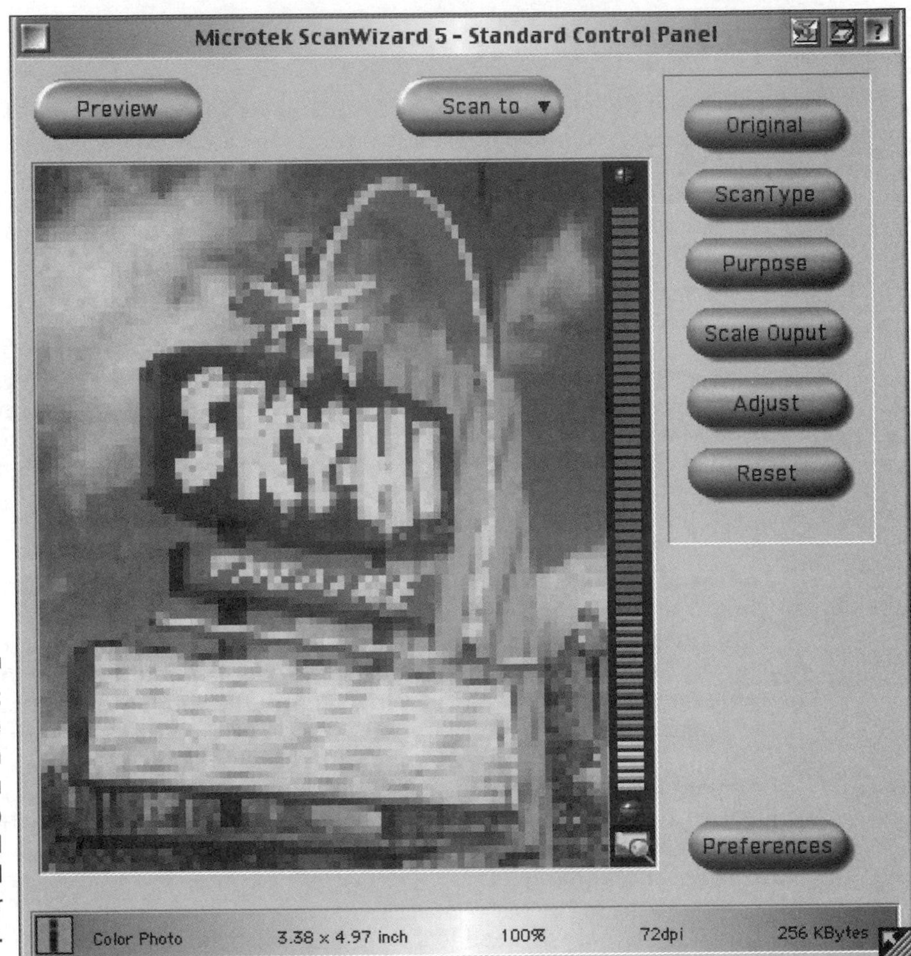

Figure 6-7: With the Zoom feature, you can get up close and personal with your preview.

Choosing a Chunk

Okay, you've set everything, and your preview is centered right where you need it. But what if the animated dotted box (called a *selection box*) is not over the right area? ScanWizard takes its best shot at guessing what you want to scan on your original, although that's sometimes not the right region. You can select a new square or rectangular region of the original to scan in one of three ways:

- **Click and drag the existing selection box:** If the box is the right size and shape (and just in the wrong place), you can move it to a new spot on the original. Move your mouse cursor over the box, and it turns into a special cursor that points in all four directions. Click and drag the cursor to move the box where you want it, and then release the mouse button to "drop" the box in its new location.

- **Resize the existing selection box:** If the box is in the right place (and just too big or too small), you can resize it. Move your mouse cursor over the edge of the box you want to change. This time, the cursor turns into a special cursor that indicates the two directions in which that edge can move. If you click over a corner, you can resize both edges (just like you can resize a window in Windows or Mac OS). Click and drag the cursor to move the edge or corner to the desired size and release the mouse button.
- **Create a new selection box:** You can also discard the existing selection box and create a new one. Move your mouse cursor anywhere outside the box, and it turns into a crosshair. Click and drag to open a new box.

Naturally, in most cases, you simply want the selection box to cover the entire original from edge to edge, and this is the assumption the program makes when it creates the default selection.

Doing the Scan Thing

Houston, everything is go! The original is in place with the cover down, the settings are correct, and you've chosen the region of the original you want to scan. It's time to do the Scanner Dance. Follow these steps:

1. **Click the Scan to button at the top of the ScanWizard panel and choose the Scan to command from the pop-up menu.**

   The Mac version of the program displays the dialog box you see in Figure 6-8. If you're using the Windows version of ScanWizard, you see the familiar Windows Save As dialog box instead. (This just makes good sense.)

2. **After you've navigated to the proper location, enter a new filename for your scanned image.**

   In this case, I named my image `relic`. You don't need to add the extension `.jpg` because the program adds it automatically.

3. **Choose the output format for the image.**

   On the Mac, click the Format drop-down list box. In Windows, click the File Type drop-down list box. Because you want photo quality and a small file size, choose JPEG.

   All is ready!

4. **Click Save to begin the scanning process.**

   The program displays a progress bar to update you on what's being done.

Figure 6-8: Selecting a destination for your new image.

After the image is scanned, you can close ScanWizard and admire your new work of art. Note that you should be able to view a JPEG without an image editor if you're running Windows 98 (or later) or Mac OS 8 (or later). Figure 6-9 shows off my image, ready for my e-mail Outbox. The image is a whopping 200K, so it fits as a message attachment with room to spare!

If your first scanned image isn't quite perfect, don't worry — remember that this chapter covers only the basic scanning procedure! In later chapters, I cover the tool you can use to enhance your images and fix problems (both great and small) in your work: the image editor, tool of scanning veterans around the world!

Figure 6-9: "Relic," copyright 2000 by Mark L. Chambers.

Look, Ma — One Button!

Before I close this chapter, I want to talk about one-button scanning, which I introduce in Chapter 2. In purely automatic mode, which is the default for most of these scanners, you can forget most of the steps I cover in the last three sections, if you've read them. The software for a one-button scanner takes care of configuring settings and usually checks the entire original to make sure that all text and graphics are included, so you probably don't even have to select a region to scan.

Although the basic scanning procedure naturally varies by manufacturer, here's a typical scanning procedure on a one-button model:

1. Load the original document and press the automatic scanning button on the scanner.
2. A program running in the background within Windows or Mac OS detects that the button has been pressed and loads the scanner's control software.
3. The scanning software automatically previews the original and selects what it considers the major area (or areas) of text and graphics.

4. At this point, you may be given the chance to adjust the selection box to better fit your needs — or the software may blissfully continue without any intervention from you. (This option depends on the manufacturer's idea of what the phrase "one-button" *really* means.) You may be able to configure your scanner software to work both ways.

5. After the scanning has finished, the software usually concludes with one of five actions (depending on what you pressed and how you've configured the scanning software):

   - **The program displays the Save As dialog box.** You're given the chance to save the image to disk, as I just described.
   - **The program runs a word processor.** As I mention earlier in this chapter, many of these scanners advertise that they can create a nearly perfect duplicate of a printed document as a document in your word processor (using simple scanning for images and a simple OCR program for the text). With this option, your computer runs Word, WordPerfect, AppleWorks, or a page-layout program and "pours" the document directly into it. From there, you can modify and edit the document just as you would do with a page you write yourself.
   - **The program creates a copy.** If your scanner has a one-button copy function, the image it scans should shoot directly to your printer without any intervention from you.
   - **The program runs a fax program.** Some scanners deliver one-button faxing as well, although this isn't, of course, a completely automatic procedure. You press the fax button on your scanner, which runs your fax program and sends the document using your computer's modem.
   - **The program runs an e-mail program.** Here's another wrinkle on the one-button idea: Pressing the e-mail button on your scanner runs your e-mail program and attaches the scanned image to a new message. Neat!

All this is neat, as long as your scanner's software allows you to do more. If you find yourself unable to use a "fully automatic," one-button scanner in other chapters because of the programs you received with it, use another TWAIN-compatible scanner-capture program (like Paint Shop Pro). You still have your buttons when you need 'em, but you can also explore the advanced image-editing and creative techniques I demonstrate in Chapters 9, 11, and 13!

Chapter 7 helps explain why all originals are not the same — and how you should handle the differences between line art, drawings, color photographs, halftones, and black-and-white photographs.

Chapter 7

Examining Your Original: The Sequel

In This Chapter

- Understanding how originals differ
- Scanning line art
- Scanning color and grayscale photographs
- Scanning halftones
- Scanning 3-D objects
- Scanning text

It's time to expand your horizons and move into more advanced material. Translated, that reads "Ready for another of my scanning rules?" Okay, here it is: *All originals are not scanned equally.* (If Shakespeare himself had owned a scanner, he would have included this weighty thought in one of those plays he was continually writing.)

What do I mean by that? Different types of original material need different treatment to provide the same quality in the finished image. For example, if you scan three different originals — a color photo, a pencil drawing, and a military shoulder patch, for example — using the same settings, you end up with three dramatically different results, and two of those images are probably of poor quality.

In Chapter 6, I tell you that you should always examine your original, and in this chapter, I discuss how to expand that examination a step further than simply checking for tape, staples, or creases. In this chapter, you study the media used to create the image itself.

So What's the Difference?

Why do originals created using different media have different requirements? You can sum up the variation between media using three criteria:

- **Shading:** Shades, tones, graduations — call them what you will, some originals have them (like photographs), and others don't (like line drawings).
- **Texture:** If you're scanning a three-dimensional object — and by that term, I mean any original that's not perfectly flat, like a plain piece of paper — it likely has some sort of texture. A certain depth to the texture is desirable, although a texture that's too deep can produce heavy shadows. Also, if a portion of the original is significantly farther away from the scanner glass, like a dinner plate, you end up with fuzzy spots in your image. (Why scan a dinner plate? I've done it: Ever attempted to describe a china pattern that's not in the book?)
- **Color:** Originals have more variety than you may think when it comes to color: Besides just simple color and black-and-white (or *monochrome,* as graphic artists call it), you also have to deal with grayscale and halftones. I get into these topics later in this chapter, in the section "Scanning Halftones."

With that in mind, three scanner settings also vary between these different media. (Weird how that works out that way, doesn't it? Perhaps those theories of visits from ancient astronauts have some truth to them.) The settings are shown in this list:

- **Color depth:** You may remember the point I make earlier in this book about scanning a blank piece of paper in stunning 24-bit color. You get a huge image file filled with more than 16 million possible shades of white, of which your image likely uses only a handful. The same rule applies here: If you're working with a monochrome original (like a black-and-white line drawing or a blueprint), you don't need the same color depth as in a color photograph. That savings translates into a smaller image file at any resolution.

  In one case, more colors with a monochrome document may make sense: You can often improve the performance of an OCR program slightly by scanning a page of text in 24-bit color, *if* the original page was printed on an inkjet printer. Why? Two reasons: First, a typical inkjet printer often doesn't produce a "true" black, especially if you're printing black with a color cartridge on an older printer. Second, subtle differences in color often exist across the text on a page, especially if your printer's cartridge is low on ink. On the other hand, because a laser printer produces a true black character, you can use fewer colors when you're scanning OCR text from a page produced by a laser printer.

- **dpi:** It's generally true that the higher the dpi, the better the image — but what if you're going to view your scanned image on your computer's monitor? Most computer monitors can display a maximum of around 72 to 90 dpi (depending on how much you spent on that high-resolution screen). Anything more is overkill. Generally, a higher dpi produces significantly better results when you're scanning line art.
- **Color balance:** The third setting that helps tailor your scan to your original image is a new setting — and it may not be offered by your scanning software, so you may have to adjust color balance with an image editor after the scan is complete. If your original image includes colors that are not true to life — for example, a color print taken under harsh fluorescent light, a faded or sepia original, or a printed image produced without color correction (like an inkjet printer using a single cartridge) — you need to adjust the balance. This process is handled differently depending on the software: Some programs can perform automatic color balancing, others let you make the changes manually, and a few require you to specify the color of "absolute white" in your image before you can make adjustments.

That covers the scanning settings used in this chapter. One or two affect only one type of original material, and I point those out when necessary.

Without further ado, then, I want to cover each major type of original material you're likely to encounter and demonstrate how to configure your scanning software for the best possible results with each material. (If you don't want me to do this for some reason — for example, if you were frightened by a piece of line art when you were a child — you can certainly turn to Chapter 8, although you'll miss some great stuff.)

Scanning Line Art

By the strictest definition of the graphics world, *line art* is material drawn in black and white with no shading or tones, like the ink-on-plain-paper masterpiece shown in Figure 7-1. (I'm no critic, but I know what I like, and anything my kids turn out is art.)

However, what's interpreted as line art in the real world can include a host of other possibilities:

- **Blueprints and diagrams:** If you scan traditional white-on-blue blueprints, you should follow the same guidelines for line art.
- **Charcoal, felt-tip pen, and colored pencil:** Regardless of the two colors used, I usually scan these as line art (as long as the contrast between the colors is high).
- **Cartoons:** A cartoon produced without shading (for example, a classic *Dilbert* or *Peanuts* cartoon) looks best when it's scanned as line art.

Figure 7-1: Look out, Leonardo — a piece of "true" line art.

Perhaps a better definition of line art would be an original with images drawn in contrasting colors, featuring crisp borders, heavy lines, and little or no shading. With this definition, the familiar graphics of a playing card that I've scanned in Figure 7-2 also (rightly) qualifies as line art.

Here are the guidelines you should follow in choosing settings for scanning line art:

- **Color depth:** A maximum of 256 colors (or 8-bit color) should be sufficient for virtually all line art. As I mention earlier in this chapter, this setting should also result in a smaller image file.
- **dpi:** For line art, I recommend a setting of 72 dpi for on-screen display. If you're sending your image to your inkjet or laser printer, 200 to 300 dpi is a good pick.
- **Color balance:** If you follow that strict definition of line art, color balance is not applicable: You have only black lines on white or one color on another.

If, however, you're scanning an original that uses multiple colors on a white background that's really *not* white — perhaps it's oyster or cream — you may need to adjust the color balance if you want a true white background. I run into this extra step most often with originals destined to be transparent GIF

Figure 7-2: Although it's not black-and-white, this playing card counts as line art.

images for Web pages. For example, if the page has a pure white background, an image scanned without this correction is surrounded by an obvious border of a slightly darker white.

Scanning Color and Grayscale Photographs

Full-color photographs are probably the most popular class of originals for most people. This category includes

- **Film prints:** Before digital cameras dropped so much in price, I got several years' worth of experience in scanning color prints. For example, Figure 7-3 is the scan I made of a scenic photograph taken atop Hoover Dam.

  Note: Please bear with me for just a second — it's time for another plug! If you want a complete guide to digital cameras for the novice or intermediate photographer, pick up a copy of my *Hewlett-Packard Digital Photography Handbook,* published by — you guessed it — Hungry Minds, Inc.

- **Continuous-tone images:** This type covers everything from originals created by expensive, thermal wax printers to oil paintings. *Continuous tone* means that the colors and detail in the image are, well, blended and continuous! To be more specific, a continuous tone image isn't created by grouping dots together — that's the definition of a *halftone* original, which I cover later in this chapter, in the section "Scanning Halftones." Most photographs produced in books and magazines are halftone images. As you may have guessed, this type also eliminates inkjet and laser printers from the color photograph category because they create images using dots.
- **Slides, transparencies, and negatives:** As I mention earlier in this book, you need either a negative scanner (for just slides and photograph negatives) or a slide/transparency adapter (for all three types of transparent originals) to properly scan these materials. The reason? The original has to be illuminated differently from an opaque original; hence, the hardware.

Figure 7-3: A scanned image from a color photograph.

If you're configuring your scanning software to capture a color photograph, I recommend these settings:

- **Color depth:** Here's where you need the full-color-depth firepower of your scanner. Use the true color setting, which should result in a minimum of 24-bit color. Naturally, your image file will be larger, but that's the penalty you pay a for photo-quality color scan.

- **dpi:** For the same reasons as line art, a setting of 72 dpi for on-screen display (which includes Web page display) is fine for your color photographs. However, I always recommend at least 300 dpi for a good-quality scan, and I have taken my system to as high as 1200 dpi for some materials.
- **Color balance:** If the colors in the original are appreciably out of balance (a green cast to a person's face, perhaps), it's time to correct the color balance in the finished image. As I say earlier in this chapter, you may be able to accomplish this balance by using your scanning software; you can also look for a control that can set white balance or perform hue correction. If your scanning software can't fix a color balance problem, you have to load the scanned image into your image editor and fix it there.

I should also mention *grayscale* photographs. They're the familiar black-and-white film counterparts to the color photographs I've been discussing. Grayscale images also provide continuous tones, although the tones are 256 shades of gray (8-bit) rather than color. Grayscale images can also be printed with colored inks (typically gray or blue as well as black) as a special effect. These "tinted" images are called *duotones.*

- **Color depth:** If your scanner allows you to capture grayscale as a selection for color depth (for example, the Microtek software I use offers Gray as a scan type), you should use this setting. However, if you're forced into a color depth, I recommend that you use 24-bit color and convert the image to true grayscale using your image editor.
- **dpi:** dpi settings for grayscale remain the same as with a color photograph: 72 dpi for onscreen display and at least 300 dpi for a good-quality scan for printing or archiving.
- **Color balance:** Naturally, you don't have to bother with balancing color in a grayscale image, although you may decide to experiment with brightness, contrast, and gamma correction. They can have a similar effect on the shades of gray. For example, you may use a combination of gamma correction and contrast to rescue an original grayscale image that's overexposed — too light. (Read more about this subject in Chapter 8.) Unfortunately, if your grayscale image is underexposed — too dark — you may not be able to save it at all because increasing the brightness doesn't add detail to a muddy image.

Scanning Halftones

As I explain in the preceding section, halftone images are composed of thousands of tiny dots of varying sizes, which the human eye perceives — at least, at a distance — as a continuous range of color or monochrome shades. (Notice that I don't call them photographs. This distinction helps keep halftone originals separate from the continuous-tone originals I discuss earlier in this chapter.)

Here are three classic examples of halftones:

- **Output from your inkjet printer:** If you've read Chapter 5, do you remember that I talk about resolution when I discuss printers? Like your monitor, today's inkjet printers produce an image with dots. These dots are so fine that they're smaller than the point of a pin, but they're there.

  "Wait just a second, Mark — you said a page or so ago that something called a thermal wax printer could print a continuous-tone photograph! How does it do that?" The answer is in the semifluid nature of the wax dye that's applied to the paper. The dye flows together to blend into continuous shades, whereas the ink from an inkjet printer dries immediately. (This is the reason that printing color images on your inkjet using glossy photo paper produces better results: The ink spreads slightly before it dries instead of soaking into the paper.) Of course, a thermal wax (or dye sublimation) graphics printer is liable to set you back $5,000 or $6,000, so you pay for that quality!

- **An image in a newspaper or magazine:** Does Figure 7-4 look familiar? It's a magnified example of the kind of halftone you've come to expect from the front page of your newspaper — no continuous tones here! The glossy pages of your favorite magazines are also halftones, although you may have to use a good magnifying glass to see them. It depends on the quality of the paper and the type of press that produced the page.
- **Images in books:** That's right — check out any of the figures in this book with a magnifying glass (except for 7-4, or else you'll wear your eyes out). Of course, the presses that produce the book you're holding are state-of-the-art, so most of us never notice.

Scanning a halftone image calls for these settings:

- **Color depth:** Like a continuous-tone photograph, a halftone benefits from 24-bit color. Anything less could accentuate the dots in the original and produce a truly ghastly image. (I've seen this done on purpose, although only as a special effect!)
- **dpi:** Here's where things get dicey. Because of the dots that make up a halftone image, scanning at too high a resolution *degrades* the quality of the image rather than improves it. I typically choose 150 dpi or less when I'm scanning a halftone; depending on the quality of the original, you may have to experiment before you hit on a value that properly preserves the appearance.
- **Color balance:** Although the shades of color aren't continuous, they can still be fine-tuned in a color halftone using the same techniques as in a photograph: the built-in color-balance controls in your scanning software or the color-balance controls offered by your image editor.

Figure 7-4: Nice kitty — at least, I *think* it's a kitten.

Scanning 3-D Objects

You may not scan solid 3-D objects very often — how many people buy a scanner to create gargantuan, high-resolution images of a toothbrush or a floppy disk? However, scanning an object can also save you the trouble of digging through your collection of clip art, trying to find the perfect picture. If the object is sitting on your desk, why not scan your own clip art?

Friends of mine have used their scanners to capture images of items for eBay auctions and to create photos for their home inventory records. A woman I know even uses her scanner as a tool in her hobbies by scanning interesting fabric patterns and objects for her photo collages. In fact, forget what I said a second ago. If you don't have a digital camera, you *may* end up scanning solid, 3-D objects often!

Are you the proud owner of a sheet-fed scanner? SKIP THIS SECTION. (By the way, that's the only sentence in this entire book that's completely capitalized.) No matter how tempting, scanning anything that's not perfectly flat and thicker than card stock is very likely to result in a *seriously damaged* sheet-fed scanner!

What makes a suitable object for scanning? Three general requirements apply:

- **At least one reasonably flat surface:** You won't be scanning the Venus de Milo any time soon — Figure 7-5 illustrates what happens when you try to capture a 3-D figure with deep crevices. (That's my bust of Samuel Clemens, also known as Mark Twain, that provides me with inspiration while I'm writing.) A scanner can't focus on surface details that are far-removed from the glass, so your object needs one recognizable surface that can rest fairly close to the glass, like the floppy disk shown in Figure 7-6. Use a digital camera for the Venus.
- **Surface detail:** "Ach, Cap'n, I just don't think the scanner can *see* anything. I need more power!" Scotty's got a point: Without at least some surface detail, your scanner can't capture anything more than a general outline. As an example, scanning a bar of soap gives you a really nice rectangle, and because it has little or no surface detail, that's it. Scanning the label on a compact disc, on the other hand, captures the text and design. Other favorite originals include textured paper products and cloth, like the woven item shown in Figure 7-7.
- **Little or no reflectivity:** Even a perfectly flat original with reflective regions causes some problems because the reflected light tends to overwhelm the scanner head, producing phantom light spots in the scanned image (an effect I like to call *white-out*). Therefore, scanning a highly reflective 3-D item, like a piece of jewelry or a shiny toy, *definitely* doesn't work. Adding distance to the mix creates a mixture of shadows and reflections as the scanner head moves across the original.

Figure 7-5: Sorry, Sam. You're my favorite author, but you're just not scanner material.

Figure 7-6: Hey, remember when software used to come on these?

Figure 7-7: Textiles can produce interesting patterns for Web page back-grounds and such.

If you do have to scan an original with reflective areas, you can use one of two work-arounds to avoid white-out. You can reduce the brightness setting in your scanner software — or, if you don't need the reflective area, simply resize the selection box and don't scan that area.

Although scanning a 3-D object probably requires more experimentation than just about any class of original in this chapter, I can at least steer you in the right direction with these guidelines:

- **Color depth:** Even if your 3-D original is made of a single material, I recommend that you use 24-bit color to capture the image — especially if the surface detail is textured, embossed, or inscribed rather than painted or printed, so that the shading can help define the surface.
- **dpi:** Unlike scanning a "herd of dots" (as my college journalism professor used to call a halftone), scanning a 3-D object calls for a higher dpi setting; you need it to capture fine detail, especially if the surface is textured.
- **Color balance:** Not a problem here. Your scanner produces a pure white light, so your colors with a 3-D object should be spot-on.

Most flatbed scanners now come equipped with a cover that can be raised to accommodate 3-D items that are several inches thick. Even though a space may exist between the glass and the cover, lowering the cover when you're scanning a thick object is still a good idea.

Scanning Text

Welcome to my discussion of that perennial office favorite, the text document. I discuss and demonstrate OCR in Chapter 13; for now, consider what types of text originals you're likely to encounter:

- **Office documents:** Although inkjet printers are making inroads into the business world, the laser printer is still the workhorse around most offices, and that means sharp, consistently black text at a snappy 600 x 600 dpi. It's not too shabby, and it's easy to scan, as you can see in Figure 7-8!
- **Faxed material:** Documents you've received via fax are more akin to halftone photographs than they are to typical text documents. Most folks have noticed that transmitting a document results in a grainy appearance on the receiving end and that text printed in all except the largest font sizes generally loses its sharpness. (This is one reason that it's often difficult to use a faxed document for OCR work.)

DATE

MEMO

Compare the laser-printed text with this writing!

SIGNED

Figure 7-8: Crisp text and nice, dark, uniform black — it must be laser-printed text!

- **Business cards:** Generally, you have no problem scanning a traditional business card with black lettering on a white background. You may need to adjust the color balance, however, if you're scanning a card with a colored background or colored text to yield a "white" background or "black" letters. For example, Figure 7-9 shows a scan of one of my business cards. It's printed with raised green lettering on a green background, and you can see that reflected in the quality of the scan. By adjusting the color balance and contrast level before I scanned the card, however, I was able to clean things up considerably, as you can see in Figure 7-10. (Alternatively, I could have scanned the card to produce a grayscale image, although the image would have still needed the contrast adjustments.)

  Logos and other artwork on a business card should be scanned as line art.

- **Books and magazines:** Scanning text from a book or magazine page can be challenging, especially if the text falls in the middle pages of a thick book, where the page curls away from the binding and you can "lose" characters. (Try to flatten the original as much as possible, but don't put too much pressure on your scanner's glass.) Also, you may have to adjust the brightness and contrast settings to pick up colored text in a magazine or text that's printed with a photograph as a background.

Figure 7-9: A "raw" scan of my business card — because of the text and background colors, it needs contrast.

Figure 7-10: New, improved, and even fresher smelling — well, at least the text is black and the background is white.

When you're scanning the most common text — black characters on a white background — use these settings:

- **Color depth:** As I mention earlier in this chapter, use 24-bit color for scanning text (even if you're not planning on using the image for OCR). One exception exists: If you're planning to fax the image of a document you're scanning, drop your image to 8-bit color to minimize the size of the file. It takes less time to transfer, and (unless the receiving end of your transmission is a color fax machine) those extra colors are wasted.

- **dpi:** I recommend 75 dpi for scanning a text document, which is all the resolution you really need. If photographs are included along with the text in the same document, however, there's no reason that you can't crank up the dpi setting as necessary.
- **Color balance:** You can use the same color-balancing techniques I suggest for color photographs to change the appearance of colored text. (In an extreme case, like hot pink letters mixed with olive drab, a grayscale scan can do the trick as well.)

If you want to use all the advanced features of your scanning software to make the adjustments I talk about in this chapter, see Chapter 8! I cover these procedures step-by-step using the Microtek scanning software.

Chapter 8

Attack of the Fine-Tuning Monster

In This Chapter

- Specifying resolution
- Setting colors and color depth
- Adjusting brightness and contrast
- Choosing an image size
- Balancing color
- Applying filters
- Flipping and rotating
- Adjusting tones
- Correcting saturation

In Chapter 6, I show you scanning in its simplest form, using the default settings. That chapter is fun, but now that you may be seasoned and more experienced, it's time to tackle those originals that may need fine-tuning before you can scan them properly. To do that, you have to explore the true power of your scanning software by using its advanced features.

In this chapter, I do just that with Microtek ScanWizard: I move from Standard mode, which you may have already used, into the more complex and powerful Advanced mode, which offers you complete control over the scanning environment. I demonstrate each of the advanced controls, and you see their effect on a representative scanned image.

Are All These Advanced Settings Really Necessary?

In a word, "No" — but *only* if one or more of the following criteria is met:

- **Your original happens to be well suited to the default settings used by your scanning software.** This situation is often the case. However, as you find out in Chapter 7, a wide range of originals require special attention to achieve the best results.
- **Your scanner sets these controls automatically.** Some scanner-control programs try their best to deduce which settings are right for the original — but I can't say that I've seen them do better than a smart monkey with a dartboard. Besides, if the software cannot automatically correct a problem, you have to know how to change the settings in this chapter anyway.
- **You don't care about the quality of your scanned image.** I know that this statement isn't true, or else you wouldn't be reading this book!

I obviously consider this chapter to be required reading. However, it's fine if you want to use your scanner's Standard mode. Just use these advanced settings whenever necessary.

Switching to Advanced Mode

Before I can start discussing a boatload of advanced settings, you have to be able to see them first. In this section, I show you how to reconfigure ScanWizard to display the Advanced mode menu.

Note: What I say in Chapter 6 about the basic controls in ScanWizard is true here, too: Your scanning software's controls may be labeled differently, but most programs do have these features, and they have the same effect on the final image. Some programs don't have Advanced mode — everything is grouped together instead. No big deal! Use the program's online help or check the software's manual to determine whether you can make a similar setting change within your program (and where that setting is located on the menu).

Follow these steps:

1. **Click the ScanWizard icon on your desktop to run the program.**

   The familiar Standard Control Panel appears.

2. **Locate the Switch button in the top right corner of the ScanWizard window. It shows a blue square with a red arrow pointing to a gray square. Click this button once.**

After a second or two, ScanWizard switches to Advanced mode, displaying the window shown in Figure 8-1. (Although this is the Windows version of the program, Mac users have the same controls in the same spot.)

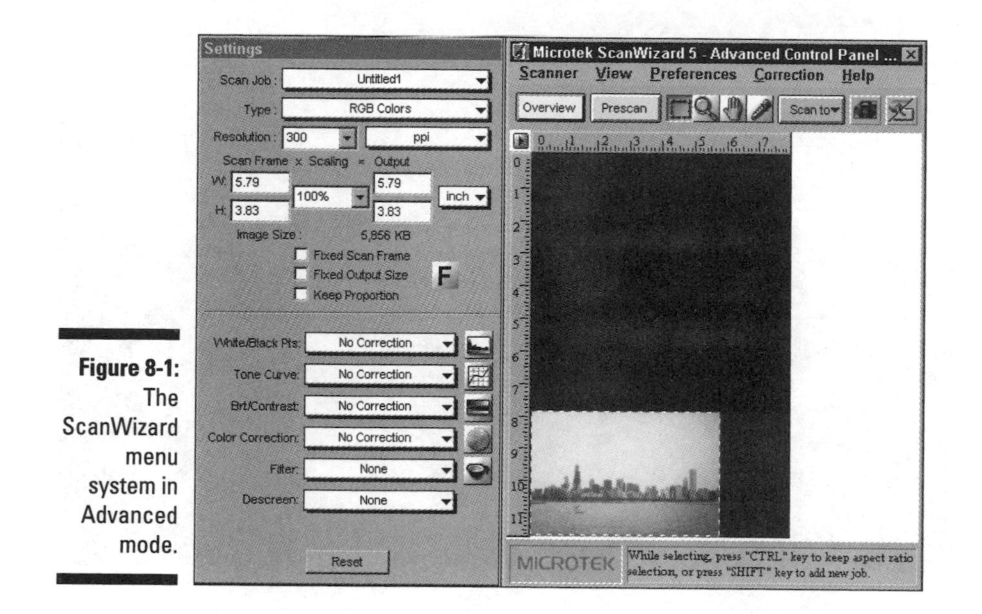

Figure 8-1: The ScanWizard menu system in Advanced mode.

To switch back to Standard mode at any time, click the Switch button again.

Oh — I Almost Forgot!

Figure 8-2 shows another favorite photograph from my album: the beautiful, scenic skyline of Chicago, complete with the world's tallest building. I chose this image because it has a wide range of shading and plenty of detail you can use.

I scanned this photograph using the default settings for a color photograph in ScanWizard so that you have a frame of reference for the different effects produced in this chapter. The settings were

- Twenty-four-bit color
- Two hundred (200) dpi
- No adjustments made to brightness, contrast, sharpness, color, or saturation

Figure 8-2: The fair city of Chicago, as scanned with untouched default settings.

Setting Your Resolution

In Advanced mode, you can set not only your resolution but also the unit of measurement. The Resolution controls are shown in Figure 8-3.

Figure 8-3: Give me a close-up on the Resolution controls!

Selecting the unit of measurement

To choose a unit of measurement for the scanning resolution, click the drop-down list box on the right side of the Res field and click the unit you want to use. I highly recommend that you stick with ppi (short for pixels per inch, which, as you already know, is another moniker for the dots-per-inch [dpi] standard I use throughout this book). However, if you want to scan by lines per inch, choose one of the lpi measurements.

Selecting a preset resolution

To select a measurement from the program's preset levels, click the button with the up-and-down arrows next to the Res field to display the pop-up menu and click the resolution you want. You can choose from 72, 100, 150, 300, 600, 1000, and 1200 ppi.

Entering a specific resolution

You can also click directly in the Res field and enter a specific resolution. The values for ppi range from 10 to 9600 dpi.

To illustrate a range of resolution, Figure 8-4 shows the Chicago skyline at a whopping 20 dpi, and Figure 8-5 shows it off at 600 dpi. Boy, those extra dots do make a difference, don't they?

Figure 8-4: Man, talk about rough edges — 20 dpi is barely recognizable!

Figure 8-5: At this image size, no difference exists between 200 dpi and 600 dpi.

By the way, I should mention that I had to resize both these images for reference so that they match the size shown in Figure 8-2. In reality, 20 dpi produced an image with a total size of only 105 x 78, and the 600 dpi image was 3012 x 2251!

Now, really, why would anyone in her right mind want to scan something at 20 dpi? Well, I give you two good reasons — and both are related to the Web. First, you may use a low resolution if you want to use images as buttons on your Web page. This trick also comes in handy if you want to offer an index of *thumbnails* (small versions of images that are about the size of your thumb); a visitor to your page clicks the thumbnail to download a larger version of the same image. Your images are still recognizable, although they're tiny, and they load in a Web browser much faster than larger images.

Note that Figure 8-5 looks exactly the same as Figure 8-2, which you may remember was scanned at 200 dpi! What effect did all those 400 extra dots per inch make? The final image at 600 dpi was much bigger, but after it's resized to the same image size of 800 x 600, the human eye can discern literally no difference. However, the differences in file sizes are incredible: The 200 dpi image was a mere 1.3MB, and the 600 dpi version was more than 21MB!

Colors and Bits, Colors and Bits

Take a look at the control shown in Figure 8-6. Although the control is cleverly disguised with the name Type, you should click this drop-down list box to set the color depth for your scan.

Type: RGB Colors

Figure 8-6: You can select a color depth from the Type control.

You use the RGB Colors setting for most work. That's yet another way of saying 24-bit or true color, which provides as many as 16.7 million colors. (I don't recommend that you use the 48-bit option unless you're sure that your image editor supports it.) The other options include

- **Grayscale:** Use this option for 8-bit, 256 shades of gray. Again, don't use the 16-bit Grayscale option unless your image editor can handle it.
- **Web/Internet Colors:** Choose this option for a 256-color image that's optimized for use on a Web page. ScanWizard uses a special selection of colors (called a *palette*) that's supported by Netscape and Internet Explorer.
- **256 colors:** Use this option for your average, standard 8-bit color depth.
- **Line Art:** As I explain in Chapter 7, you use this setting for black-on-white drawings (or any other high-contrast color on a solid background color).
- **B&W Diffusion:** You and I know this option as a black-and-white halftone that simulates shades of gray — not to be confused with true grayscale. Figure 8-7 shows the demonstration photograph scanned with this setting.

Figure 8-7: A black-and-white halftone version of the photograph.

The Light and the Dark

I don't say much elsewhere about brightness and contrast because your scanning software may not allow you to adjust these two settings. However, I have good news: If you find that your scanning program doesn't support them, you can always use your image editor to make changes to them instead!

If you're using ScanWizard, you can control brightness and contrast before the scan. Follow these steps:

1. **Click the button to the right of the Brt/Contrast drop-down list box to display the Advanced Image Correction dialog box, as shown in Figure 8-8.**
2. **If the Thumbnails and Preview check boxes aren't enabled, click both to check them.**
3. **Move either slider control by clicking and dragging it. Alternatively, you can click in the Percentage field and enter an exact value.**

Notice that ScanWizard automatically updates the image on the right as you change the value, allowing you to gauge the effect the setting will have on your scan.

4. **After you've made the changes to the levels and you like what you see, click OK to accept the settings and return to the Advanced menu.**

   If, on the other hand, you don't like the results, click Revert to return to the original settings.

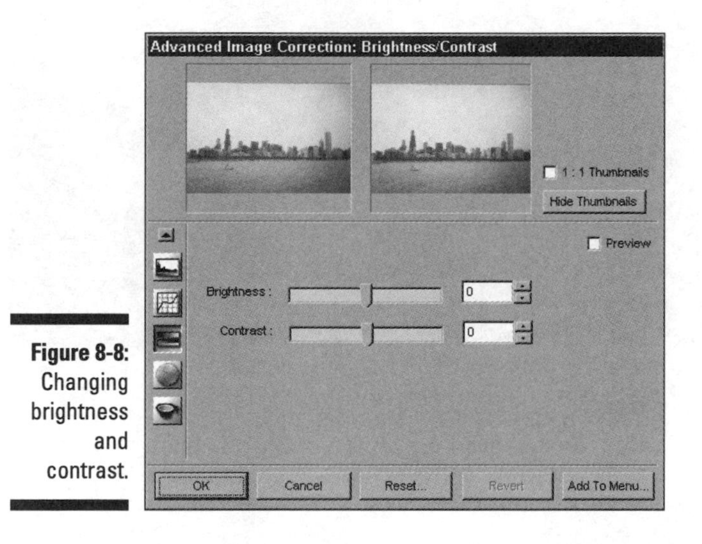

Figure 8-8: Changing brightness and contrast.

The brightness of an image indicates the concentration of light (in the positive) or the intensity of dark (in the negative) throughout the entire image. Raising the brightness level can accentuate details in the dark areas of an image, and lowering the level can cancel the effects of overexposure (a photographer's 10-cent term for "too much light"). Figure 8-9 illustrates the image with a –50 percent brightness setting, and Figure 8-10 shows the effects of a 50 percent setting.

The contrast level controls the contrast between light and dark shades in your image. This feature is a great tool for bringing out detail in an image, although you shouldn't overuse it because it can degrade the overall quality of your image at higher levels. Figure 8-11 illustrates the Chicago skyline with a 50 percent contrast enhancement. I would call this too much contrast (for example, look at the glare of the sky), but I wanted you to be able to see the difference in the buildings.

Figure 8-9: Lowering brightness darkens the entire image.

Figure 8-10: Increasing brightness yields a lighter scan.

Figure 8-11: Use contrast to enhance detail in your scanned image.

Size Really Does Count

Now consider height and width — no, not *yours.* I'm talking about your scanned image! (Sorry — I couldn't help that one.) The image dimensions and size controls are probably the most straightforward settings you can make within your scanning software. For example, ScanWizard uses three values to compute the final size of your scanned image:

- The height of the region you've chosen with the selection box
- The width of the region you've chosen with the selection box
- Scaling

Scaling works just like the size-percentage control on a typical copy machine — 100 percent yields the same size, 50 percent yields a scanned image half the size of the original, and 200 percent doubles the size of the original, for example. Click the Scaling list box to choose one of the standard scale levels or click directly in the field and enter your own. Notice that ScanWizard automatically adjusts the output size if you specify a different scaling value.

In most cases, you want to keep the proportions (also called the *aspect ratio*) of the image the same so that the image you scan doesn't turn out "pinched" or "pulled," like a piece of taffy. To make sure that the proportion stays the same even if you make a change to the height or width, click the Keep Proportion check box to enable it before making any modifications to the image dimensions. Notice that the program automatically adjusts the other dimension to provide the same aspect ratio.

By default, the measurement units are inches, although you can also choose other units, including

- Centimeters (cm)
- Millimeters (mm)
- Points
- Pixels

To change the unit of measure, click the drop-down list box to the right of the output fields and click the unit you want.

After you've set your image size, you also notice that ScanWizard does its best to estimate the total file size. The estimate is displayed in the Image Size field. For example, selecting a 50 percent scale may drop an image from 2.9MB to 725K.

Making Green Bananas Yellow

It's time to balance that color! Again, you can take care of color balancing before the scan (using your scanning software, if it supports this feature) or after the scan (using your image editor). In Chapter 11, I show you how to alter the color of a single element in your scanned image. This procedure alters the color range for the entire image, making it the perfect method of fixing an original with a tinge from fluorescent or colored lighting.

Note: I think that it's important to keep in mind that if your original uses a well-balanced palette of colors (for example, if you're scanning a simple text document, a page from a magazine, or a photograph taken in sunlight), your color levels shouldn't require any adjustment. You should use these controls only if you need to correct an obvious color defect in the entire image or if you want to exercise your creativity.

Follow these steps:

1. **Click the button to the right of the Color Correction drop-down list box — it looks like a colored circle — to display the Advanced Image Correction dialog box, as shown in Figure 8-12.**

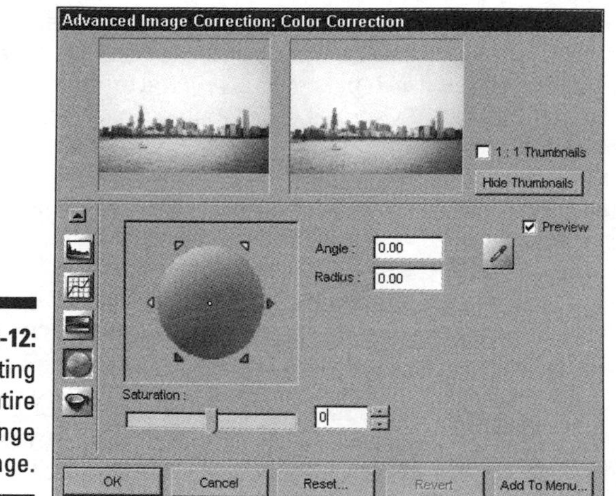

Figure 8-12: Adjusting the entire color range of an image.

2. **If the Thumbnails and Preview check boxes aren't enabled, click both to check them.**
3. **Click and drag the pointer in the center of the palette circle in the direction directly away from the color you want to reduce.**

   For example, if the image has too much red in it, you move the pointer to the left, toward the cyan area of the circle. You can see the results immediately as ScanWizard updates the thumbnail image on the right.

   For more precise movement in a specific direction, click the colored arrows on the outside of the palette circle; this draws the pointer directly toward that color.

4. **After the correction has been made and you're impressed with the results, click OK to accept the settings. To start over, click Revert.**

I don't show you an example of color correction here; the sample image was taken outside on a somewhat overcast day, yielding an almost perfect color palette (and this book uses black-and-white halftone figures, so it would be hard to tell the difference). Suffice it to say that you should try this using your own scanning software. You'll be surprised by the results!

Basic Filters 101

First, here's a definition of *filter:* It's a mathematical formula applied to an image within an image editor, a digital camera, or a scanning program. A filter can make both subtle and dramatic changes in the appearance of a digital image.

I'll be honest with you: I don't use the filters that are built-in to ScanWizard. Why? I like to apply filters and effects to an image *after* it has been scanned, using Paint Shop Pro, where I have more precise and powerful tools available, and I show you how to do just that in Chapter 11. (I also display a gallery of my ten favorite filters and effects in Chapter 17.)

However, I also like to be through, so here's a quick rundown of what these filters can do for your image:

- **Blur:** Yes, believe it or not, sometimes you want a scanned image to turn out blurry and hazy! This filter gives an image a soft, out-of-focus look by lightening the pixels next to any sharp border in the original.
- **Edge enhancement:** This filter increases the contrast level along the boundaries of gray and color regions in your image. As you can tell from Figure 8-13, the results can be spectacular from a graphic artist's point of view.
- **Emboss:** Turns your original into an embossed metal work of art! I like this one. Emboss is illustrated in Figure 8-14.
- **Sharpen:** I discuss how to use the Sharpen filter in detail in Chapter 9. Suffice it to say that this filter is the opposite of the Blur filter, darkening the pixels next to the borders in the original instead. A wide range of images benefits from at least a small amount of sharpening, so you'll probably use this filter often.

Figure 8-13: I've enhanced the edges of Chicago.

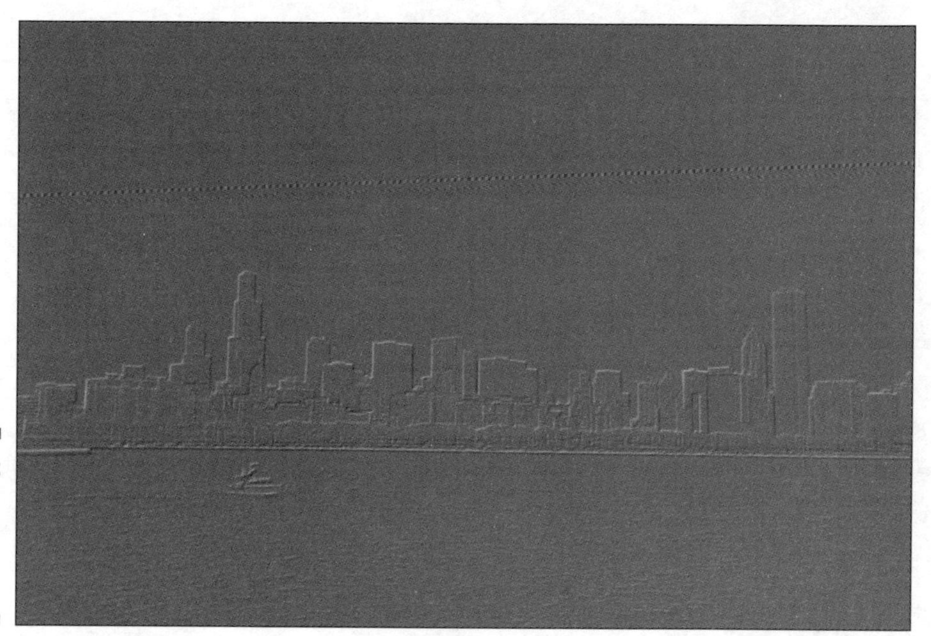

Figure 8-14: Embossing puts the skyline on a metal sheet.

To apply a filter in ScanWizard, follow these steps:

1. **Click the button to the right of the Filter drop-down list box to display the Advanced Image Correction dialog box, as shown in Figure 8-15.**
2. **If the Thumbnails and Preview check boxes aren't enabled, click both to check them.**
3. **Click the Filters drop-down list box and choose the effect you want. The effects of the filter are displayed automatically on the right thumbnail image.**

   Selecting Blur More or Sharpen More increases the effect of the filter by a factor of two.
4. **Ready to accept the filter effects? Click OK. To start over, click Revert.**

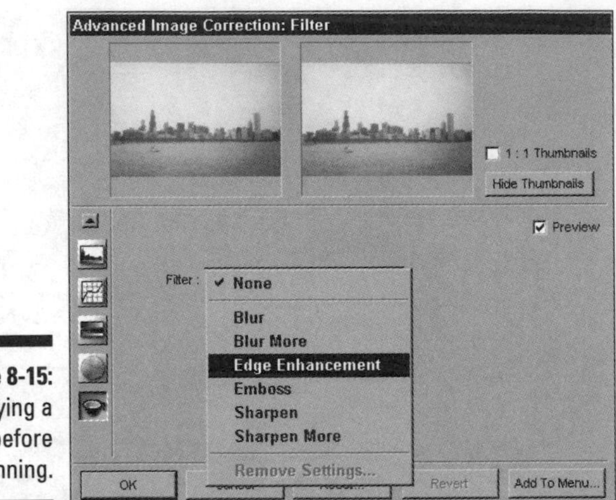

Figure 8-15: Applying a filter before scanning.

Flipping and Rotating: The Scanner Dance Craze

Naturally, your scanner has no idea which end is "up" on your original. That's why your scanning software gives you the ability to rotate or flip *(mirror)* the image. The horizontal and vertical mirror settings are particularly useful where the original is reversed or if you have to reverse an original. For example, when you're creating a T-shirt design and you're scanning a photograph to use, you may have to flip it — either the entire design has to be reversed, or your inkjet printer has to print it in reverse. After you've learned which way is "up" when aligning your originals with your scanner's home corner, this stuff doesn't come up often, although being able to flip or rotate when you need it is handy.

To flip or rotate the scanned image, click the Transform button (it looks like an *F* button) to display the alignment grid. The direction in which the F is facing relative to the normal alignment indicates the effect that the transformation will have on the completed scan. Click a button to select it.

As an example, look at the image shown in Figure 8-16. The original was arranged on the scanner in the default manner, with the F in its normal orientation. However, clicking the F "lying on its back" produces an image that's rotated to the left 90 degrees, as shown in Figure 8-17. Clicking the backward F produces the mirrored image shown in Figurc 8-18.

Figure 8-16: A beautiful woman with beautiful flowers.

Figure 8-17: Applying a 90-degree rotation to the left.

You can also take care of rotating and mirroring an image with Paint Shop Pro, and I show you how in Chapter 9.

Figure 8-18: Is she a clone? Or is it all done with mirrors?

Pitching a Tonal Curve

As with the color balancing I demonstrate earlier in this chapter, you can also adjust the balance of the tones in both color and grayscale images — either all the tones or you can choose to adjust just the red, green, or blue components of the colors in your original.

You take care of these changes with a special control that's familiar to most folks who work in publishing and the graphic arts: a *tone graph.* Again, this procedure generally isn't necessary as long as your original has a correct range of tones. I use it more as a special effect.

Follow these steps:

1. **Click the button to the right of the Tone Curve drop-down list box to display the Advanced Image Correction dialog box, as shown in Figure 8-19.**
2. **If the Thumbnails and Preview check boxes aren't enabled, click both to check them.**
3. **To alter all three color channels, set the Channel drop-down list box to Master. To restrict your changes to a single channel, click the Channel drop-down list box and choose Red, Green, or Blue.**

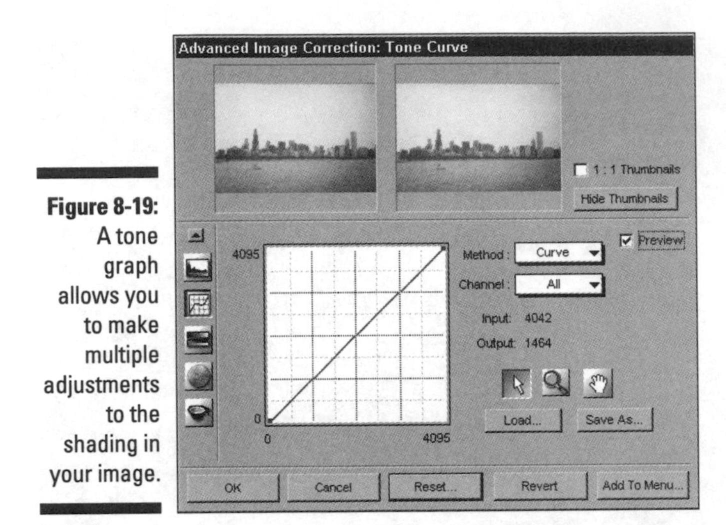

Figure 8-19: A tone graph allows you to make multiple adjustments to the shading in your image.

4. **Click and drag the pointer anywhere along the tone graph to "push" or "pull" the line.**

   Pulling the line below the diagonal enhances the darker tones in your image (as shown in Figure 8-20), and pushing the line above the diagonal enhances the lighter tones. Note that you click more than one point along the line. The results are immediately updated so that you can see the effect of your changes.

Figure 8-20: I've enhanced the darker tones in the sample image.

5. **When you've made your adjustments, click OK to accept the settings. To start over, click Revert.**

"I'm Saturated with Color!"

You may want to adjust the color saturation before you scan an original. Color *saturation* controls the intensity of a specific color (or, in other words, the amount of color in a single hue of the original's palette). If that sounds like verbal spaghetti, think of it this way: The more saturated a color, the more you see of that particular color in the image. Green grass looks greener, and a blue sky looks bluer, for example.

To modify the amount of saturation for a specific color in ScanWizard, follow these steps:

1. **Click the button to the right of the Color Correction drop-down list box to display the Advanced Image Correction dialog box, as shown in Figure 8-21.**

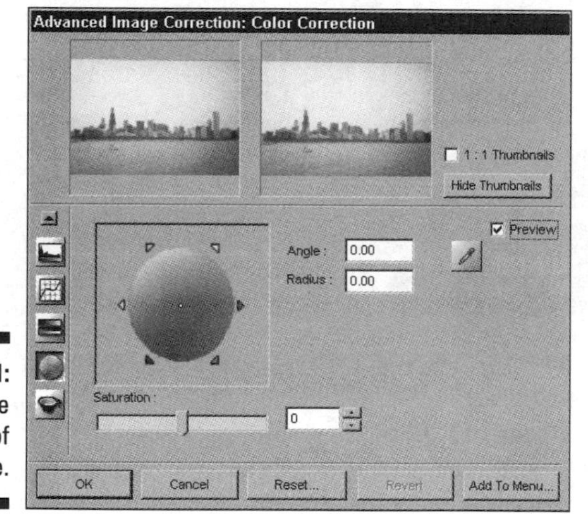

Figure 8-21: Altering the saturation of an image.

2. **If the Thumbnails and Preview check boxes aren't enabled, click both to check them.**
3. **Click and drag the pointer in the center of the palette circle in the direction of the color you want to reduce.**

4. **Move the Saturation slider control by clicking and dragging it.**

   You can also click in the Saturation field and enter an exact value. The image on the right is updated.

5. **After you've set the saturation level as you like it, click OK to accept the settings. (Click Revert to return to the original settings.)**

Figure 8-22 illustrates a 75-point red hue saturation applied to the sample image.

If you're familiar with both the basic controls on the Standard menu and the more powerful settings on the Advanced menu (or whatever your scanner-control software calls them), you can turn your attention to another tool on the scanning expert's belt: the image editor. In Chapter 9, I introduce you to Paint Shop Pro, and you use it to adjust and improve your images — *after* you've scanned them!

Figure 8-22: A thoroughly saturated image.

Chapter 9

Image Editing: The Easy Way

In This Chapter

- Introducing Paint Shop Pro
- Opening and saving image files
- Browsing a folder
- Cropping an image
- Sharpening an image
- Resizing an image
- Creating a mirror or flipped image
- Correcting gamma levels
- Adding a picture frame
- Removing red-eye
- Rotating an image
- Converting to grayscale
- Converting to another format

A scanner is indeed a wonderful piece of equipment, and, if you've read the preceding chapters in this book, I think that you'll agree with me. I rank my scanner right up there with inventions like the light bulb, the baseball, and the Rolling Stones. Yet, even with all the tips and tricks you may have learned, you can do only so much with a "raw" image saved straight to your hard drive. Often, an image still needs a bit of tweaking (even with the scanning software adjustments I discuss in earlier chapters) before you can use it.

Ladies and gentlemen, you're no longer raw recruits. In this chapter, I introduce you to the *image editor.* Consider it your development lab, creative digital easel, and versatile cutting board, all rolled into one! After you've experienced the power of an image editor, I think that you may find it hard to imagine a mundane scanning existence without one. Personally, I like to manipulate pixels like a composer manipulates musical notes!

Throughout this chapter, I use my favorite image editor — Paint Shop Pro, from Jasc Software, Inc. — to demonstrate how you can apply the necessary finishing touches before importing your scanned image into a document, sending it through e-mail, or preparing it for use on your Web page. As in Chapter 8, I provide step-by-step procedures and show you their effects.

Why Edit What's Already Perfect?

Hey, don't mess with perfection! If your scanned image is already *exactly* as you need it, or if perfection isn't a necessity (for example, if you've scanned a document in order to send it with your computer's fax-modem), you have no need to use an image editor, and you can march proudly onward.

However, other images *do* require first aid, and for a number of different reasons:

- In some cases, the problem may be one of *composition* — something that's there isn't supposed to be there.
- Perhaps you may decide that a *post-scanning process* (like an orientation or mirror procedure) needs to be done after scanning an original.
- You can make simple *aesthetic* changes to enhance a scan, too, like converting it to grayscale or adding a picture frame.
- Finally, an out-and-out *creative urge* brings a wild look to your eyes — and wild results to your hard drive! With filters and special effects (which I discuss in detail in Chapter 11), you become a true artist.

In this chapter, I stick with the first three types of image-editing work — including the chores that some people take care of with adjustments to their scanning software (as I show you in previous chapters), as well as one or two new tricks.

Introducing the Tool of Choice: Paint Shop Pro

Paint Shop Pro (`www.jasc.com`) has been a fixture on my PC for many years — in fact, since the days when it was a simple shareware program available on bulletin-board systems. Today, Paint Shop Pro ranks with Adobe Photoshop as one of the best-known image editors on the market. Paint Shop Pro provides most of the same features as Photoshop, although it costs many hundreds of dollars less. Also, readers of my other books have told me that they find Paint Shop Pro much, much easier to understand and use than Photoshop. (Like anyone else who has to program a VCR when the power goes out, I'm in favor of simplicity.) The trial version of Paint Shop Pro is included on the companion CD in this book.

Figure 9-1 illustrates the Paint Shop Pro main window, which is composed of four major parts:

- The familiar menu system
- The toolbars at the left side and top of the window
- The color palette at the right side of the window
- The editing area

I refer to these areas (and the controls you see) throughout the rest of this book.

Figure 9-1: Displaying an image in Paint Shop Pro.

I want to mention one other feature of the program: Paint Shop Pro includes a great online help system that provides complete details on every function, feature, switch, and setting. Plus, you also find additional image-editing tips and tricks for just about everything the program can do. Dig into this gold mine whenever you try out a new procedure.

Opening a File

Every journey begins with a first step. In this case, tweaking a scanned image begins when you open the file. Follow these steps to open an image in Paint Shop Pro:

1. **Click the Paint Shop Pro icon on your Windows desktop to run the program.**

   Alternatively, you can click the Start button and choose Programs⇨Jasc Software⇨Paint Shop Pro.

2. **Click File and click Open to display the Open dialog box, as shown in Figure 9-2. Navigate to the folder where the scanned image is located and click it once to display a thumbnail preview and basic information about the size and color depth of the image.**

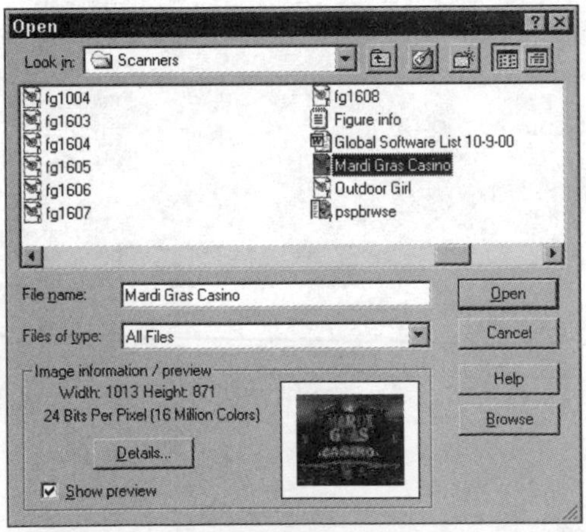

Figure 9-2: The Paint Shop Pro Open dialog box lets you preview an image — pretty doggone convenient, eh?

TIP: Need even more information on an image without opening it? You can display the full description of an image — including compression level, exact size, and the creation or modification date — by clicking the Details button.

3. **Click Open to open the highlighted file within Paint Shop Pro. The image is displayed within a new editing window.**

By the way, if you allow Paint Shop Pro to configure itself as the default viewing program for image files during installation, you can simplify things dramatically. Open an image file by simply double-clicking it! You know that Paint Shop Pro is registered within Windows as the default application for an image if the scanned file is represented by an artist's palette icon. The file also carries the Paint Shop Pro Image type within Windows Explorer.

Shall We Browse?

As you continue to build your library of scanned images, you eventually find yourself digging through a folder containing hundreds of files for a particular scan of a llama next to a grass hut. It's a frustrating chore that brings new meaning to the tired, overworked, worn-out cliché "looking for a needle in a haystack." (You would *think* that a picture like that would stand out, but to your computer, everything's ones and zeros.)

Paint Shop Pro includes a feature that can save you literally hours of opening images. You can browse a folder's worth of files by viewing a catalog of thumbnail images. It's much easier to locate that llama visually than try to remember the filename.

Here are two methods of browsing a folder using Paint Shop Pro:

- The easiest method is to right-click directly on a folder in Windows Explorer; one of the menu items is Browse this folder using Paint Shop Pro. Choose this menu item, and the program automatically starts and opens the Browse window, as shown in Figure 9-3.
- If Paint Shop Pro is already running, click File and choose the Browse menu item. Then select the folder you want to browse.

Fence those images in, pardner!

I always recommend that folks dedicate a folder on their hard drive to store their scanned images (rather than save them here and there or simply dump them in the C:\ root directory). Why? It helps you keep track of where your images have been saved — and, if you use Paint Shop Pro to browse that directory, it can also save you time in the future! Here's the deal: Whenever you use Paint Shop Pro to browse a folder, the program saves a small data file, named PSPBRWSE.JBF, within that folder. This index file holds a "snapshot" of information about which images were included in the browsing session. The next time you browse that same folder, Paint Shop Pro can use this index file to automatically update the Browse display with any new images you've added since the last browsing session, and it's *fast!*

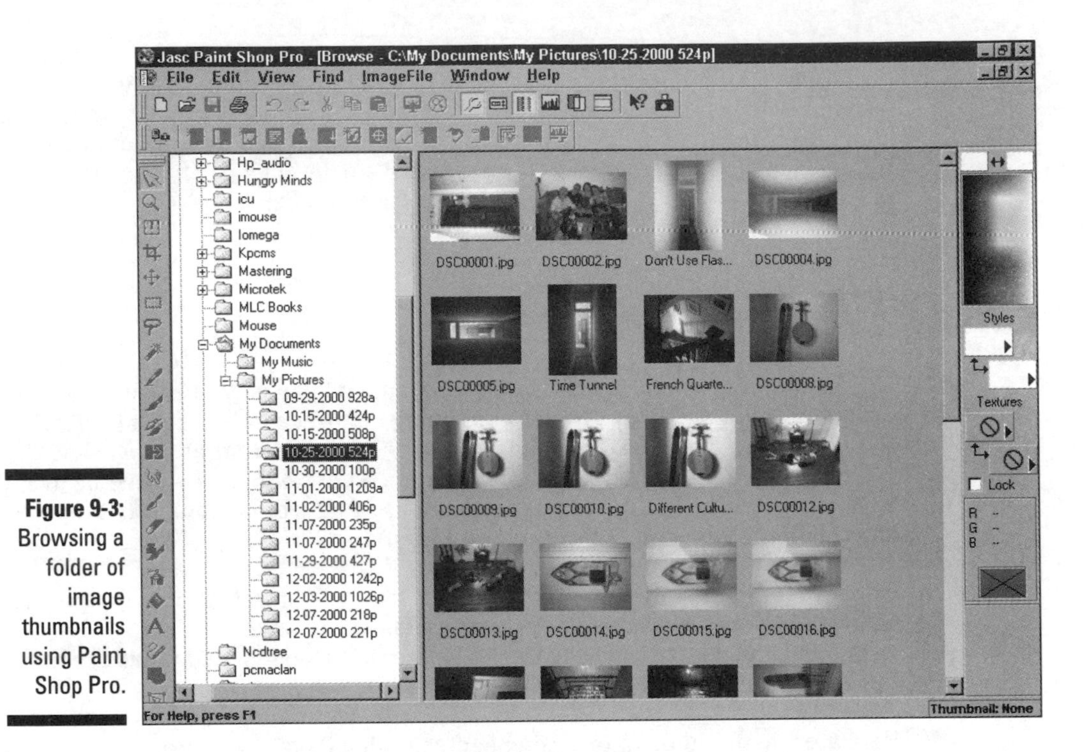

Figure 9-3: Browsing a folder of image thumbnails using Paint Shop Pro.

After the contents of the folder are displayed, you can load any image by clicking directly on the thumbnail. It's surrounded by a highlighted border, and Paint Shop Pro loads it into a separate editing window.

To keep your images sorted alphabetically by filename, right-click in the Browse display and choose Sort by Filename.

Cropping a Scanned Image

So you've got the perfect scan from that magazine page, but all you want is the photograph, and not the text around it. (Or perhaps your finger intruded into the frame of that priceless family reunion photo.) No problem: You can *crop* the image, which removes the portion of the border you specify. (It works just like the ScanWizard selection box.) Because cropping an image also reduces its dimensions, you get the bonus of a smaller file size!

Follow these steps:

1. **Click File and choose the Open menu item to load your image.**
2. **Click the geometric selection tool (which looks like a dotted rectangle) on the toolbar on the left edge of the screen.**

   Your mouse cursor changes from an arrow to a crosshair, indicating that you're in selection mode.
3. **Click in the top left corner of the area you want to save, and hold the mouse down to drag the selection rectangle to the lower right corner of the area you want to save. Release the mouse button to select the area, which is surrounded by an animated dotted line, like the one shown in Figure 9-4.**

Figure 9-4: Selecting the portion of an image to keep.

4. **Click Image and choose the Crop to Selection menu item.**

   For those of you who still favor the keyboard, you can also press the Shift+R shortcut. The area outside the selection box is cut, as shown in Figure 9-5.

Figure 9-5: The cropped image looks much better, don't you think?

5. **To save the cropped image, click File and choose Save (to overwrite the old image) or Save As (to save a new image). You can use Save As to create a copy of the image with another filename or format.**

Need to undo something that didn't work in Paint Shop Pro? Choose Undo from the Edit menu to cancel the effects of the last task you performed.

Sharpen That Line, Mister!

You may remember the sharpening feature of ScanWizard that I mention in Chapter 8. Paint Shop Pro provides a sharpening feature as well — I often use it to add focus to a scan of a hazy or blurry original. In effect, this sharpening increases the contrast at all the lines and edges within the image, which usually means the subject of a photograph. Sharpening usually isn't necessary with simple line art or a text document because those types of scanned images already offer a high level of contrast.

Note: Sharpening an image *does not* create additional detail! (That would be like a neat trick, rather like the interpolation I talk about in Chapter 1 — creating pixels out of nothing.) Therefore, use this technique sparingly. Too much sharpening can turn an image into a grainy mess.

Follow these steps:

1. **Click File and choose the Open menu item to load your image.**
2. **Click Effects and choose Sharpen (or Sharpen More, which significantly enhances the effect).**
3. **Save your changes. Click File and choose Save or Save As.**

To give you an idea of the effects of sharpening, Figure 9-6 illustrates an image in need of serious focus, and Figure 9-7 shows the same image after the application of the Sharpen More operation.

Figure 9-6: Notice the edges in this scanned image. They need sharpening.

Figure 9-7: With Sharpen More, the image looks much better.

It's Just Plain Too Big!

A scanner can turn out a huge image at higher dpi settings, so you often need to resize the image before printing it, importing it into another document, or using it on your Web site. Resizing the image dimensions also helps trim the size of the image file.

What is an aspect ratio?

When you're resizing an image, *aspect ratio* (the ratio of height to width) is very important. A picture can be badly stretched or pinched if the aspect ratio is changed while you're resizing it. When the Maintain aspect ratio check box at the bottom of the dialog box is enabled, Paint Shop Pro automatically enters the second value when you enter one number in either the width or height fields. Leave this box checked unless you need to force an image to a new aspect ratio. The moral of the story is "Preserve that ratio!"

Follow these steps to resize an image:

1. **Click File and choose the Open menu item to load your image.**
2. **Click Image and choose Resize to display the Resize dialog box, as shown in Figure 9-8.**

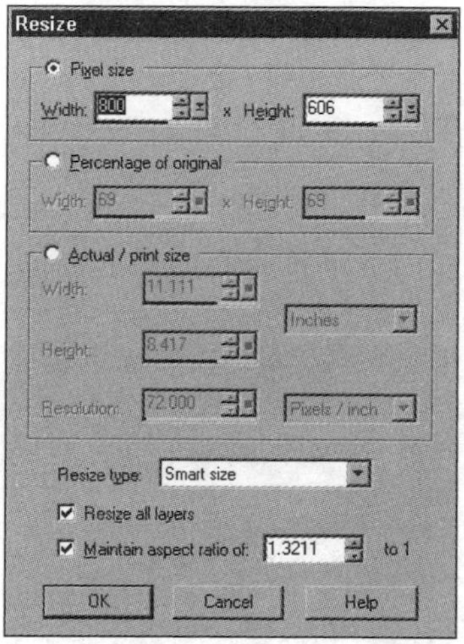

Figure 9-8: The Paint Shop Pro Resize dialog box.

3. **Choose one of the three measurement modes: by pixel resolution, as a percentage of the original size, or the actual size of the final image.**

   If I'm resizing an image to fit in a specific size on a Web page, I usually use pixel resolution, where you enter the new width and height for the image in pixels. If you're importing the image for use in another document, using the actual size of the final image is a good idea.

4. **Click the Resize type drop-down list box and choose Smart size.**
5. **Click OK. (Note that the larger the change in the image size, the more time resizing takes.)**
6. **Save your changes — click File and choose Save or Save As.**

Mirror, Mirror, on the Wall

Paint Shop Pro can easily reverse or flip an image — a good trick when you're creating a "reverse" image for a T-shirt transfer. Follow these steps:

1. **Click File and choose the Open menu item to load your image.**
2. **Click Image and choose Flip (to reverse the image from top to bottom) or Mirror (to reverse the image from left to right).**
3. **Save your changes — click File and choose Save or Save As.**

Figures 9-9 and 9-10 speak volumes about the effect the mirror operation can have on a typical scanned image.

Figure 9-9: An image that needs to be reversed.

Figure 9-10: After the mirror operation, things look much better!

The Light and the Dark

Scanning an overexposed or underexposed original can result in an image that needs a contrast adjustment — and the easiest way to lighten or darken an entire image is to use the gamma correction setting in Paint Shop Pro.

Follow these steps:

1. **Click File and choose the Open menu item to load the image.**
2. **Click Colors and choose Adjust and Gamma Correction from the pop-up menu to display the Gamma Correction dialog box, as shown in Figure 9-11.**
3. **Enable the Link check box.**
4. **Click and drag any of the three slider controls to the right (to lighten the image) or the left (to darken the image).**

   The window on the right displays a preview of the correction.
5. **When you're satisfied with the correction, click OK.**
6. **Save your changes. Click File and choose Save or Save As.**

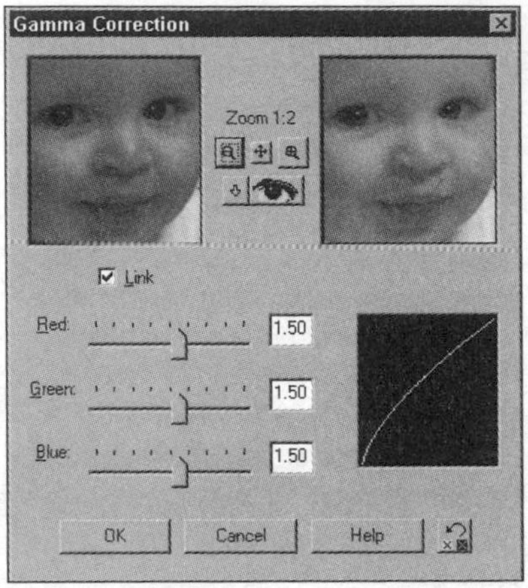

Figure 9-11: Adjusting the Gamma Correction for an image.

Wouldn't a Frame Look Nice?

Paint Shop Pro allows you to add a decorative frame to an image. Figure 9-12 illustrates a frame border I added to a scanned snapshot of me posing with my favorite President. (Okay, I created the photograph in Paint Shop Pro — but it does make a great portrait, doesn't it?)

Figure 9-12: The author poses with Mr. Lincoln.

Follow these steps:

1. **Click File and choose the Open menu item to load your image.**
2. **After you've opened the photograph, click Image and choose the Picture Frame menu item to display the Picture Frame Wizard dialog box, as shown in Figure 9-13.**

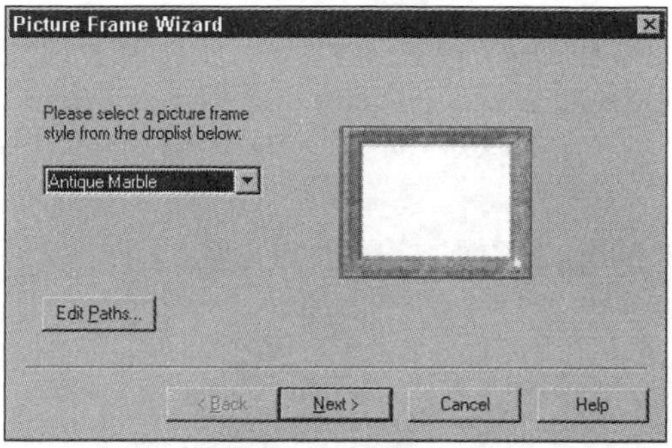

Picture Frame Wizard
Please select a picture frame style from the droplist below:
Antique Marble
Edit Paths...
< Back Next > Cancel Help

Figure 9-13: Selecting a picture frame.

3. **Click the Style drop-down list box and choose the type of frame you want surrounding the image. Paint Shop Pro displays a preview of the frame. Click Next when you've selected the frame you want.**
4. **The Wizard displays the dialog box shown in Figure 9-14, where you specify whether the frame should fall inside the edges of the image or be added outside the edges of the image.**

   Naturally, placing the frame inside the edges keeps the original image dimensions, but the frame hides more of the image itself.
5. **Choose the frame position and click Finish.**
6. **Save your changes. Click File and choose Save or Save As.**

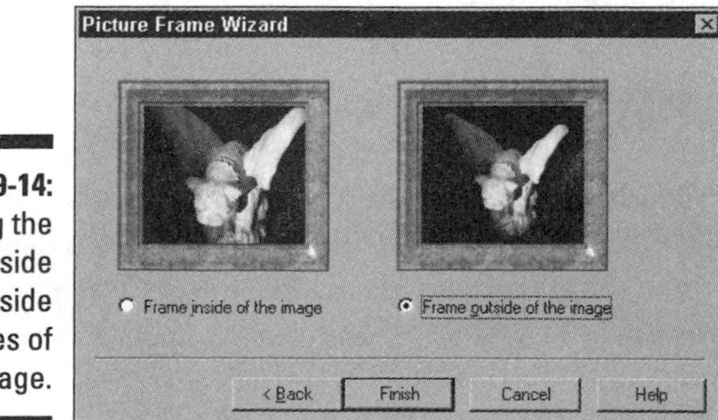

Figure 9-14: Locating the frame inside or outside the edges of the image.

Removing Uncle Milton's Red-Eye

Today's automatic point-and-shoot cameras may advertise a red-eye reduction feature, but you may still have to remove that irritating red shine from your subject's eyes after scanning a photograph.

Follow these steps:

1. **Click File and choose the Open menu item to load your image.**
2. **Click Effects and choose Enhance Photo and Red-eye Removal from the pop-up menus to display the dialog box, as shown in Figure 9-15.**

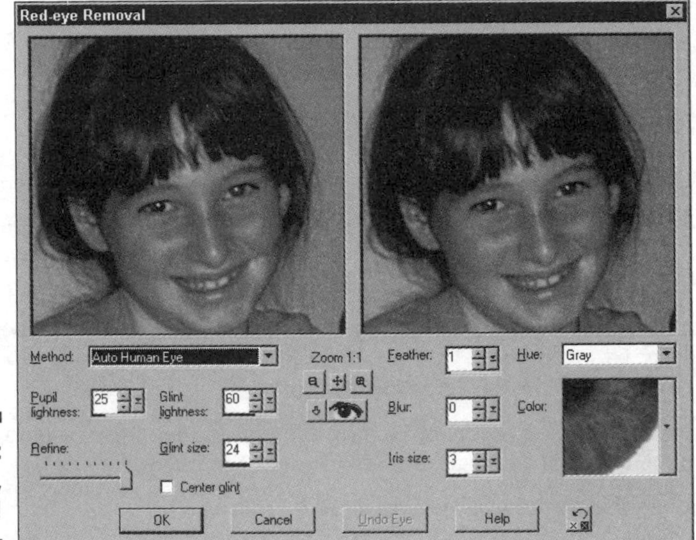

Figure 9-15: Red-eye, begone!

3. **Click within the right window and drag the image in the desired direction until the subject's eyes are in the selection windows.**
4. **Click the mouse cursor in the center of one eye in the left window to select it.**

   Paint Shop Pro surrounds the colored portion of the eye with a selection box.
5. **Click the Hue drop-down list box and the arrow next to the Color box to choose the proper hue and color.**
6. **Click OK to fix the image.**
7. **Repeat steps 2 through 6 to fix the remaining eye (or eyes).**
8. **Click File and choose Save or Save As.**

Rotating 101

If you snap a photograph holding your camera on its end, you may need to change the orientation of the image before it's displayed correctly. Follow these steps with Paint Shop Pro:

1. **Click File and choose the Open menu item to load your image.**
2. **Click Image and choose Rotate to display the dialog box, as shown in Figure 9-16.**

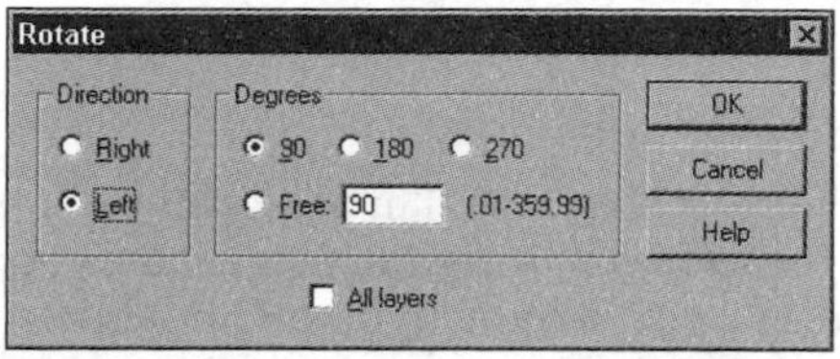

Figure 9-16: The Rotate dialog box.

3. **Click Left or Right to choose the direction of rotation.**
4. **Click the number of degrees to rotate (usually either 90 or 180 degrees).**
5. **Click OK to rotate the image.**
6. **Click File and choose Save or Save As.**

Who Needs Color, Anyway?

You may be wondering why anyone would convert a perfectly good color image to grayscale. More reasons exist than you may think! For example:

- **To hide mismatched colors:** There goes Aunt Harriet again, choosing a robin's egg blue kimono when the rest of the family was dressed in festive red and green for the holidays. In grayscale, though, she matches once again!
- **For artistic reasons:** If you're bitten by the creative bug, a grayscale version of a color image may appeal to your photographer's eye.
- **For specific publications:** If you're busy publishing a black-and-white newsletter using the office copier, a grayscale image likely looks better in the final copy.

The procedure is simple and painless. Follow these steps:

1. **Click File and choose the Open menu item to load your image.**
2. **Click Colors and choose Grey Scale.**
3. **Because you can't return from a grayscale conversion, I recommend that you click File and choose Save As (to save the grayscale creation under another filename).**

A Little Alchemy: Changing Image Formats

Time to talk more about alchemy. In this case, I'm not talking about digitizing images, but rather changing the *format* of a digital image. I don't delve deeply into image formats here because I cover them in detail in Chapter 10. However, because Paint Shop Pro makes the process of conversion from one format to another so doggone easy, I take the time to show you how to change a format now.

Follow these steps to convert a file from one format to another — for this example, I convert a JPEG image (the native format that's produced by default by my scanner) to a TIFF image:

1. **Click File and choose the Open menu item to load the image.**
2. **Click File and choose Save As to display the dialog box shown in Figure 9-17.**

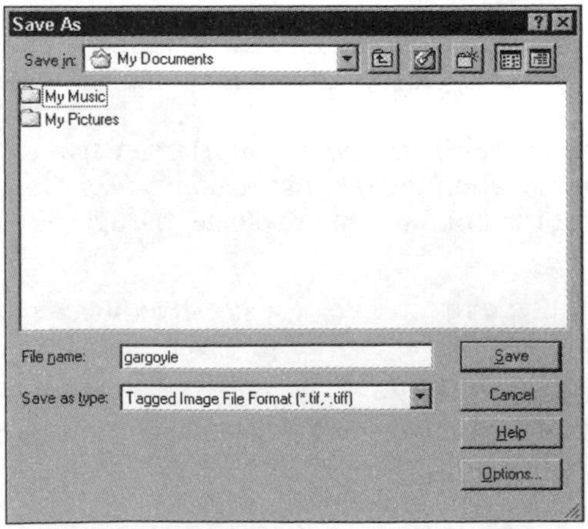

Figure 9-17: Saving a file to disk using Paint Shop Pro.

3. **Click the Save as type drop-down list box and choose the format for the new image. In this case, choose Tagged Image File Format (*.tif).**
4. **If you like, type a new filename in the File name field. (Again, I recommend that you save the original image, just in case.)**
5. **Click the Options button to select the settings the program uses in converting to the new format. Most of the image settings are different for each format; Figure 9-18 illustrates the Save options for the TIFF format. Leave them at their defaults unless you specifically need to change them, and click OK to return to the Save As dialog box.**
6. **Click Save to start the conversion and save the new file to disk.**

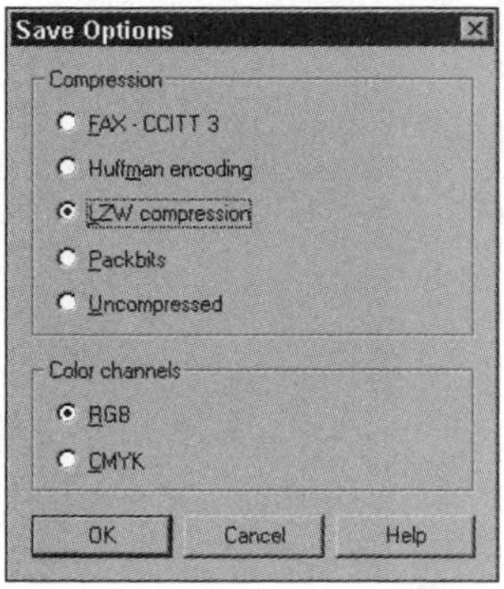

Figure 9-18: Adjusting settings while saving a TIFF image.

Part IV

The Lazy Expert's Guide to Advanced Scanning

In this part . . .

This part turns your attention to more complex material, including details on image formats, images for e-mail messages and Web pages, and advanced image-editing techniques. I'll provide you with a comprehensive discussion of scanner maintenance and trouble-shooting and show you how to use your scanner for craft and business projects.

Chapter 10

So You Want to Be an Internet Graphics Guru

In This Chapter

- Understanding image formats
- Choosing color depth for Web images
- Adding compression to JPEG images
- Optimizing images for the Web
- Choosing the best image size
- Sending an image through e-mail
- Considering legal issues

"The Internet has revolutionized. . . ." Blah, blah, blah. I refuse to type that stuff. You've heard it so many times during the past two or three years that there's nothing left to explain! Everyone's fighting to get online if they're not already there. A business isn't truly on the fast track to success without a Web site, and your Christmas cards are just as likely to list your e-mail address as your mailing address. I don't waste your time by noting how the Internet started as a military communications network, nor do I describe in excruciating detail how your peanut butter fudge recipe gets to Aunt Harriet in Boise by hopping from your modem to an e-mail server across the Internet to her ISP and back again. (If you want to pull back the curtain and see how the Great Oz does these things, I recommend buying the appropriate edition of *The Internet For Dummies,* written by John R. Levine, Margaret Levine Young, and Carol Baroudi, and published by Hungry Minds, Inc.)

What's *really* noteworthy about the Internet — and what's especially interesting to your elite group, the Scanner Owners of the World Club — is the *visual* aspect of the Grand Design! Naturally, the World Wide Web comes to mind first; it's the fastest-growing part of the Internet, and it offers a chance for just about anyone to publish the information she wants for the world to see — in 24-bit color, no less. However, don't forget about your e-mail account; I'm just as likely to find myself transferring scanned images as e-mail attachments to my friends and family. (In fact, every figure in this book was transferred to my heroic project editor through e-mail.)

In this chapter, I turn the magnifying glass on the Internet — specifically, how you can produce images that are optimized for use on your Web pages and enclosure in your e-mail messages. I also cover a number of subjects that are of interest to Web page designers, lawyers, and the average preschool child. (You can't say that I don't appeal to a wide audience.)

A GIF Isn't a Snack Food, and It's Not Spelled Jaypeg

Although the two image formats most commonly found on the Internet are GIF and JPEG (with PNG on the rise), I want to cover the advantages and disadvantages of all the well-known formats here. After all, you may find yourself scanning images for use on "that *other* operating system."

By the way, keep in mind that no hard-and-fast rule says that you have to use GIF or JPEG images on your Web site. You can just as easily offer Windows bitmap or TIFF images for downloading. However, in the descriptions that follow, I explain why an unwritten agreement stipulates that GIF, JPEG, and PNG are the best choices for the Internet.

Joint Photographic Experts Group

Commonly called JPEG, this format is the most popular now in use; it's also called JPG because these images usually end with the .JPG extension under Windows. You do indeed pronounce it "JAY-peg."

JPEG images deliver high resolution with very small file sizes; a typical one-page document with mixed text and graphics, for example, can take less than 300K worth of hard drive space. The savings result from the built-in compression that's part of the JPEG format. You can find out more about this topic later in this chapter, in the section "Compression in the 21st Century."

On the flip side, a JPEG image can lose detail and image quality at higher compression rates or if it's repeatedly compressed. Compression like this is commonly called *lossy* compression because pixels (and therefore details) are removed to deliver better compression. (Again, I cover this topic within a couple of pages.)

JPEG images, with their small size and great quality, are the standard for pictures used on the Web and images sent through e-mail; smaller file sizes mean less time required to send or receive these images over your computer's modem.

So what exactly *is* an image format?

An *image format* is a standard file layout (or template) that's used to store the data that makes up the image. I could spend a chapter or two quoting the specifications for a typical format, but, to tell you the truth, details about the low-level structure of a digital photograph fall into the realm of computer programmers and technowizards. (In other words, the details would be gibberish to both you and me.) If you're interested in how the bits and bytes are stacked together, you can find information on the Web that details the standards used by programmers to read and write image files. Here are a couple of sites to visit:

For JPEG: `www.jpeg.org/public/jpeglinks.htm`

For PNG: `www.libpng.org/pub/png/`

It's no accident that today's digital cameras also save images to their RAM cards in JPEG format. Smaller files mean more exposures on a "roll" of "digital film."

Graphics Interchange Format

The GIF file format is one of the oldest (and most common) image formats still used today. GIF files usually end with the .GIF extension under Windows. Although many uninformed folks persist in pronouncing GIF with a hard "g" sound, as in guffaw, the inventor of the GIF format (as well as the author of this book) pronounces it correctly, with a soft "g," as in giraffe.

As for the other great international CTPF (that's short for *c*omputer *t*erm *p*ronunciation *f*lub), the word *Linux* is pronounced like Linus, the name of the man who wrote the operating system — and the character from *Peanuts.*

GIF images originated on the old king of the online services, CompuServe, and were popularized on the bulletin-board systems (or *BBSs*) common throughout the 1980s and early 1990s. At the time, the Internet was a "weird" system that colleges and scientists used and was barely known in public circles. I'm showing my age again, I admit, but I have fond memories of those times. I operated a popular multilane BBS for 15 years. I still have thousands of GIF images stored on CD-R. They're lurking somewhere around my office, although it would take a bulldozer to find them.

These days, GIF images are used almost exclusively on the Web. Unlike a JPEG, a GIF image can be animated, so it appears to move when it's displayed by your browser. Two common types of GIF images exist. The specifications are cryptically named 87a and 89a (after the dates they were released), but only the 89a GIF images can be made transparent, so they're now the most popular by far. *Transparency* means that you can see the background color or pattern of a Web page around the edges of the graphic, just as though it were part of the page itself. Many Web sites use this trick to "build" a Web page that looks like a cohesive whole, when it's actually a background covered with text and transparent GIF images. GIF files are also quite small because they're compressed. (A GIF image doesn't lose quality like a JPEG does when it's compressed over and over.)

"Then why aren't GIF images as popular as JPEG images?" Ah, that's a good question with an easy answer: GIF images can include only a maximum of 256 colors (or 8-bit color), so when they're displayed on-screen or printed, the 16.7 million colors supported by a 24-bit JPEG image are *far* superior. (Also, GIF images can't produce true grayscale.) Therefore, GIF images have been relegated to cartoons, basic Web graphics, and animation.

I'll miss GIF images when they finally disappear, but they're now in vogue because most people still connect to the Internet through an analog telephone modem. After the majority of folks have moved to broadband connections, like DSL and cable modems, image quality will be the name of the game!

Windows bitmap

If you use Windows, you've likely encountered an image in bitmap format. For example, you may have changed your background image on your desktop or used clip art from some Microsoft products. These images end with the extension .BMP.

Bitmap images provide the best image quality of any of the common formats, in both 24-bit color and grayscale. Plus, bitmaps are supported by every Windows operating system from Windows 3.1 to the latest Windows Me and Windows 2000, so you can bet that another person using Windows can open a bitmap image you send.

Unfortunately, because this quality stems partly from a lack of compression, bitmap images are many, many times larger than their JPEG counterparts. For example, a typical desktop background image at 1024 x 768 resolution may measure more than a full megabyte in size! For this reason, bitmaps are scarce on the Internet. (If you do download them, they're usually compressed beforehand with a program like WinZIP.)

Most folks store scanned images in bitmap format for archival purposes. These images, with their compatibility and image quality, can be read from a CD-R and converted into whatever format you need at the time.

Tagged image file format

Cross-platform appeal is the claim to fame for the TIFF format. It's recognized by just about any image editor under the sun under Windows, Mac OS, Linux, and even operating systems like BeOS and that rascally OS/2. TIFF images end with the extension .TIF in the Windows world.

The TIFF format delivers a little of the best of all formats: You can choose to apply different types of compression, although picture quality is excellent with both 24-bit color and grayscale. Graphic artists and publishers appreciate the support TIFF provides for color separations, too. On the downside, however, TIFF images are still larger than JPEG, even with significant compression, so TIFFs aren't a big favorite for Web or e-mail use.

Table 10-1 summarizes the image formats I discuss in this chapter. The sizes I list represent a 24-bit color image at 1024 x 768 resolution from my collection, which I converted to each format.

Table 10-1 The "Compressed" Pros and Cons of Image Formats

Format	*Compression*	*Size*	*Color Depth*	*Grayscale*
JPEG	Yes	110K	16.7 million (24-bit)	Yes
GIF	Yes	N/A	256 colors (8-bit)	No
Bitmap	No	972K	16.7 million (24-bit)	Yes
TIFF	Yes	403K	16.7 million (24-bit)	Yes

What the Sam Hill Is a PNG?

A little-known image format has been threatening to burst onto the Internet scene for the past two or three years, but it just hasn't quite made it yet. The format is named *p*ortable *n*etwork *g*raphics — or PNG ("ping"), for short — and these images typically carry the .PNG extension under Windows.

Why treat PNG differently? Here are three reasons:

- **PNG is the only format designed from top to bottom especially for the Internet — specifically, the Web.** PNG offers the same transparency feature as a GIF file (although a PNG image can't be animated), and it delivers the same 24-bit color as a JPEG. The first ancestor of the PNG format appeared in 1995, so it's a relative toddler compared to the other formats I discuss.

- **PNG offers a *lossless* compression.** Unlike with a JPEG, the compression used to shrink the file size doesn't remove pixels or detail.
- **PNG was supposed to revolutionize the very fabric of the space-time continuum.** (Yes, I'm a *Star Trek* fan, but only of the original series — well, and the first two movies. In my opinion, any form of the show after the second movie is a travesty.)

As you may have guessed from the direction I'm taking, that last reason doesn't hold water. The developers of the PNG format forgot that simple human nature makes people stick with what works until someone develops something better, and that something has to be accepted as a standard by everyone or else it just doesn't get very far off the ground. Although PNG is indeed a better format than GIF, the file sizes PNG provides aren't as small as they are in JPEG format. Therefore, Web page developers still continue to use GIF and JPEG images, and PNG sits on the sidelines like a third-string quarterback.

The PNG format is supported in today's popular browsers, and it still may catch the eye of programmers in the future. After all, it took a few years for people to get excited about that Wright Brothers contraption. (Or so I've read. I'm not *that* old.) For now, though, don't hold your breath waiting for PNG to replace the Big Two.

Choosing Color Depth for Web Images

Here's where things get interesting for your preschooler: Ask the next 4-year-old you meet, "What's the best size for a box of crayons?" That little boy or girl almost certainly will grin widely and say "The biggest one, of course!" And in just about every case, that's the right answer. After all, who wants to use a measly 16-color box of crayons when you can have the 256-color deluxe box instead?

There *is* one case. . . . (You knew that I would say that, didn't you?) Like English grammar, an exception to every rule always exists in the world of computer technology. As I say in Chapter 1, most Web developers tend to choose 256-color images for pages that are visited often. This choice cuts down on the time it takes to download images, including these types:

- Buttons, clip art, and borders.
- Three-dimensional titles. For example, Figure 10-1 illustrates one of my sites (dedicated to the classic 1960s TV series *Batman*). The title on this page is a fair-size piece of rendered three-dimensional artwork, but the image was reduced to 256 colors and loads in five or six seconds on a 56 Kbps modem connection.
- Thumbnails (for Web sites that allow a visitor to click on thumbnails to download larger versions).
- Advertising banners and animated graphics.

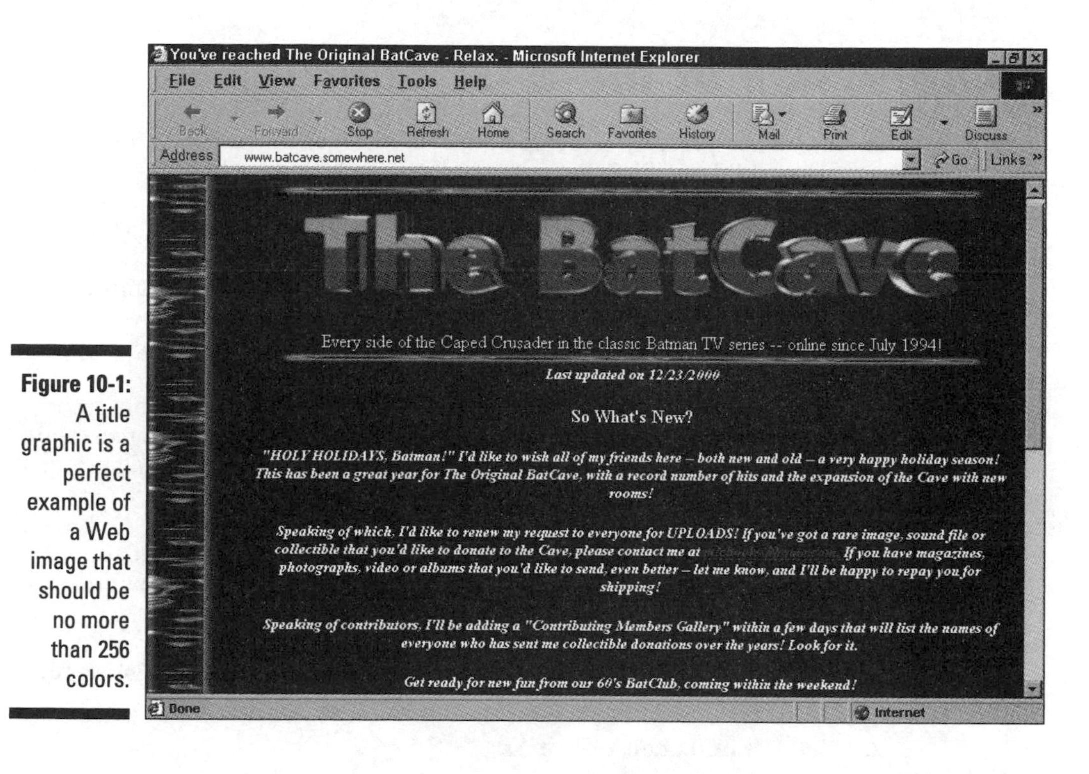

Figure 10-1: A title graphic is a perfect example of a Web image that should be no more than 256 colors.

On the other hand, in two cases, 24-bit color is called for on a Web page:

- **When quality is the thing:** If your site presents high-quality images as its primary function, you need the high-quality appearance of 24-bit color. For example, if your Web site is dedicated to medieval European tapestries of the 14th century, you *have* to deliver 24-bit color to your visitors. (If these images are 800 x 600 or larger, I recommend placing a warning on your home page explaining to those with modem connections to the Internet that downloading may be tedious. Most sites with this kind of content list the typical download time for an image at various speeds, which can help visitors decide whether the entire idea is worthwhile.)

  This type of site is the perfect candidate for thumbnails. That way, your visitors can decide with a glance whether they want to download "Men in Tights" or "Knights in White Satin" *without* having to suffer through an interminable wait just to discover that they picked the wrong image.

- **When your visitors are in the fast lane:** If you run a business site that caters to other businesses (which are likely to be using high-speed connections to the Internet, like a T1 line or a cable modem), you make a better impression with flashier, high-quality images. This statement is especially true on an office intranet, where you know that everyone accesses the site over the office network.

For most people, then, the rule is simple: Stick with 256-color images unless you have a specific need for a larger box of 16 million crayons.

Compression in the 21st Century

The topic of compression pops up in this chapter whenever I mention image formats like JPEG and PNG. Because these image formats allow you to pack a 24-bit image into a smaller space, why not crank compression higher and reduce them even further? In this section, I show you a series of images that help illustrate what I mean by *lossy* compression (where pixels are removed using a mathematical formula) and *lossless* compression (which compresses the image without removing pixels), and I help you to understand why too much compression is not a good thing.

The sample shown in Figure 10-2 is the starting point: It's an uncompressed Windows bitmap image, with plenty of detail and shadows you can use (and an attractive subject to boot). At 1100 x 1057 and 24-bit color, the image occupies about 3.5MB of hard drive territory.

You can experiment with compression to convert this bitmap image into a compressed JPEG. As a first step, you apply a simple 15 percent compression (practically nothing) by following these steps in Paint Shop Pro:

1. **Click File and choose the Open menu item. Highlight the existing file and click Open.**
2. **Click File and choose Save As.**
3. **Click the Save as type drop-down list box and choose the JPEG format.**
4. **Type a new filename in the File name field.**
5. **Click the Options button to specify JPEG settings, which displays the dialog box shown in Figure 10-3. Click Standard encoding and then click and drag the Compression factor slider control until it reaches 15.**
6. **Click OK to return to the Save As dialog box.**
7. **Click Save to start the conversion and save the new file to disk.**

As you can see in Figure 10-4 — well, you can't really see much difference (at least none that you can tell with the naked eye, or even at a significant zoom factor!) I generally apply 15 percent compression to all my JPEG images, and it has never affected the quality of the images appreciably. However, check the new file size — *whoa!* The same file at the same size and same color depth is now (drum roll, please) a measly 196K — hence, the popularity of the JPEG format. That's a combination of the more efficient image format and the compression level you chose.

Figure 10-2: An uncompressed bitmap version of a scanned photograph.

Crank up the compression and apply 65 percent to the sample image. Finally, you can begin to see in Figure 10-5 the effects of lossy compression as the image starts to lose detail. The file size is reduced further, to a mere 62K.

Avoid the pit of repeating compression!

You can easily fall into the Pit of Repeating Compression. That's the case with a JPEG image you open and edit repeatedly (perhaps to add or update a piece of text or to experiment with the gamma level). If you save the image each time using that typical 15 percent compression ratio I mention in the main text, each copy you save suffers another repetition of the compression procedure (thereby unnecessarily degrading the quality of the image a little bit further). To avoid this situation, set your image editor to reduce compression to 1 percent for successive saves. You generally can't turn off compression altogether when you're saving a JPEG, although you can reduce it to the bare minimum.

Just for kicks, go all the way and increase the compression to the maximum 99 percent. This amount is ridiculous, of course, but you can do it in Paint Shop Pro. And, as you can see in Figure 10-6, the JPEG format still provides something that's almost recognizable! At this point, the image is only 27K in size!

Now you can convert the sample image to PNG format. Although the image looks exactly the same as the original bitmap image shown in Figure 10-2, its size drops to about 1.7MB. The lossless compression used in a PNG image is far less effective than even a minimum 1 percent compression level applied to a JPEG image, which produces about an 800K image.

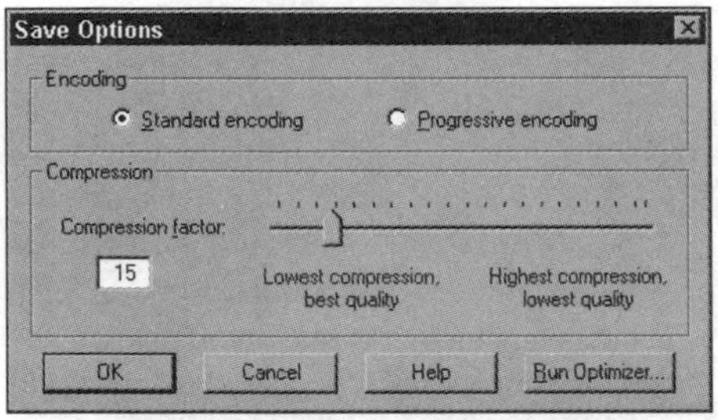

Figure 10-3: Choosing a mild level of JPEG compression with Paint Shop Pro.

Figure 10-4: Wait — I know that 15 percent compression is applied here, but I can't see it!

Figure 10-5: At 65 percent compression, the image starts to lose a noticeable amount of quality.

Figure 10-6: Well, what did you expect at 99 percent lossy compression? A Rembrandt?

That Color Doesn't Look Right

The Web can be a colorful place — at least, if you've decided to use 24-bit color images. Then again, for all the reasons I mention in preceding sections, you may decide to opt for 256 colors, which means that you've decided on the GIF format for a particular Web image. The problem is, *which* 256 colors look "right" in every visitor's browser? Imagine all the different combinations of commercial, freeware, and shareware browsers out there, matched with Windows or Mac OS or Linux! (On second thought, don't imagine it. Like mine, your head probably hurts already.)

Luckily, the HTTP powers that be (read "Internet Explorer and Netscape Navigator") have decided on their own color palette that's supposed to be the best possible compromise between the Windows system color palette and the Mac OS system color palette. The result is an "optimized" Web palette of 216 colors that delivers a good range of colors — everything from a 256-color VGA display all the way up to a 16.7 million-color display. People who design Web pages for a living are well familiar with the Web palette.

Paint Shop Pro makes reducing your GIF images to this "Web safe" palette easy by loading what it calls the Jasc Safety Palette. Follow these steps:

1. **Click File and choose the Open menu item to load your image.**
2. **Click Colors and choose Load Palette. Double-click the Palette folder to open it and choose the SAFETY.PAL file from the list. Paint Shop Pro reduces things for you.**
3. **Save your changes: Click File and choose Save or Save As.**

Remember that Web palette optimization is for *only* 256-color GIF images. Applied to a 24-bit photograph, the Web palette destroys the quality by reducing 16.7 million possible colors to a whopping 216 colors, and the result is barely recognizable!

What Size Is Best for the Web?

As you may already know, no single "correct" size exists for a Web image. If a visitor to your site downloads an image that's bigger than her screen resolution, her browser still displays it. However, she has to scroll the image from top to bottom or side to side (or both) to view the entire thing, which is really not the best solution.

Therefore, keep these guidelines in mind while you're deciding on the dimensions of your Web images:

- **Most folks still use lower screen resolutions.** Although today's video cards and monitors allow absolutely ludicrous on-screen resolutions, how many people actually hang out at 1600 x 1200? Most site visitors are likely to use a resolution of 800 x 600 (with some a little higher, at 1024 x 768, and some still clinging stubbornly to 640 x 480). Therefore, if you want your images to be displayed without scrolling and downloaded in a bearable period of time, they should be significantly smaller than 800 x 600.
- **Use a common aspect ratio.** A computer monitor uses an aspect ratio of approximately 1.33 to 1. Therefore, most visitors have problems if you try to display an image that's 450 x 900. Instead, try cropping or resizing to bring such an image more in line with the standard aspect ratio.
- **Thumbnails are not to be taken seriously.** Can you really expect anyone to appreciate an image that's only 100 x 75 (*especially* if it includes text)? Unfortunately, I've visited more than one Web site where the designer expects you to buy a product based on a thumbnail image! Thumbnails should be used only as part of a visual catalog, and if your visitors deserve a better look, give them a look at your image at 400 x 300 or 640 x 480 instead. As you find out in the section "Wait a Second: Is This Legal?" (later in this chapter), this Catch-22 occurs if your images are the star of the show. If you offer a version of an original photograph that's too large, it can be stolen by others who don't care about copyrights and used for their purposes.

If an image absolutely has to be larger than 800 x 600 or the aspect ratio must remain somewhat outrageous, consider using WinZIP to archive that image into a zip file, and allow your visitors to download the ZIP file rather than the image itself. They save time — plus, after they've unarchived the image, they can load it into their own image editor program and modify it to their liking. Everyone's happy this way!

Sending Your Scans through E-Mail

Sending a scanned image as an e-mail attachment is convenient and quick. All that's required on both ends is an Internet connection and an e-mail account that can receive binary attachments. To illustrate the process, I show you how to send an image to a friend using Microsoft Outlook.

Follow these steps:

1. **Run Outlook by clicking the Outlook icon on your Windows desktop. (Outlook Express works fine as well.)**
2. **Click File and choose New and Mail Message from the pop-up menu to display a new message window, as shown Figure 10-7.**
3. **Click your cursor in the To field and type an e-mail address. (Or, if you're using the Address Book, click the To button and choose an entry.)**

4. **Click in the editing pane and enter the text of your message.**
5. **Click Insert and choose File to display the Insert File dialog box, as shown in Figure 10-8.**
6. **Locate the image on your hard drive and click the filename to select it.**
7. **Click on the arrow next to the Insert button and choose Insert as Attachment from the pop-up menu; an attachment pane is automatically added to the bottom of the window, showing you the attached file, as shown in Figure 10-9.**
8. **Click the Send button on the toolbar to send the message.**

After the recipient of your message receives your e-mail, he can easily save the attachment to disk. If they're using Outlook as well, he can right-click on the attachment icon and choose Save As to display the Save As dialog box, choose a location, and save the file. Outlook preserves the filename (including the extension) on the receiving end.

Converting your images to JPEG format before you add them as attachments is always a good idea. Your Internet Service Provider is likely to have a maximum allowed size for attachments, and a 3MB bitmap or TIFF file may be rejected by your e-mail server when you try to send it. (Plus, you would be covered in cobwebs by the time your 56 Kbps modem finished sending it.)

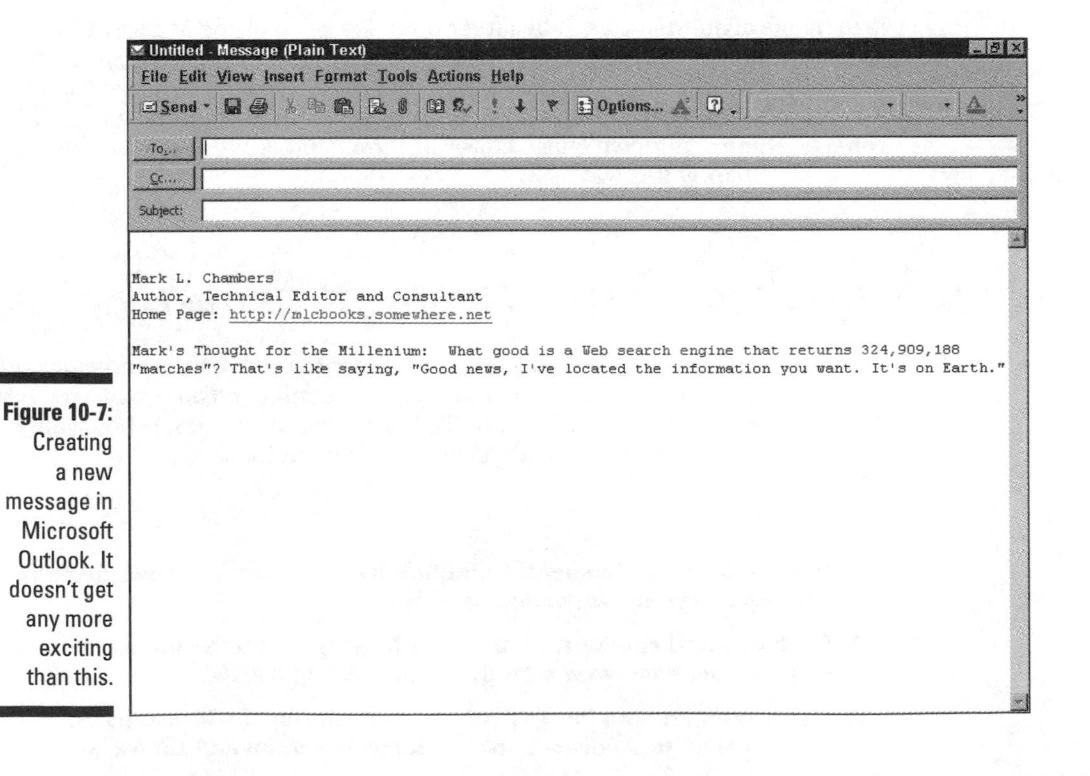

Figure 10-7: Creating a new message in Microsoft Outlook. It doesn't get any more exciting than this.

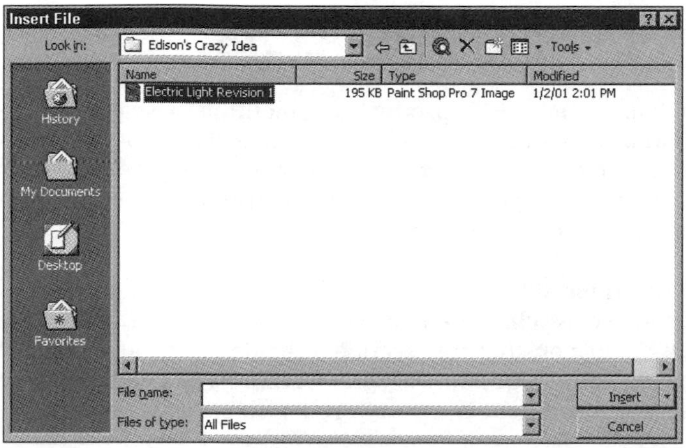

Insert File

Look in: Edison's Crazy Idea

Tools

Name	Size	Type	Modified
Electric Light Revision 1	195 KB	Paint Shop Pro 7 Image	1/2/01 2:01 PM

History

My Documents

Desktop

Favorites

File name:

Files of type: All Files

Insert

Cancel

Figure 10-8: Selecting a file to attach to the message.

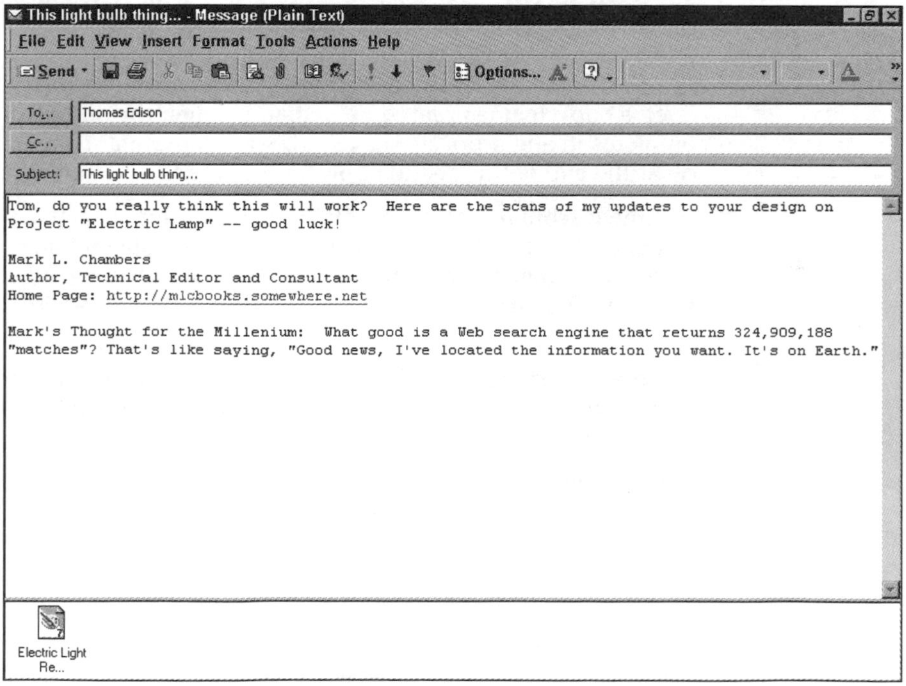

This light bulb thing... - Message (Plain Text)

File Edit View Insert Format Tools Actions Help

Send Options...

To... Thomas Edison

Cc...

Subject: This light bulb thing...

```
Tom, do you really think this will work?  Here are the scans of my updates to your design on
Project "Electric Lamp" -- good luck!

Mark L. Chambers
Author, Technical Editor and Consultant
Home Page: http://mlcbooks.somewhere.net

Mark's Thought for the Millenium:  What good is a Web search engine that returns 324,909,188
"matches"? That's like saying, "Good news, I've located the information you want. It's on Earth."
```

Electric Light Re...

Figure 10-9: The image is ready to be sent along with the e-mail message.

Wait a Second: Is This Legal?

And well you should ask! Reproducing something by scanning it for your own, personal use is one thing. Often, the material is yours anyway, but communicating it to the outside world in any way could involve you in a legal wrestling match. The problem is one of copyrights — and the question is far more complex than most people think.

Let's get one thing straight: *I am not a lawyer.* I have friends and relatives who are lawyers, I've watched them on TV, and I know a half-dozen good lawyer jokes, but *do not* consider this section to be definitive legal advice! The guidelines I provide here are simply general warnings, so if you have copyright questions that need to be answered, you *must* employ a knowledgeable copyright lawyer!

Now that you're all cognizant that I'm not Perry Mason, I can furnish you with a few rules every scanner owner should know:

- **A work doesn't have to carry a copyright mark to be copyrighted.** In effect, a copyright is granted immediately when the author of a work completes it, and it doesn't have to bear a copyright. (However, I show you at the end of this section how to add one to a scanned image.)
- **Movement from document to digital is moot.** Just because the original is a paper document and you've scanned it as a digital image, it doesn't suddenly become your property. (If so, I would be the genius behind everything Mozart ever composed, Shakespeare ever wrote, and Escher ever drew!)
- **The source is immaterial.** Web sites, Internet newsgroups, your neighbor's trash, or the daily paper — no matter how you got it, if it's not your original work, you must receive permission from the author to use it.
- **Permissions must be individually obtained.** Even if the author of an original document has granted you permission for other, similar works in the past, no shortcut is allowed; you must receive permission for each work individually.
- **Changing an original doesn't change the copyright.** Substituting your face for the *Mona Lisa*'s kisser with your image editor doesn't change a thing. The rule is simple: If the work wasn't your creation, modifying it doesn't make it yours.

If you do decide to distribute a scanned image of your original work, I definitely recommend that you add a visible copyright to it! Follow these steps within Paint Shop Pro:

1. **Click File and choose the Open menu item. Highlight the existing file and click Open.**

2. **Click the Text icon on the toolbar on the left side of the screen (it looks like a letter A), and then click the cursor where you want the line of text to begin.**

   Paint Shop Pro displays the Text Entry dialog box, as shown in Figure 10-10.

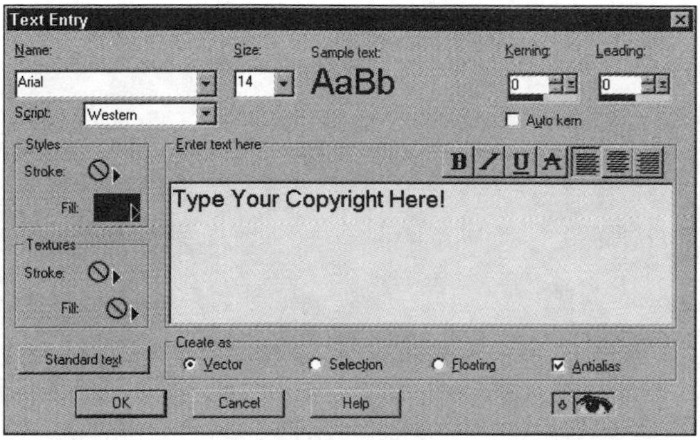

Figure 10-10: Entering a copyright message in the Text Entry dialog box.

3. **Choose a font from the Name drop-down list box and a font size from the Size list box, click in the Text box, and type the following line where it's visible:**

   Copyright (c) [year] by [name], All Rights Reserved.

   where [year] is the year in which you created the work and [name] is your name or the name of your company.

4. **Save your changes: Click File and choose Save or Save As.**

Should I Keep This to Myself?

Let me be brutally frank here: Most travelers on the Web don't know (or don't care) about copyright law. If you're the creator and copyright owner of an image, *never offer it on your Web page or send it to another person if you want to keep exclusive rights!* As an author with a professional relationship with my publishers, I know that my rights are protected under contract. If you simply add an original high-resolution image to your Web page for anyone to download, however, don't be surprised if that work shows up on other Web sites and Internet newsgroups. Usually, you aren't credited, and to most people your image becomes part of the "public domain" (although, as I just discussed, it most certainly *isn't*).

"So how do I distribute an image without losing control?" Unfortunately, if you don't have a legal agreement or contract, about the only method you can depend on is to "cripple" the image by either adding a line of text over it (as shown in Figure 10-11). You can also reduce its size to something that's worthless to redistribute, which means that your visitors get treated to something not much bigger than a thumbnail. Even these safeguards aren't guarantees. Other people have image editors too.

Figure 10-11: Although this text doesn't prevent a patient person from restoring the image, it should prove troublesome.

Chapter 11

Advanced Image Editing 101

In This Chapter

- Introducing filters and effects
- Using the Effect Browser in Paint Shop Pro
- Installing plug-in effects and filters
- Copying and pasting pixels
- Coloring pixels
- Exploring other image applications

Are you ready to try the deep end of the scanning pool? If so, you're considering testing the waters that many scanner owners never reach. Those folks are satisfied with a simple crop or a resizing, and they never wonder what an image would look like if the subject were swirling down a drain or pressed into aluminum — or even set on fire!

The moral of the story is a simple one, and it forms the foundation for this chapter. To wit: *You don't have to settle for the images your scanner produces!* Take my word for it: The artist inside you is just waiting for a chance to emerge. After you know how, the rest is simply finding all the time you need to experiment.

I already cover minor image surgery in Chapter 8; in this chapter, I introduce you to the procedures and tools you need to apply major changes and enhancements to your scanned images (as well as a number of additional software tools you may find valuable).

Making Magic with Scanned Images

All right, let me come clean: I never *really* sat for the portrait with President Abraham Lincoln you see in Figure 11-1; Figure 11-2 shows the original photograph of the Hero of the Republic, and the original scanned image of me is shown in Figure 11-3.

Figure 11-1: Sitting with the President was such a thrill!

Figure 11-2: Honest Abe, before I joined him.

Figure 11-3: An ordinary author, with no Presidential companion.

So how did I do it? By using my image editor to "combine" the two portraits, using the same familiar type of cut-and-paste commands you've grown to know and love with applications like your word processor. Rather than cut paragraphs, though, I cut my image and pasted it into Lincoln's photograph. (I also converted my image to grayscale because brilliant color wasn't a feature of the cameras available back in those days.)

Such magic is easy, and you find out how to do it later in this chapter, in the section "Copying and pasting (without scissors)." First, I want to introduce you to filters and special effects, which are probably the most powerful tools available in your image editor.

Introducing Filters and Effects

Whenever you feel creative, it's time to turn to the two big-name stars featured within most image editors: *filters* and *effects.* They both do the same thing: modify your image by applying a mathematical formula. Some filters and effects change only the pixels in a certain area of your image, and others modify the entire image.

What about text?

You may be wondering whether filters and effects can be applied to scanned images with text, like a newsletter page you've scanned. The answer is yes (filters and effects can be used with *any* image), although in most cases you can't read the text! If you use a twist effect on that newsletter page, for example, the text appears to spiral into the center of the image. This trick can work, however, if you're using an effect that can be controlled; a slight twist may leave the text intact while imparting a, well, a wacky feel! Trust me on this one.

What's the difference between a filter and an effect? (Pay close attention — you can win your next trivia contest with this question.) An effect can typically be controlled, so you can specify just how much you want to change your image — and therefore it requires your input. On the other hand, a filter is usually automatic. You simply apply it and forget it. Other than that, filters and effects are virtually indistinguishable from each other, so you can promptly forget this if you want.

I cover some of my favorite filters and effects elsewhere in this book. For now, just remember that they can change an ordinary snapshot into something that looks like it was taken in the Twilight Zone!

Going Wild with the Effect Browser

If you're reading this chapter from beginning to end, you should be on speaking terms with filters and effects. Let's visit our old friend Paint Shop Pro and see how the program applies them.

Here I go, waxing enthusiastic about my favorite image editor again. This program is so doggone cool, though, that I can't *help* it! Paint Shop Pro provides a browser that makes it easy to see the changes you can make to an image with any effect. (Note that the Effect Browser has nothing to do with Web pages or the Internet. Instead, it's a separate window displayed within the program. I've visited some mind-boggling Web pages, although not within Paint Shop Pro.)

To use the Effect Browser, follow these steps:

1. **Click Effects and choose Effect Browser to display the window shown in Figure 11-4.**

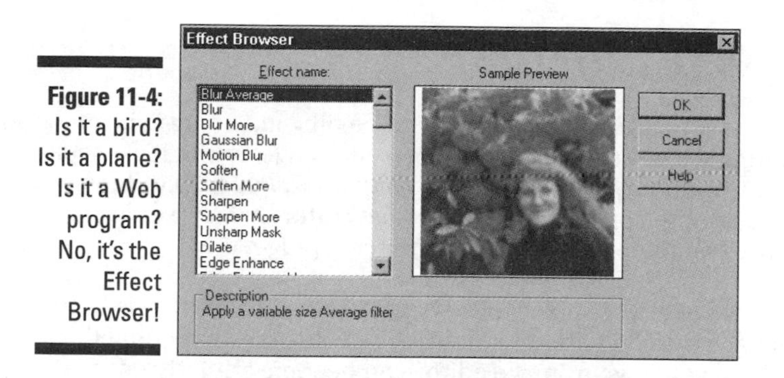

Figure 11-4: Is it a bird? Is it a plane? Is it a Web program? No, it's the Effect Browser!

2. **Click the Contours effect in the list.**

   Paint Shop Pro displays a thumbnail preview image that demonstrates what type of changes the effect produces. You also get a quick description of the effect on the status line at the bottom of the browser.

3. **After you've chosen the effect you want, click OK to apply it or click Cancel to back out without making any changes.**

   Figure 11-5 shows an image after Contours has been used. Wow!

Figure 11-5: The artistic result produced by the Contours effect.

I know that the preview window provided by the Effect Browser may not give you an exact idea of what an effect does. A thumbnail can show only so much detail, so keep in mind that you can use the Undo feature to reverse any effect you apply! You can choose Undo from the Edit menu.

Let's Hear It for Plug-Ins!

I want to introduce you to a good friend of mine, the plug-in. A *plug-in* is an extension program that's not actually built-in to your image editor. It's a separate piece of software you buy. A plug-in is typically produced by a different developer than the folks who produced your image editor; in fact, some software companies are completely devoted to producing plug-ins.

To give you some idea of how popular these beasties are, I have friends in the graphic arts who have installed literally hundreds of plug-ins! Extending the craziness available to you in your image editor can become addictive. It's much like those folks you probably know who are "hooked" on fonts.

Before I wax too enthusiastic about plug-ins, check your image editor's documentation. Although most well-known programs support them, exceptions exist. The most popular type of plug-in is designed to be used with Adobe Photoshop, and Paint Shop Pro supports this standard type. Other plug-ins you encounter may be designed for a specific image editor, so they may not work on your system; check the system requirements in the documentation for the plug-in to make sure that it works with your editor.

If your image editor does indeed support plug-ins and you've bought or downloaded one or two compatible modules to experiment with, you're ready to install them and get down to business.

In Paint Shop Pro, follow these steps to add a new plug-in:

1. **Click File, choose Preferences, and click File Locations from the pop-up menu to open the File Locations dialog box.**
2. **Click the Plug-in Filters tab to display the settings shown in Figure 11-6.**

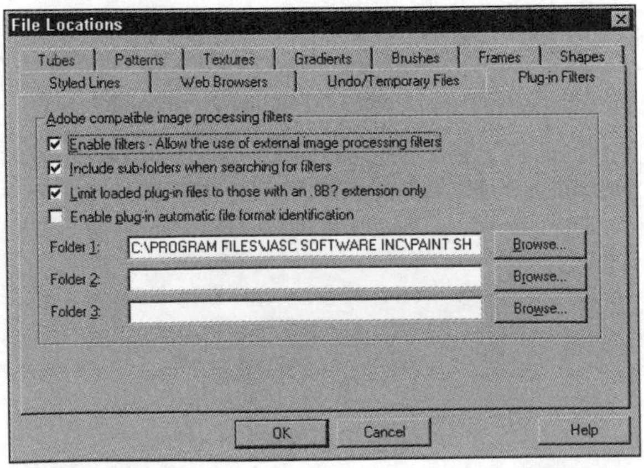

Figure 11-6: Adding a plug-in is fun and educational. Well, at least it's not hard.

3. **Click the Enable filters check box to enable external plug-ins in Paint Shop Pro.**

4. **Some plug-ins come with their own installation program. If that's the case with your new toy, run the install program and smile quietly to yourself. Otherwise, copy the file into the folder \Plugins under your Paint Shop Pro home folder.**

   Alternatively, click the Browse button next to the Folder 2 field and select the folder where you've installed your new plug-in files.

   Some people like to keep different sets of plug-ins from different developers in different folders so that they can add or remove them more easily. Personally, I prefer the easy route.

5. **Click OK to save your new settings and return to Paint Shop Pro.**

Photoshop users find that things work much the same:

- If the plug-in comes with an installer, run the program.
- If the plug-in needs to be installed manually, copy it into the Plug-ins folder inside the Photoshop home folder.

To set up an alternative folder for a plug-in within Photoshop, follow these steps:

1. **Click Edit, choose Preferences, and choose Plug-ins and Scratch Disks from the pop-up menu. Photoshop displays the dialog box shown in Figure 11-7.**

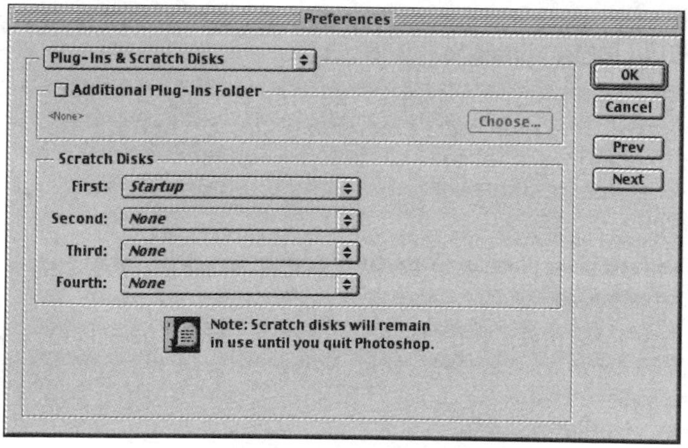

Figure 11-7: Adding a Photoshop plug-in folder. Feel the power.

2. **Enable the Additional Plug-Ins Folder check box, click Choose, and highlight the folder where you installed the additional plug-ins.**
3. **Click OK (or Choose, depending on the operating system) to save your changes.**
4. **Restart Photoshop so that the program can recognize the new plug-ins.**

Editing Tiny Pieces of Your Images

Earlier in this chapter, I discuss all sorts of filters, effects, and plug-in fun. Now I want to turn your attention toward the manual joys of image editing. I show you how to change images by copying and pasting and by changing the colors of pixels.

Copying and pasting (without scissors)

As I mention earlier in this chapter, I used this trick to hang out with President Lincoln, but you can use it for more practical purposes, like copying a piece of an image and pasting it in another place (either in the same image or another image). You can use it to replicate (adding multiple "copies" of people in the same scanned photograph, for example) or eliminate (by copying a blank area over an offending object). To practice cutting and pasting within Paint Shop Pro, follow these steps:

1. **Click File and choose the Open command to load your image.**
2. **Click the geometric selection tool on the left side of the program's window. (Remember that it looks like a dotted rectangle.)**
3. **Click on the top left corner of the area to copy, and hold the mouse down while you drag the selection rectangle to the lower right corner of the area you want to save. Release the mouse button to select the area, which remains surrounded by the animated rectangle (as shown in Figure 11-8).**
4. **Click Edit and choose Copy to place the image you selected in the Windows Clipboard.**
5. **To paste the piece you copied into the current image, click Edit and choose Paste as New Selection. Move the mouse to place the selected area where you want it, and click to "drop" it when you're ready, as shown in Figure 11-9.**

Figure 11-8: Selecting an area of an image to copy.

Figure 11-9: Just call it cloning for the common man.

To paste into another image the piece you copied from the Clipboard, follow these steps:

1. **Click File and choose Close. (Click No when you're prompted to save changes, unless you actually did make changes to the source image you want to save.)**
2. **Click File and Open to open the target image and then click Edit and choose Paste as New Selection.**
3. **Move your mouse to move the piece anywhere in the image, and click once to drop it where you want it.**
4. **Click File and choose Save or Save As to save the new image with another filename or format (or both).**

Changing colors (without crayons)

Face it: Pixels aren't always perfect, and most of the time the problem has to do with coloring. You can encounter a wide range of color problems in your scanned images, including

- Elements in the image that need to be changed or erased (but can't be cropped out), like a sign in the background of a photograph or a stray line of text in a document.
- Cosmetic imperfections in the original, such as "flecks" in a photograph or a thumbprint on a business card.
- Just plain downright wrong colors. Aunt Harriet wore yellow and purple together again, didn't she?

Follow these steps to change the color of individual pixels (or a group of pixels) in an image using Paint Shop Pro:

1. **Click File and choose Open to load your image.**
2. **Click the zoom tool on the left side of the program's window; the tool resembles a magnifying glass.**
3. **To get a better look at your pixels, click the area of the image you want to edit.**

   Each click zooms in closer, so keep clicking until you can easily see the area of pixels you want to change. Figure 11-10 illustrates a block of pixels that needs to be "painted" white.
4. **Move your mouse cursor to the color selector in the upper right corner of the program window. As you move your mouse cursor over the color you want, the cursor changes to an eyedropper to indicate that Paint Shop Pro is ready to "pick up" that color. Click once to set the foreground color and right-click once to set the background color.**

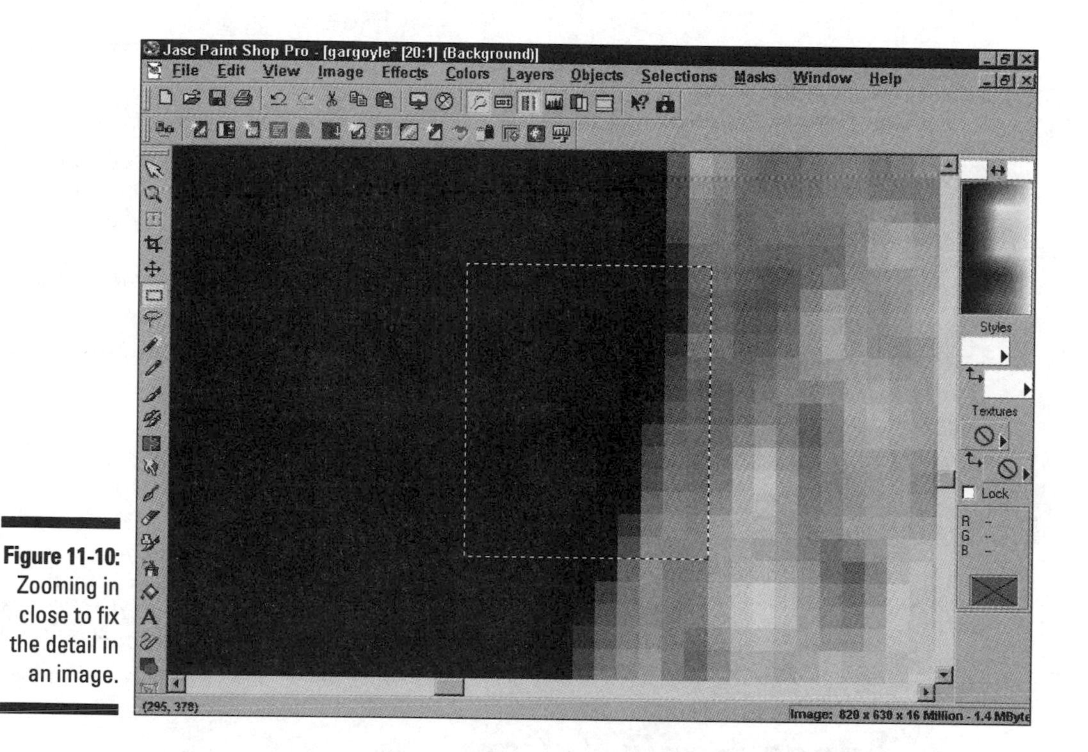

Figure 11-10: Zooming in close to fix the detail in an image.

5. **Click the paintbrush tool on the left side of the program window. Move the paintbrush cursor on top of the pixel (or pixels) you need to change and click to paint the pixel with the new colors. Repeat as necessary.**
6. **Click File and choose Save or Save As to save the new image with another filename or format (or both).**

Naturally, these basic techniques are nowhere near a complete catalog of everything you can do in a powerful image editor like Paint Shop Pro or Photoshop — but then, covering everything you can do with such programs is far beyond the scope of this book, which is supposed to be about scanners (no matter how much I like image editing). Several complete books the size of this one — and many that are *much* bigger — are completely devoted to Photoshop and Paint Shop Pro.

For a complete guide to Photoshop (which is something akin to a complete guide to every grain of sand on Pismo Beach), I recommend all 900-plus pages of *Photoshop 6 Bible,* by Deke McClelland. It comes in two flavors — one edition for Windows and another for Mac OS — and it's published by Hungry Minds, Inc. For an in-depth guide to Paint Shop Pro (with a *...For Dummies* attitude), turn to my comrade-in-arms, David C. Kay, the author of *Paint Shop Pro 7 For Dummies* (also published by Hungry Minds, Inc.).

Talk about seamless!

What's that you say, Bunkie? You're having a hard time matching the color surrounding a pixel by using the color selector? Well, I've got good news: If you want, you can duplicate the exact colors in surrounding pixels! Paint Shop Pro provides an eyedropper you can use to match the colors of a single pixel in your image. Click the eyedropper tool on the left side of the screen and move the eyedropper cursor over the pixel with the color you want to use. Click once with the left mouse button and once with the right to lock in the colors.

Imaging Tools You Can't Resist

Before I close up shop for this chapter, expand your horizons and leave "pure" image-editing software behind! In this section, I familiarize you with other types of image applications you may want to use with your scanned images as well as cover a few of the best-known plug-ins on the market. These programs can add convenience and versatility to your digital toolbox!

Image manipulation

First on a wish list of image software is the *image manipulation* genre. This category covers a wide range of programs, all of which are designed to apply some sort of special appearance or perform a single type of editing procedure on an image. If you like, think of these programs as stand-alone plug-ins that run without an image editor.

Corel KnockOut

KnockOut is a *masking* program: That term means that you can use the program to isolate and remove just one element from an image and then copy that image the same way you pasted a rectangular selection if you've read the first part of this chapter. However, KnockOut provides much more precise selection tools than a plain image editor. For example, you can isolate and manipulate a tree from a scanned photograph, complete with every leaf intact, or even subjects with blurred or hazy edges. Imagine being able to "grab" an image of a Persian cat from one photo and seamlessly insert it into another image, without losing a single hair! The program has a street price of about $200, and it runs on both Macs and PCs. Figure 11-11 illustrates KnockOut at work.

For more information on KnockOut, visit the Corel site, at `www.corel.com`.

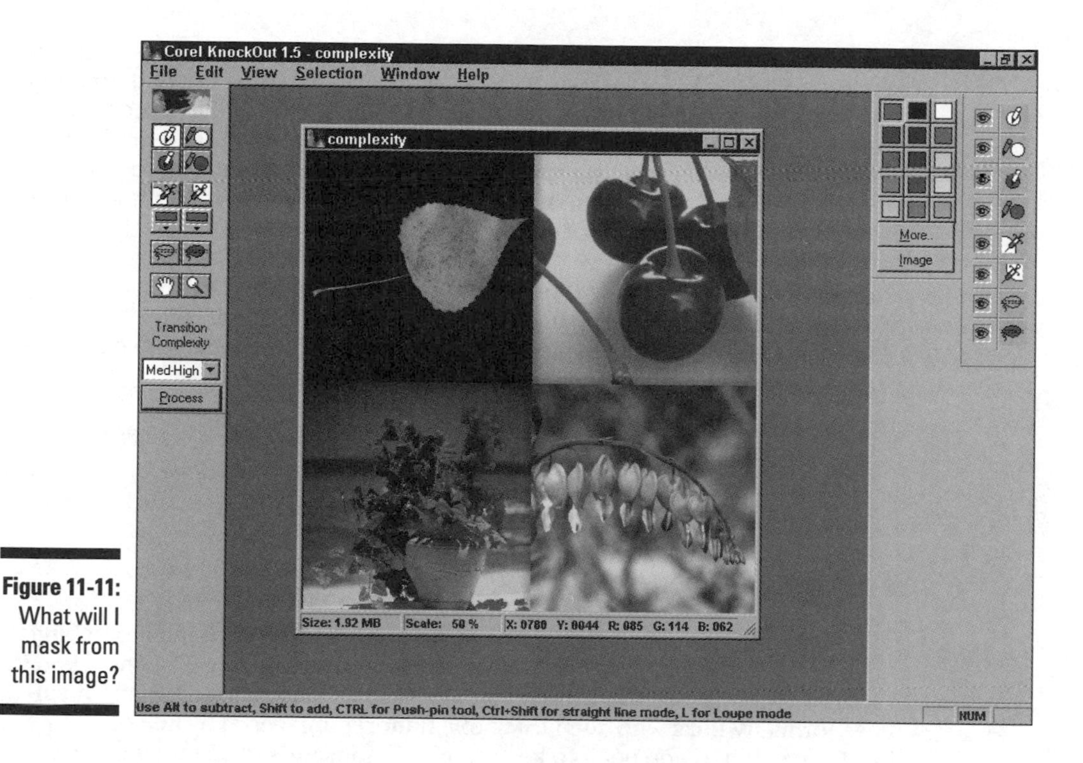

Figure 11-11: What will I mask from this image?

Kai's SuperGoo

SuperGoo has been a favorite of my kids for years. This easy-to-use image manipulator has several built-in filters that allow you to see the effects of what you're doing in real time, while you're working. You can turn an innocent portrait into a wacky shot of an unearthly alien — all with no previous knowledge of image editing. Smudge a face this way or bash it that way or stretch a subject in a photograph like taffy! You can also animate your changes to an image and produce the resulting "goo" as an AVI or QuickTime movie. SuperGoo is a steal at $20, and it can run on both Macs and PCs.

Visit the SuperGoo home page, at `www.scansoft.com/products/goo`.

Image correction: Kai's PhotoSoap2

Another type of common image application is specially designed to fix specific errors within your images — a nasty case of red-eye, for example, or the scratches typically found on those old photographs kept in shoeboxes. These image-correction programs aren't used as often as your image editor, but when you do need them to rescue an image that's otherwise unusable, they're worth every penny you spend.

PhotoSoap2 shares many of the same ease-of-use features as its sister product SuperGoo. Scanner owners from 10 to 100 can easily use it, and no previous image editing experience is needed. You can correct images scanned from wrinkled or scratched originals, brighten and sharpen, add or change colors, and even remove the speckles from a text document before you use an OCR program. All these tasks are done with intuitive animated tools, like brushes and pencils, in real time!

PhotoSoap2 also includes more traditional editing chores that I cover in my discussion of Paint Shop Pro, like cropping, rotating, and resizing. PhotoSoap2 also provides a basic image album feature so that you can store your images and retrieve them when you need them.

For more information or to order PhotoSoap2 online, visit `www.scansoft.com/products/soap`.

Image cataloging

The more you use your scanner, the more you may find yourself scratching your head and wondering "Exactly where did I put that image?" I show you in Chapter 9 how to use the Browse function within Paint Shop Pro, and it suffices for many folks who keep track of a hundred images at a time on their hard drive. But, if you need to keep track of thousands of scanned images, you need a more powerful image cataloging tool.

Media Center Plus 3

From the same folks who brought me my favorite image editor, Jasc Software, comes Media Center Plus 3, a program that can even keep images organized for someone like me. (I'm about as methodical and neat as a panda bear.) Figure 11-12 shows the main window from Media Center Plus 3.

To use a catalog, you display thumbnails (again, much like the Paint Shop Pro Browse screen) and double-click on a thumbnail to load the file. An image cataloging tool can also store much more, however, including audio (like MP3 and WAV format files) and video (like MPEG and Microsoft AVI movie files)! Even though you're concerned only with images in this book, you can think of this program as a Swiss army knife for storing all your digital media. You can acquire images from your scanner directly from MCP 3, display any image and print it directly from your catalog, or create a slideshow presentation (rather like the slideshow CD-ROM I show you how to create in Chapter 13) complete with background music. You can "attach" text keywords and descriptions to any media file so that you can search an entire catalog for a Glorious Eagle That Symbolizes Freedom from Oppression. (I have that image somewhere.) To make life easier, MCP 3 can even convert images from one format to another — no need to fire up Paint Shop Pro!

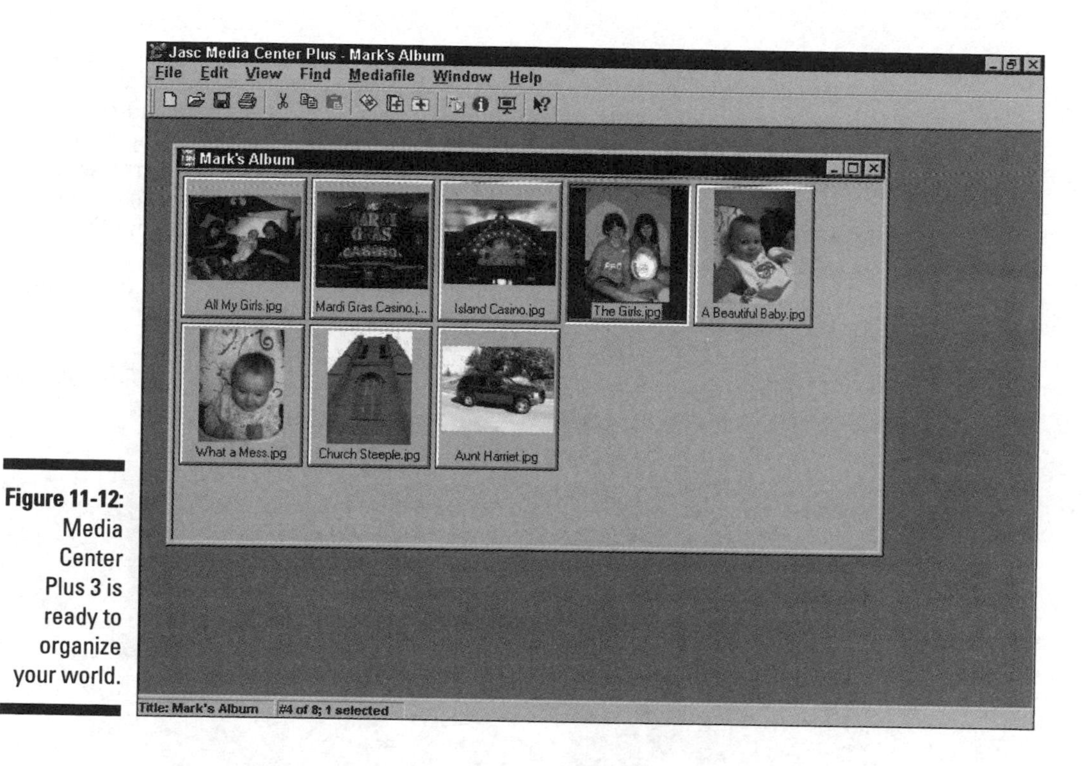

Figure 11-12: Media Center Plus 3 is ready to organize your world.

Like Paint Shop Pro, MCP 3 is available directly from Jasc Software, at `www.jasc.com`. The program costs about $30 for the download-only version and about $40 for the boxed version. That's a bargain!

ImageAXS Professional

ImageAXS Professional offers the same media database tools you find in Media Center Plus 3, and it offers a number of different tricks as well. For example, you can use the e-Z Card export feature to quickly create a slideshow floppy disk for people with no image display software handy. The program can handle an amazing number of different audio, video, and image formats, and you can create Web pages with thumbnails or full-size images with the built-in HTML wizard. The program retails for about $200. For more information on ImageAXS Professional, visit `www.scansoft.com/products/imageaxs/`.

Plug-in software: Eye Candy 4000

I have an easy way to demonstrate just exactly how many plug-ins are available for image editors like Photoshop or Paint Shop Pro: Just drop by your favorite online software store (or visit `www.yahoo.com`) and type **photoshop plug-in** for your search criteria! Some plug-ins simply add effects, and others add new commands and functionality.

Alien Skin Software has produced a number of fantastic plug-in suites over the past several years, and Eye Candy 4000 is the company's latest work. The package includes 23 Photoshop-standard filters, including Glass (adds a realistic glass layer or fonts on top of an image, with accurate reflection and refraction effects), Marble (which can create original marble patterns with full control over coloring, veins, and shape), and Smoke (which can create smoke, haze, and fog for those London shots that didn't turn out right).

Figure 11-13 illustrates what I did in just 30 seconds with the Glass filter, and Figure 11-14 shows off the Marble effect!

You can buy Eye Candy directly from the developers for less than $200 by visiting their site, at www.alienskin.com.

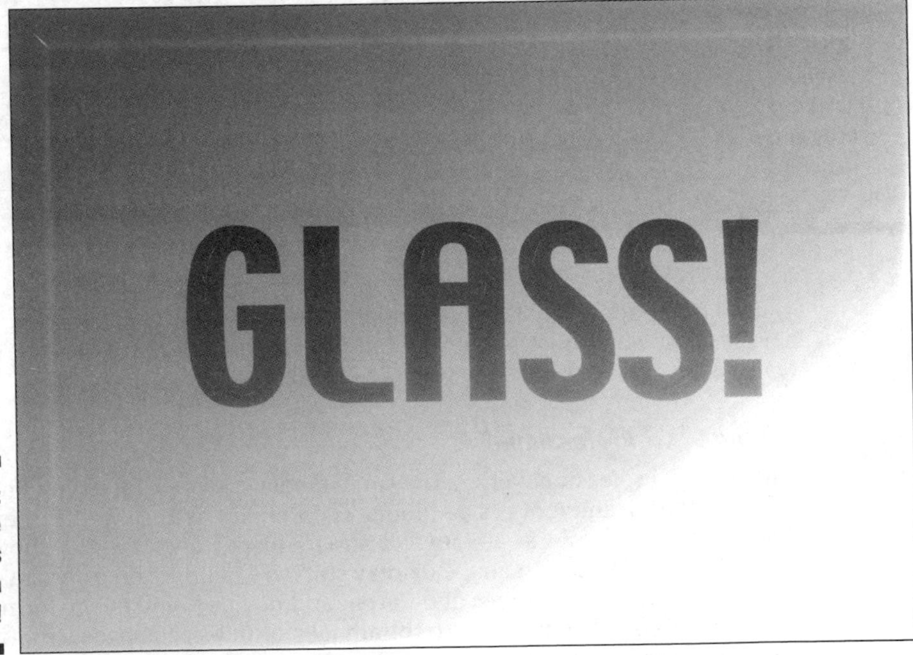

Figure 11-13: The Eye Candy Glass filter is a treat!

Figure 11-14: Who would guess that this stone masterpiece was computer generated?

Chapter 12

Maintaining the Scanner Beast

In This Chapter

- Calibrating your scanner
- Cleaning your scanner
- Troubleshooting and solving hardware problems
- Troubleshooting and solving software problems
- Calling technical support

Compared to other pieces of rather recalcitrant hardware you can attach to your computer, like a printer or digital camera, a scanner is, I'm happy to say, practically a walk in the park when it comes to maintenance. It has no batteries, ink cartridges, or paper to change and no clogged inkjet nozzles or spilled toner dust. Jamming a sheet-fed scanner is possible (I tell you more about this topic in a bit), but a flatbed is practically a sealed unit.

That doesn't mean, however, that you can simply ignore your scanner like it's a lawn gnome. You should follow basic steps that help keep your scanner (and the images it produces) in tiptop shape. Although most scanners these days sell for less than $200 or $300, that certainly doesn't make them disposable.

In this chapter, I provide all the information you need to keep your scanner clean, perfectly calibrated, and reasonably happy. I also cover the common problems that crop up most often with scanner hardware and software and provide possible solutions — and tell you what to do in case you need expert help from the manufacturer's technical support department.

Calibrate Your Way to Happiness

When you consider just exactly what a scanner does, digitizing thousands of pixels in a precise pattern from an original, you can easily understand why some scanner manufacturers recommend that you *calibrate* your scanner regularly.

Would the real "calibration" please stand up?

You can perform another type of calibration, although it doesn't affect your scanner. Instead, you can calibrate your system's printer and monitor to more accurately reflect the colors in the scanned original. Under Windows 98, Windows Me, and Mac OS 9, colors are calibrated between different pieces of hardware using a *color matching system.*

In the Macintosh world, the Mac OS features a system named ColorSync, which sets a definition for each color supported by each piece of hardware that matches the international color palette called the CIE XYZ standard. Most Macintosh hardware comes with its own, unique ColorSync profile.

On the Windows side, Microsoft supports a color matching system called ICM/ICC. Again, the hardware you buy that can scan, print, and display images is likely to have an ICM/ICC profile that's copied to disk during the installation process.

For most people, worrying so much about color matching is basically "too much sugar for a nickel." Hot pink doesn't have to look exactly the same on the computer screen as it does when it's printed. For a graphics professional, however, the story is altogether different, and computer-savvy folks who work with print media rely heavily on color matching.

To be more specific, calibrating a scanner is somewhat akin to aligning the printer cartridges on your inkjet printer or even adjusting the timing for your car's engine: You're correcting the "drift" that occurs over time and returning the scanner's mechanism to its factory alignment.

Only sheet-fed scanners (including those that are built-in to an "all-in-one" multifunction printer) usually need to be calibrated. Check your scanner's manual to see whether it mentions this process. Some older flatbeds can be calibrated as well. If you don't need to calibrate your scanner, I invite you to skip this section and save yourself a section's worth of reading.

If you're still with me, your sheet-fed scanner likely requires calibration from time to time. Signs that you need to calibrate include

- Vertical black or white streaks in scanned images
- Images with pixels "lost" from the margin or margins, even from originals that were correctly aligned
- Empty areas in scanned images where text or graphics should be

Also, calibrating a scanner at least once a year is a good idea if it's used often, as in an office environment.

Although the exact steps you take vary according to your scanner's brand and model, here's the general procedure for calibrating a sheet-fed scanner:

1. **Run your scanner's control program and choose the Calibrate command. (On an all-in-one multifunction device, you may need to choose Calibrate from the front panel menu.)**
2. **Load a blank white sheet of standard 8½-x-11-inch printer paper into the all-in-one's document feeder. (If you're using a stand-alone sheet-fed scanner, the manufacturer typically provides a preprinted calibration page. If you use one of these pages, skip Step 3.)**
3. **The printer prints a calibration test page using the sheet of paper.**
4. **Take the calibration test page and load it into the scanner's document feeder. The scanner loads the page and performs the calibration procedure using the pattern.**

The Right Way to Clean Your Scanner

Want to find out how to clean the surfaces inside and outside your scanner? As I mention elsewhere, dust, smudges, and fingerprints can make an impression on your scanner — and therefore on your scanned images! It takes only a couple of minutes every few weeks to keep your scanner clean, and you benefit every time you produce a scanned image.

Never disassemble any piece of computer hardware without specific instruction from the owner's guide (or the company's technical support department)! Taking your scanner apart to clean it may expose you to a shock hazard. It can also damage your scanner and invalidate your warranty. (Besides, nothing deep inside your average scanner is *meant* to be accessible for cleaning!)

I don't discuss how to wipe down the exterior of your scanner. It's a process called *dusting,* and most adults already have more than enough training to accomplish the task. However, I provide a number of guidelines in this section that can help prevent problems.

On the outside

I've met many, many computer owners who feel that both a computer's case and external peripherals are indestructible, which is why their systems usually look like a work of modern art. You may notice coffee cup rings, at least one Unknown Stain, and several dozen pieces of tape. As long as the fan and the CD-ROM drive aren't completely covered with sticky notes, it's all acceptable! (Personally, I use Microsoft Outlook to keep things straight.)

Never use solvents!

When it comes to cleaning, you quickly find that your computer and your scanner are, well, all too human! Your scanner most likely has a plastic body, and you can discolor or damage it with many types of household cleaners.

A number of companies make antistatic cleaners especially for computer hardware; these cleaners are fine (they help repel dust, and they don't hurt your hardware). Take care, though, in using a spray or any uncontrolled aerosol around your scanner. I tell you more about this topic in the section after next, "On the inside."

Use the right tool

For the outside of your scanner, as well as the rest of your computer hardware, all you really need during spring cleaning is a soft cloth. I recommend either a computer antistatic cloth or an old T-shirt.

If, on the other hand, an accident occurs and something stains the outside of your scanner, you probably can remove it with a slightly moist paper towel. Again, don't spray anything on your scanner!

On the inside

I suppose that this section may not apply to all scanner owners because they don't open a hand scanner or an inexpensive sheet-fed model; their scanners are permanently sealed. However, it does concern owners of all flatbed and most sheet-fed scanners, where you can actually reach under the cover or inside the body of the scanner.

Abrasives are out!

Although this advice is self explanatory, I want to mention it anyway: If you use the wrong type of cleaner, you can scratch the glass in your flatbed scanner. This problem is almost as bad as a crack or a broken glass because (depending on the location and the size) a scratch can easily show up at a higher dpi setting! What's worse, a single scratch rarely occurs by itself, unless something sharp accidentally hits your scanner's glass.

Treat your scanner like the precision device it is, and take the same care with the glass as you do with those expensive sunglasses or that telephoto lens for your 35mm camera! As a matter of fact, a friend of mine uses a photographer's lens cloth to wipe down his scanner's glass.

Never spray liquids!

This piece of advice is a biggie! I have personally seen what happens when someone uses a glass cleaner delivered by an aerosol pump on a flatbed scanner: The liquid works its way between the edge of the scanner's glass and the body of the unit. In this case, the liquid that seeped through didn't cause problems with the scanner's electronics (although that *can* happen if enough liquid is applied). Instead, it resulted in enough condensation to produce a "fogging" effect whenever the temperature in the room changed by a few degrees! Anyone who drives a car on a cold morning has almost certainly encountered something similar on the inside of the windshield. Scanning through this mess proved impossible.

As you can imagine, a fogged scanner glass forces you to do either of the following:

- **Open your scanner yourself:** For those with technical knowledge and experience with electronic hardware, this task is no big deal. Most folks would consider it a tricky operation, though. Remember that opening your scanner is sure to void your warranty.
- **Take the unit to a repair shop:** (Insert sound of cash register ringing here.) If you spent around $100 for your flatbed scanner, is it worth spending $35 to have it fixed?

The moral of the story? Keep substantial amounts of any liquid — *including* water — away from the interior of your scanner. If you have to apply a liquid (for example, to eliminate streaks on your glass), apply a small amount to a cloth and *then* wipe down the glass.

While you're at it, wiping down the foam pad on the bottom of your flatbed scanner's cover is also a good idea.

Consider the monitor wipe

"Isn't there a simple way to take care of my scanner's glass?" You bet! Use what I use: an antistatic computer monitor wipe. Technonerds like myself get ridiculously hooked on these things. I guess it comes from spending so much time in front of a monitor.

Anyway, these wipes are non-abrasive and safe for your glass, and they carry just enough liquid to eliminate streaks and fingerprints (without risking the fogging problem I mention in the preceding section).

Cleaning a sheet-fed scanner

As I mention earlier in this chapter, most inexpensive sheet-fed scanners on the market are sealed; paper goes in, and paper comes out — end of story. However, more expensive sheet-fed units, and the scanning units within most multifunction devices, *can* be opened, and you should do so regularly to inspect and clean the interior clockwork.

How often? Usually your owner's manual gives you an idea of the time period between regular cleanings. If your manual is mute on this point, however, I recommend once every three months or so. As you may remember from

Chapter 1, sheet-fed scanners move the original past a stationary scanning head, so they're more prone to ink smudges, dust, and dirt than a typical flatbed scanner.

Naturally, your manual provides the procedure for opening your sheet-fed scanner. Often, you tip forward a door on the front or back of the unit, or you may remove the top cover entirely. For example, Figure 12-1 illustrates a typical laser all-in-one device; in Figure 12-2, the access door on the front has been opened to expose the innards for cleaning.

Exactly what you clean varies by model and manufacturer. If you're the proud owner of a multifunction device, what you encounter also depends on the type of printing engine that's used. For example, although laser all-in-one units are great, they get dirtier because of the toner that's used; devices based on inkjet printer engines are easier to maintain.

Some multifunction devices use a single *paper path*. That's the path the paper takes through the machine, for both scanning and printing. These units need to be cleaned more often than a device that has separate paper paths for scanning material and printing it.

Figure 12-1: A multifunction device in its natural environment.

Don't blow in my ear!

When you're cleaning the inside of your sheet-fed scanner, I also highly recommend a can of compressed air. This stuff can blow dust out of the tiniest cracks and crevices inside your scanner as well as out of your other computer hardware (including troublesome parts of your system, like the fan and the keyboard) without damaging anything electronic or mechanical and without leaving any residue. If you can find the variety with the long, plastic nozzle for reaching the tiniest nooks and crannies, all the better!

Keep that compressed air can away from the kids, though, because the urge to use it inappropriately is a strong one. (I've even seen grown men and women succumb to temptation and blast a friend on the arm.)

Figure 12-2: The same device, ready for cleaning.

In just about every case, however, you end up cleaning the following parts within your sheet-fed scanner:

- **Rollers:** The rollers that move the paper in a sheet-fed scanner can get unbelievably "gunked" over time by the residue on your documents, so the rollers are usually the primary cleaning targets. Make sure that you look closely for scraps of paper and other unsightly debris while cleaning. If necessary, you can use tweezers to remove pieces lodged at the bottom of the unit. As a general rule, you can use a cotton swab soaked with a *small* amount of isopropyl alcohol solution to clean the grime from your rollers; use a side-to-side wiping motion, and switch cotton swabs often. Figure 12-3 illustrates the CSSCP, short for *c*otton *s*wab *s*canner *c*leaning *p*rocedure. (I can't help it. I work with weird acronyms all day long.)
- **Scanning lens:** The scanning lens in a sheet-fed scanner is a thin strip of glass or plastic set into one side of the paper path. Use the same caution as you would with a flatbed's scanning glass. Again, a monitor wipe is your best friend in this situation.
- **Pressure sensors:** These plastic sensors may look like speed bumps or wires; they tell your sheet-fed unit when you've loaded paper and when a sheet has passed through the scanner. Because they come in direct contact with your documents, they can receive the same grime and gunk as the rollers, so give them the cotton swab treatment as well.

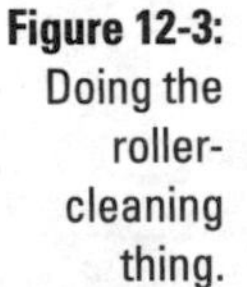

Figure 12-3: Doing the roller-cleaning thing.

Hardware Nightmares and How to Fix Them

Suppose that the unthinkable happens and your scanner is suddenly silent or acts strangely. What do you do? Are you stuck with an expensive service call or a visit to your local computer repair shop?

In this section, I describe the common hardware problems that can occur with a scanner and how you can fix them. In many cases, you can fix a hardware problem without professional help by following my suggestions, and I can also identify those problems that *do* require you to call for technical assistance.

Do not panic!

This is Rule Number One when it comes to any type of problem with your scanner: Unless the scanner is smoking or on fire, *take your time in diagnosing the problem*. Most of the parts that make up your computer system are quite simple (especially when compared with your income tax forms), so if you work through things methodically, you're likely to hit on both the problem and the solution.

Check your manual first

Although I try to be as specific as possible with the problems and solutions in this section, I can't cover everything specific to your brand and model of scanner. Therefore, always check the troubleshooting section in your scanner's manual for more information before you try my suggestions!

Another good source of troubleshooting information is the support area on the company's Web site. Don't forget to check for FAQ (Frequently Asked Questions) files, which often contain problems and solutions reported by your fellow scanner owners.

On to the fun stuff

With those two important rules in mind, let's get started with scanner hardware troubleshooting. If nothing works in this section, skip forward to the "Help!" section, at the end of this chapter, for critical information you need when you're contacting technical support.

Nothing works!

No lights, no sound, no signs of life from your scanner. Consider these possible causes:

- **Power cable unplugged:** Sure, you've heard all the jokes, but let me tell you that even the most seasoned and experienced computer technician has wondered why a piece of hardware is acting as though it's not getting any power, only to discover that it's not plugged in!
- **Malfunctioning AC adapter:** Many scanners use AC adapters, and they have been known to break. If you suspect the AC adapter and you bought your scanner locally, visit the store and ask a salesperson whether you can borrow an adapter to try. Alternatively, you can always buy a universal AC adapter, set it to match the scanner's adapter, and test the hardware.

- **Malfunctioning or tripped surge suppressor:** Of course, if absolutely nothing that's plugged into a surge suppressor strip is working, the strip itself is the suspect! If your scanner is plugged into a surge suppressor strip, make sure that the strip is turned on. Also, check to make sure that the strip's built-in circuit breaker or fuse hasn't been tripped. If it has, your AC wiring was likely hit by a decent-size electrical surge during a storm. Reset the breaker and see whether the strip works correctly.

One-button copy/scan/fax doesn't work

Although this problem seems to be in the hardware, it may be related to a software problem instead. Check these potential problem areas:

- **Background task not loaded or disabled:** When you press one of the buttons on your scanner, the scanner sends a signal to your computer — in effect, telling your computer, "Hey, someone just pressed the Copy button." To recognize the signal, your computer has to be running a special program that was installed with the scanner software. Under Windows 98 and Windows Me, you can usually see this program running on the right side of the taskbar. If an icon for the program is there, right-click on the icon to determine whether it's enabled. In the worst case, you have to reinstall your scanner software.
- **Scanner not connected:** Although your scanner may be turned on, check to make sure that it's connected to your computer. Cables can work loose, especially if you've recently moved your computer to a new location.
- **Buttons are jammed or broken:** The problem could be with the button itself — for example, if the button is jammed in the down position. If one or two of your buttons work on your scanner but another one doesn't, you may have a malfunctioning button on your hands. Again, if you bought your scanner from a local store, take it by and let one of the salespeople check it for you.
- **Software or driver problems:** Check the following section for tips and tricks to fix a possible software problem.

Do jams happen often?

If you're continually fixing paper jams while you're using your sheet-fed scanner, something is definitely wrong. In normal home use, you should encounter no more than one paper jam every month or so. First, make sure that the guides that adjust the paper path are correctly set; they should be snug against the paper in the document tray so that the paper is fed correctly into the machine. Also, it may be time for you to clean your scanner's roller system.

Finally, verify that the items you're scanning aren't too thick for your scanner. The owner's manual may tell you the maximum thickness of paper your model can accept.

Jammed sheet-fed scanner

Not much diagnosis is required here because a paper jam in a sheet-fed scanner is obvious! However, you have two possible solutions:

- **The document is still visible:** If the document is still visible outside the machine, you're in luck. (It may not seem lucky, but take my word for it.) Grab the paper by both top corners and pull in the opposite direction from the paper path. Note that this direction is usually *not* straight up, but rather toward the back of the machine. Use a steady pull, and don't try to jerk the paper out of the machine.
- **The document is inside the scanner:** Remember how I said that things could be worse than a visible paper jam? Well, if the document is lost deep in the bowels of your sheet-fed scanner or multifunction device, it's worse. Follow the instructions in your owner's manual to open the unit's case, and locate the paper release lever. (If you're using a laser multifunction device, you may have to remove the toner cartridge.) The paper should then be free to move, and you should be able to pull it gently through the roller system and out into the open.

Flatbed scanning head doesn't move

Although flatbed scanners are less prone to problems than sheet-fed scanners, they're still not perfect! If your unit is receiving power but the scanning head doesn't move when you attempt to scan something, here's a list of possible reasons:

- **Travel lock is engaged:** Most scanners come with a travel lock, which is a mechanical lever that holds the scanner head in place to avoid damage while you're carrying the scanner. If the lock has accidentally been engaged, you can damage your scanner's internal motor and drive system by repeated scanning attempts. Therefore, check this one first!
- **Broken or misaligned drive belt:** Most scanners use a belt system to transfer motion from the motor to the scanning head. Shine a flashlight through the scanner's glass and check to make certain that the belt hasn't broken or "jumped" the pulleys.
- **Threading problems with a screw drive:** Some scanners use a screw drive, where the motor turns a screw shaft to move the scanning head. Again, use a flashlight to check the scanning head to make sure that it's still moving freely on the screw and that the screw is turning when the motor is working.
- **Misaligned or damaged rails:** No matter what type of drive your flatbed scanner uses, the scanning head travels up and down the length of the machine on two rails. If the scanner was dropped or damaged during a move, these rails can become misaligned so that the scanning head "sticks" between them. Sometimes, the rails simply need a little lubrication with a few drops of light oil, and you have to open your scanner's case to reach them.

- **Software or driver problems:** Check the following section for tips and tricks to fix a possible software problem.
- **Burned-out motor:** A bad scene — and hard to test. Check to see whether your scanner motor works when you turn on the machine. Most models recalibrate themselves automatically when you turn on the scanner. If you're sure that the connection is working between your scanner and the computer (and your software is working properly), run your scanning control software and try a quick preview.

Scanning light doesn't work

The scanning light on your flatbed should come on when you turn on the unit. (Some models also turn it off until your computer sends the command to start scanning.) If it doesn't light when the scanning head is moving, one of these problems may be the culprit:

- **Loose cable:** Your scanning head receives power (and sends image data) through a cable. Use a flashlight and look through the scanner's glass to verify that the cable is still properly connected.
- **Burned-out bulb:** Depending on the manufacturer, you may be able to buy a replacement bulb; check the manufacturer's Web site or contact technical support. If the scanning head and bulb are combined into a single sealed unit, however, you're probably out of luck.

Parallel-port problems

If you're using a parallel port scanner and your computer reports that it's having trouble connecting to your scanner, check these possible problems:

- **Loose cable:** This check should be SOP (*s*tandard *o*perating *p*rocedure) for any connection problem. (Hey, it's not even a computer acronym!) Make sure that you check both ends of the cable, too.
- **Daisy-chaining isn't working:** If you're trying to plug your scanner into your parallel port Zip drive or other parallel port external device, you may encounter problems. The software and drivers for some scanner models require a direct connection to the computer. Try removing the other device and connecting your scanner directly to the computer. (If the scanner works then, try connecting the Zip disk to the scanner's second parallel port.)
- **Wrong port mode:** Your computer's parallel port must be set to ECP/EPP mode before a scanner can use it to communicate with your computer. Your computer's manual should tell you how to display the BIOS settings that control your port mode. Usually, you press F1 or Delete when you're prompted right after you turn on your PC.

- **Faulty card:** If a standard parallel port printer also has problems on this port, it may be malfunctioning. Right-click on My Computer, choose Device Manager (as shown in Figure 12-4), and make sure that your port is identified properly by Windows. If the port has a yellow question mark or a red X through it, Windows is having trouble accessing the port, so bring it to your local computer shop for a checkup.

Always reboot after a potential parallel port fix because Windows checks for parallel port operation during the boot sequence.

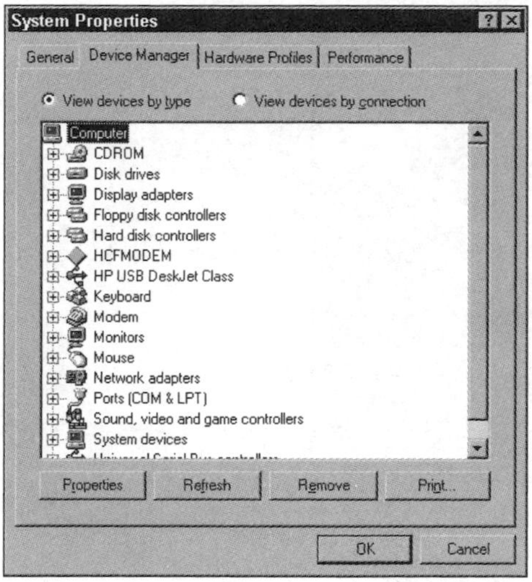

Figure 12-4: Investigating the Windows 98 Device Manager.

Send out a probe!

Your scanner probably shipped with a program designed to test the connection between it and your computer. For example, Figure 12-5 illustrates the program that came with my Microtek scanner. If you suspect a problem with your scanner's connection, run your probe program first, and let it test your system and offer advice on what's wrong.

USB (or FireWire) isn't working

Because both USB and FireWire are similar in operation, they share the same potential trouble areas and solutions:

- **Loose cable:** Check both ends of your cable — just in case.
- **Device driver problems:** Both USB and FireWire devices require specific drivers, and these drivers can be accidentally overwritten or deleted from your system. Reinstalling your scanner's software (which includes the drivers) should fix the problem.

- **Bus problems:** No, I'm not talking mass transit here. If your USB or FireWire scanner is connected to your computer through another device and that device is turned off, your computer may not recognize your scanner. Turn all USB and FireWire devices on and reboot, or disconnect the other device and connect your scanner's cable directly to your computer.

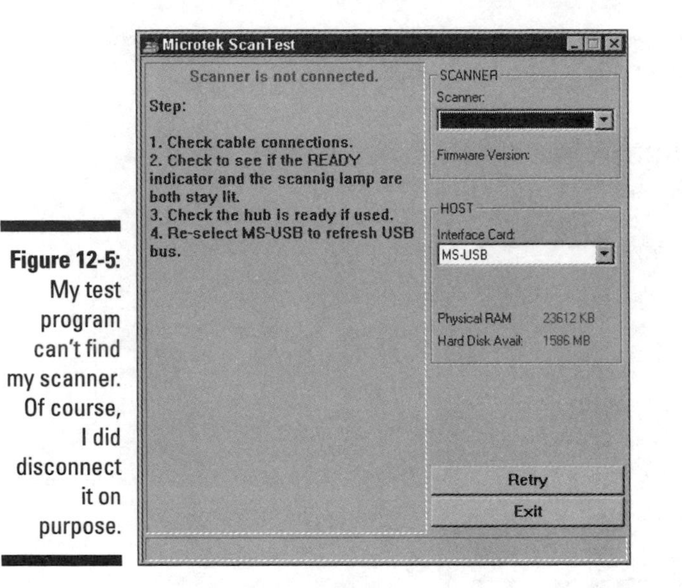

Figure 12-5: My test program can't find my scanner. Of course, I did disconnect it on purpose.

SCSI isn't working

Unfortunately, this major problem is likely to affect not just your scanner but also every other SCSI device inside and outside your computer. Thus, the entire system may grind to a permanent halt until you've tracked down the configuration problem and fixed it.

Therefore, run — do *not* walk — to Chapter 4, where I harp on and on about what needs to be set correctly for your SCSI device chain to hum like a well-tuned Cadillac.

Software Nightmares and How to Fix Them

I have good news and bad news. Because I always ask for the bad news first, here it is: Software nightmares are harder to diagnose than hardware nightmares, and in my experience they tend to happen more often.

On the other hand, here's the good news: You have more to work with because software problems usually generate at least some sort of error message you can use to point you in the right direction.

With that in mind, in this section I cover a number of common software errors and what they mean and give you tips and tricks you can use to solve them.

Reboot — just reboot!

First and foremost, if you experience a software error while using your scanner, follow the hardware technician's first solution to absolutely everything: *Reboot!* (I spent a number of years as a hardware technician for a major hospital, and I wish that I had a dime for every time I've heard someone say "Oh, okay, it's working now!" after simply rebooting her computer.)

Why does this work so well? For a number of reasons:

- Software you're running can occasionally lock up, and it may not necessarily be your scanning software, so you may not immediately be aware of it. For example, if you're running Microsoft Outlook in the background and you lose your Internet connection, your system is likely to freeze up.
- Some external devices, particularly those on a parallel port connection, can get "confused" when your computer communicates with several pieces of hardware at a time. The classic example is a parallel port Zip drive and a parallel port scanner daisy-chained together; they may work perfectly when they're accessed separately, but may lose track of their own existence when you try to write to a Zip disk and scan a document at the same time.
- Both Windows and Mac OS can sometimes crash themselves. (Yes, I *know* that you don't believe me, but I've heard stories from the victims.)

A reboot can solve these problems by resetting everything to its normal state, so try it first, before you think "Nightmare."

Keep that software current!

Here's another tip that applies to every one of your computer's peripherals, including your scanner: Keep your drivers up-to-date. Check the manufacturer's Web site regularly (once a month is usually about right) for software and driver updates, and apply them immediately when they appear.

This advice is especially important for people who are continually upgrading their operating system or hardware. Often, a driver that was installed when you bought your scanner isn't completely compatible with a new operating system, so what worked under Windows 98 may not work under Windows Me.

Manufacturers try to get their drivers updated as soon as possible because compatibility means a decrease in customer support requests, so minimize your software problems by keeping your system current.

Okay, it is a software nightmare

Arrgh! Rebooting didn't help, and you're using the latest drivers. The manual doesn't say anything about your current predicament, and the manufacturer's Web site is clueless. You have a software nightmare, so you should examine the problems and solutions.

Scanner software doesn't load

If nothing happens when you run your scanner software, check these possible problems:

- **Scanner offline:** Make sure that your scanner is powered on and connected. You can't control something that's not working.
- **Missing program files or drivers:** This problem can rear its ugly head in one of two ways: Either a program you ran "cleaned up" your hard drive (in fact, cleaned it *too* well) or you've erased important files by accident. Reinstalling your scanner software should correct the problem, although (depending on the extent of the damage to your system) you may find that other programs or hardware devices aren't working either.
- **Software incompatibilities:** Have you just installed another program or even upgraded your operating system since the last time you used your scanner? First, try reinstalling your scanner software. If that doesn't work, call the manufacturer's technical support department for help because the incompatibility is buried deep in the lower levels of the operating system.

Scanner software doesn't recognize the scanner

Your scanner software appears but then promptly informs you that you need to purchase a scanner. Your scanner, however, lies dormant. You may be experiencing difficulty with the following:

- **Scanner offline:** Again, check your scanner and its connections to make sure that all is well.
- **Changes in USB, FireWire or SCSI configuration:** If you've recently swapped devices around in your USB, FireWire, or SCSI configuration (and you haven't rebooted), I can practically guarantee that your software thinks that the scanner is still operating in its old location. Although the persnickety nature of SCSI makes this diagnosis easy, this problem is

not supposed to happen with USB and FireWire. Unfortunately, my experiences have shown that these connections are not quite as automatic as they say, especially if your USB hub is supplying additional USB devices. (By the way, check that hub to make sure that it's plugged in, too.)

- **Software incompatibilities (again):** Once more, if you've just finished installing a new piece of software, you may end up reinstalling your scanner software to overwrite the changes and restore things to normal.

Scanner freezes in mid-job

This software problem is a really nasty critter. If your scanner is halfway through a scanning job and everything grinds to a halt, potential causes include

- **A hardware conflict:** If your scanner has been working well and you've just installed a new piece of hardware or changed your old hardware configuration, the culprit is likely to be an "argument" between the two components for the same system resources. You can either remove the new component and restore the old system configuration, which is generally not the option you want, or call the technical support department for your scanner and have someone there help you isolate which Interrupt Request (or IRQ) is causing the problem.

  "What system resources can cause problems?" In Windows, a beastie called an IRQ is the likely culprit. Windows needs a separate IRQ to communicate with a device, and if two devices are trying to use the same IRQ, the scanner or the entire system may lock up. IRQ problems can also occur with modems, sound cards, and SCSI adapters.

- **Low memory or hard drive space:** Remember that your scanner can create a whopping-big image file, and it can take quite a bit of processing power, hard drive space, and system RAM to make a high-resolution 1200 dpi image a reality. If your computer runs out of either hard drive space or system RAM, Windows or your scanner program (or both) are likely to lock up and your scanner can stop dead in its pixels. Check your scanner's manual for the recommended amount of system RAM and hard drive space. If this problem occurs only when you're scanning the largest originals at the highest resolutions, you may need to upgrade your computer system.

- **Software incompatibilities (again):** You know the drill — reinstall your scanner software, and make sure that you're using the latest drivers for your hardware.

Help!

You've checked, rechecked, and covered all your bases. You've tried every possible solution that I list in this chapter, plus a few you thought up on your own, and still nothing helps.

You have reason for hope, though, because no matter what piece of hardware or software falls ill — scanner, software, operating system, or even your entire computer system — help is available! In this case, though, you're likely to need technical support from only one source: your scanner manufacturer.

So what do you need (besides a telephone and a dialing finger)? Just in case you do need to call for help, let me give you a pointer or two on what those fighting men and women need from you! (Remember — I've been in their shoes.)

You're likely to be asked for this information:

- The model number of your scanner
- The interface that connects the scanner to your system
- The version of operating system you're using
- The version of the scanner software you're using
- The brand of computer you're using and any peripherals you've added
- The serial number of your scanner and software
- Any error messages you've received
- Precisely what you were doing when the error occurred (and any steps you took afterward)

You should find the technical support number for your scanner in the manual. The number is probably listed on the company's Web site as well.

Chapter 13

Scanner Projects for Crafty People

In This Chapter

- Printing a custom wine label
- Creating a custom T-shirt
- Creating a slide show
- Using optical character recognition
- Faxing a scanned image

When you think of your scanner, *handicrafts* may not be the first word that leaps to mind. That's because most people add scanners to their systems for something practical, like business or schoolwork. (If you're a parent, try convincing the kids exactly *why* you bought a scanner.)

Therefore, you may be surprised when you take a walk through your local shopping mall. If you keep your eyes open, you see just how versatile a tool your scanner really is. You may see stores (and even kiosks) creating custom T-shirts from your photographs, recording computer CD-ROMs with your photographs, or printing custom calendars and greeting cards. Heck, one store owner I know uses a basic computer system with a good inkjet printer, a scanner, and a digital camera to fashion custom wine labels for parties and special occasions!

To be truthful, those entrepreneurs may be pretty angry with me because in this chapter I expose their secrets: You find out how to create some of those same items using the same techniques (but without the expense). I even make an effort to stay friendly with the "practical" business crowd by showing you how to send a scanned image as a fax and how to use an OCR program.

Creating a Custom Wine Label

If your computer system includes an inkjet printer, you're ready to create the perfect gift for any wine connoisseur — and the lucky recipient won't even know that you bought that $6 bottle! (At least, not until the tasting — after all, I can't help you change the vintage.) You also need a length of double-sided tape, a pair of scissors or a paper cutter, and one or two sheets of glossy photo paper.

Run Paint Shop Pro and follow these steps:

1. **Open the scanned image you want to use for the label.**
2. **Resize the image to about 5 inches x 4 inches. (To be sure, measure the existing and allow for at least half an inch of overlap on all sides.) Click Image, choose Resize, click Actual size, and enter** 5 inches **in the Width field, as shown in Figure 13-1. If the existing aspect ratio doesn't work, you can either crop the image to change the ratio or disable this field and allow Paint Shop Pro to alter the image to fit. Click OK to resize the photo.**

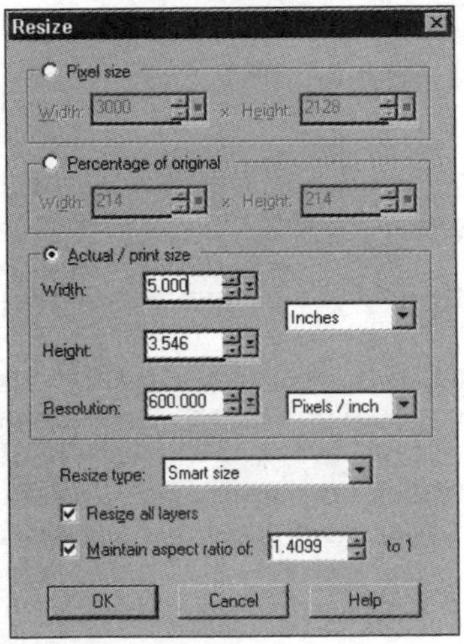

Figure 13-1: Resizing a scanned image to 5 inches x 4 inches.

3. **Click the Text icon on the toolbar on the left side of the screen (which looks like a letter *A*). Click the cursor where you want the line of text to begin. Paint Shop Pro displays the Text Entry dialog box, as shown in Figure 13-2. Select a font from the Name drop-down list box and a font size from the Size list box. Click in the Text box, type your message, and click OK to create the text.**
4. **Set your printer for Photo paper and the best possible print quality.**
5. **Load a sheet of glossy photo paper in your printer.**
6. **Click File and choose Print to print the label.**
7. **Using a paper cutter or scissors, trim around the edges of the label.**
8. **Turn the label face-down and add double-sided tape around all four edges.**

9. **Center the label so that it completely covers the existing label on the wine bottle and press down to apply.**
10. **Smooth the new label with a cloth, moving from the center of the label to the outside edges.**

The double-sided tape makes the label easy to remove later and save.

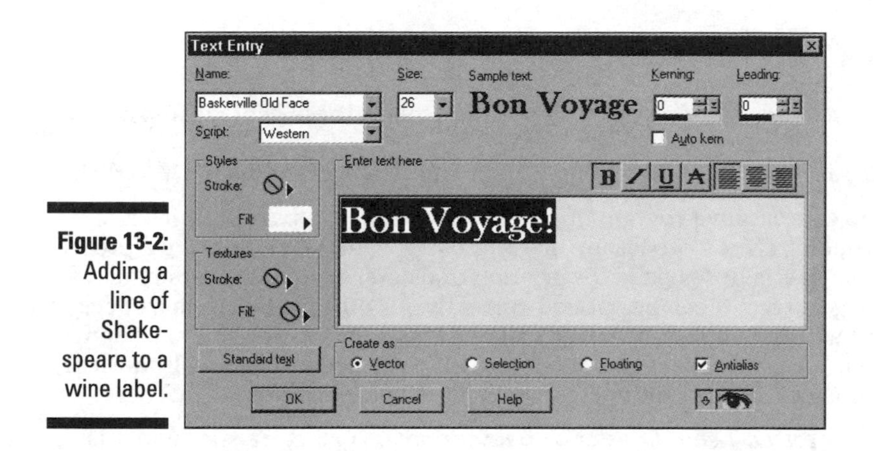

Figure 13-2: Adding a line of Shakespeare to a wine label.

A T-Shirt with a Personal Touch

Adding a scanned image to a T-shirt (or a fabric item, like a canvas book bag) is great fun, and you end up with a unique gift that pleases kids and adults alike. And (unlike what some people may have told you) this is not rocket science. Because I'm a big fan of NASA, however, I treat things in stages.

I recommend a T-shirt or fabric item made of pure cotton, a mixture of cotton and polyester, or canvas. You also need an iron, a pair of scissors, an inkjet printer, some T-shirt transfer paper, and a sheet or pillowcase.

Kids and a hot iron don't mix. You need adult supervision for this project!

Stage 1: Preparations

First, follow these general steps to prepare the item for the transfer:

1. **Wash the item in cold water.**

   For example, applying a transfer to a brand-new T-shirt usually causes problems when the shirt is washed for the first time.

2. **Machine-dry the item at normal temperature (*without* using any fabric softener or other additives during the drying cycle).**
3. **After prewashing and drying, the item may be ironed (without starch or steam) to remove wrinkles in the fabric.**

   Allow the item to cool to room temperature before applying the transfer.

Stage 2: Printing

To print your transfer on your inkjet printer, follow these general steps:

1. **Import your scanned image, design your transfer, and save it to disk.**

   You can use any program that prints in color to prepare your design, including a word processor, like Microsoft Word. If you're using a program specially designed for printing transfers, it should reverse the image so that it can be applied correctly; for other applications, check to see whether your printer has a Mirror Image or Flip Horizontal option you can enable to reverse the image. (If your machine has an Iron-On or Transfer Paper paper type, it may flip the image automatically.)

   Never print a T-shirt transfer on a laser printer. T-shirt transfer paper isn't designed for laser printers, and you may damage that expensive toy. (Plus, if it's your *company's* expensive toy, you could be in deep trouble.)

2. **Print a test page using regular paper to make sure that your design fits on the item.**

   Leaving two or three inches of border all around the design is a good idea. If you're creating a T-shirt, this "test fit" also allows you to ensure that the design doesn't wrap around, effectively appearing on the other side of the shirt! Use your design program to resize things if necessary, and then print another sample page to check the fit.

3. **It's time to load the transfer paper. Place a single sheet on top of a few sheets of regular paper and load them into the printer.**

   Typically, each sheet should have some sort of markings that indicate which side is the front and which is the back. (To make sure, though, don't forget to read the instructions that accompany the transfer paper. You may have to take specific steps to prepare a transfer sheet for printing, or you may have to follow some loading instructions.)

4. **Depending on the program you use to print the design, you may have to enable a printer setting to reverse the image. Choose the Transfer Paper or Iron-On paper type and choose the best possible print quality.**
5. **Choose the Print command from the program's File menu to send the design to the printer.**

6. **Trim around the edges of the design with scissors.**

   For a professional look, maintain a consistent distance from the border of your design. Be sure to leave a "flap" of border that's a little wider to allow easy removal of the transfer after you've applied it.

Stage 3: Liftoff!

First (don't you just hate these pauses in the countdown?), an important word about ironing! Depending on the brand of T-shirt transfer you're using, you may need different iron settings or a different amount of time to apply your transfer. Check the instructions that came with your transfer, and follow those instructions whenever they differ from my steps.

Follow these general steps to apply the transfer:

1. **Choose a smooth, hard table or countertop in your home wide enough for the entire item; a kitchen countertop is a good candidate. *Do not* use an ironing board, which can cause wrinkles. Cover this surface with a sheet or pillowcase, and smooth all wrinkles from the backing.**
2. **Fire up your iron on the highest setting it provides, and let it preheat for at least ten minutes.**

   Remember: No steam or starch!
3. **Arrange the item in the middle of the backing, with the side that receives the transfer facing up.**
4. **Align the transfer on top of the item, printed side down. Because the design is reversed, it should now be facing in the correct direction, as shown in Figure 13-3.**
5. **Move the iron slowly from the top of the design toward the bottom along one edge of the transfer, applying constant pressure. The iron should be in contact with the transfer for at least 30 seconds.**

   Make sure that the iron overlaps the transfer so that the edge of the transfer bonds to the fabric. If you're applying the transfer to a cloth with a heavy weave (such as canvas or rough cotton), you should press harder to ensure proper bonding between the cloth and the transfer.

   To avoid scorching, *never* allow the iron to rest in one place for more than a second or two!
6. **Repeat Step 5 with the other three edges of the design.**

   Completely sealing the edges of the transfer is important so that the item can survive a trip to the washing machine.

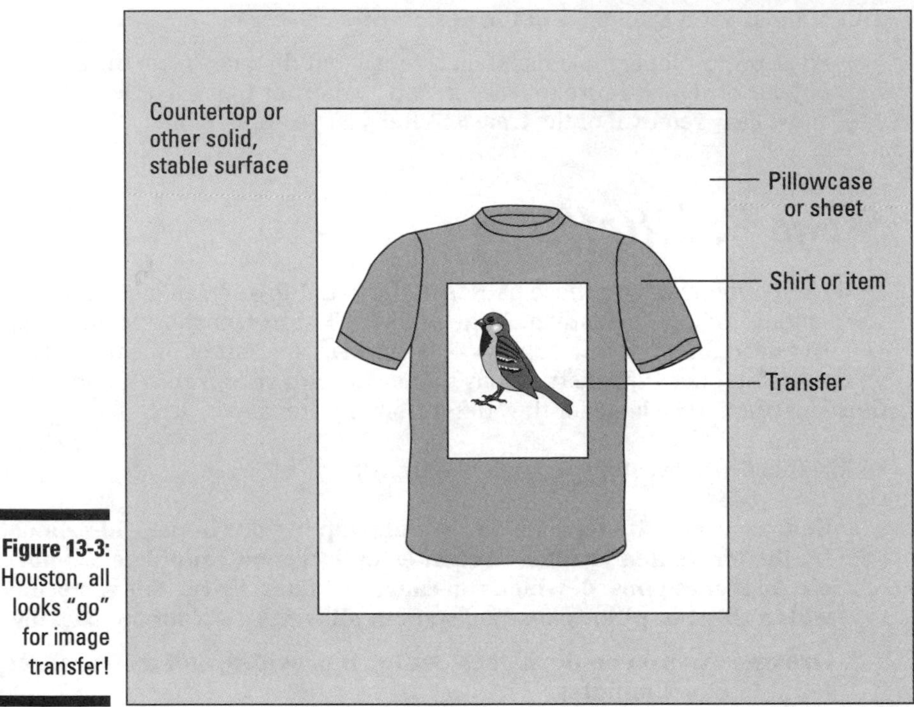

Figure 13-3: Houston, all looks "go" for image transfer!

7. **After all four edges are sealed, it's time to take care of the middle. Move the iron slowly in a circular motion around the middle of the transfer, again applying constant pressure and keeping the iron in motion.**
8. **Time to remove the transfer! Turn your iron off and set it down safely. Pull the transfer backing from the fabric immediately with a slow, steady motion, beginning at the wider edge.**

   Do not allow the transfer to cool before you have removed the paper backing, or else you can ruin the design when you try to peel it off!
9. **That's it! Hang the completed item on a hanger and set it aside to cool.**

Creating a Slide Show CD

As I mention in Chapter 5, I recommend archiving your scanned images by recording them on a CD-ROM. A CD-ROM is also the perfect method of distributing an entire "album" of images or documents, ready to be loaded into any computer with a CD-ROM drive.

What if you're sending to a computer novice (you know — someone who's not the technowizard you've become) some scanned photos on a CD-ROM you've recorded and she can't view those images? Perhaps she doesn't have an image editor or she doesn't know how to run the built-in image viewer in Windows 98. That's no problem for a compu-guru like yourself. Simply create a custom slide show disc!

For this demonstration, I use Broderbund's popular Print Shop Photo Organizer, although you can use any photograph-management program that includes a slide show feature, where your images are displayed in sequence, much like a screen saver. Naturally, the steps aren't exactly the same, although this example helps you understand the procedure.

Follow these steps:

1. **To run the Photo Manager program from the Windows 98 Start menu, click Start and choose Programs⇨Print Shop Photo Organizer⇨ Photo Organizer.**

   The program's main window appears, as shown in Figure 13-4.

   The next step is the creation of a collection of pictures, or, as this program calls it, a "photo album."

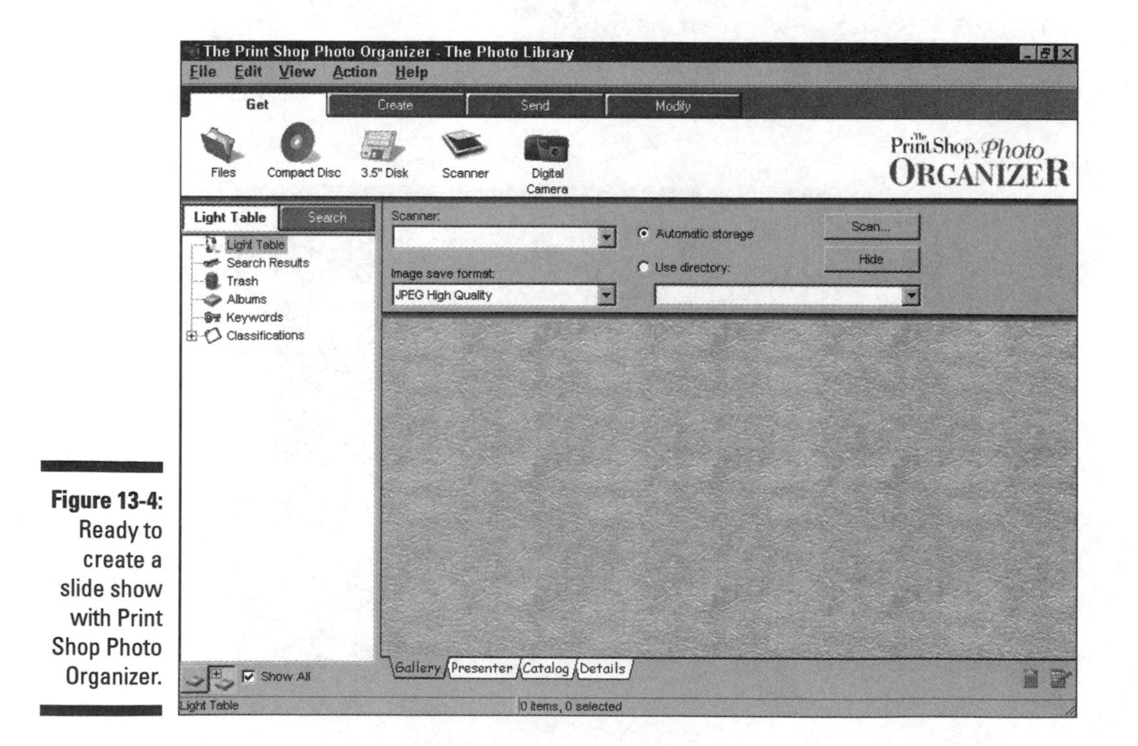

Figure 13-4: Ready to create a slide show with Print Shop Photo Organizer.

2. **Click the Create tab at the top of the screen and click the Album toolbar button to display the Create Album dialog box, as shown in Figure 13-5.**
3. **Enter a name for your album and click OK. You see the album icon appear at the left side of the screen; click it once to select it as the destination for the images.**
4. **Click the Get tab to fill the album. This program can acquire directly from the scanner, although I think that a better method is to use it after all the scanned images are saved to disk (and edited to perfection). Therefore, click the Files toolbar button.**
5. **Figure 13-6 shows the Import Photographs dialog box. Click the Look in drop-down list box and specify the folder containing your pictures. You can click individual images to select them or hold down the Ctrl key to choose multiple images. If you want all the pictures in this folder, click the Select All button. Click Next to continue.**

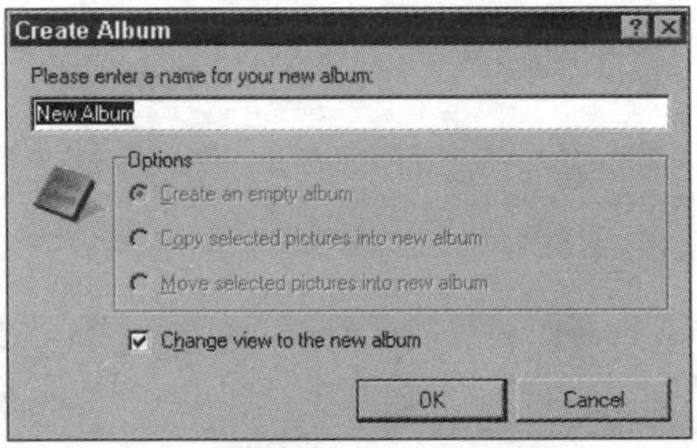

Figure 13-5: You have to name that album, pard'ner.

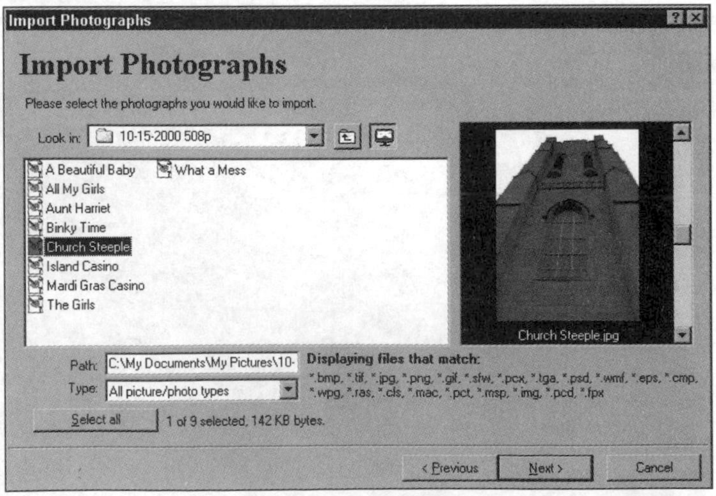

Figure 13-6: Selecting images for a Photo Organizer album.

6. **Photo Organizer displays the Specify Photograph Attributes dialog box, where you can enter a photographer's name and search keywords, the scan date, and other comments. Because the slide show doesn't display this information, however, you can simply leave these optional fields blank and just click Next.**

7. **Specify the current album as the destination for the images and click Finish to add the pictures.**

   The album window displays thumbnails of all the images you've added, as shown in Figure 13-7.

8. **Click the Create tab and click the Slideshow toolbar button to display the Publish Slideshow wizard. Click Next to continue.**

9. **Because the new album was still selected, it's automatically the source for your slide show images. You've filled your album with only images you want to add to the slide show, so click Select All in the Select Photographs dialog box (see Figure 13-8) and click Next to continue.**

10. **Click Folder, select a directory where the presentation should be stored, and click Next.**

    By storing your images temporarily in a folder, you can add other documents or files to your slide show CD before you record it.

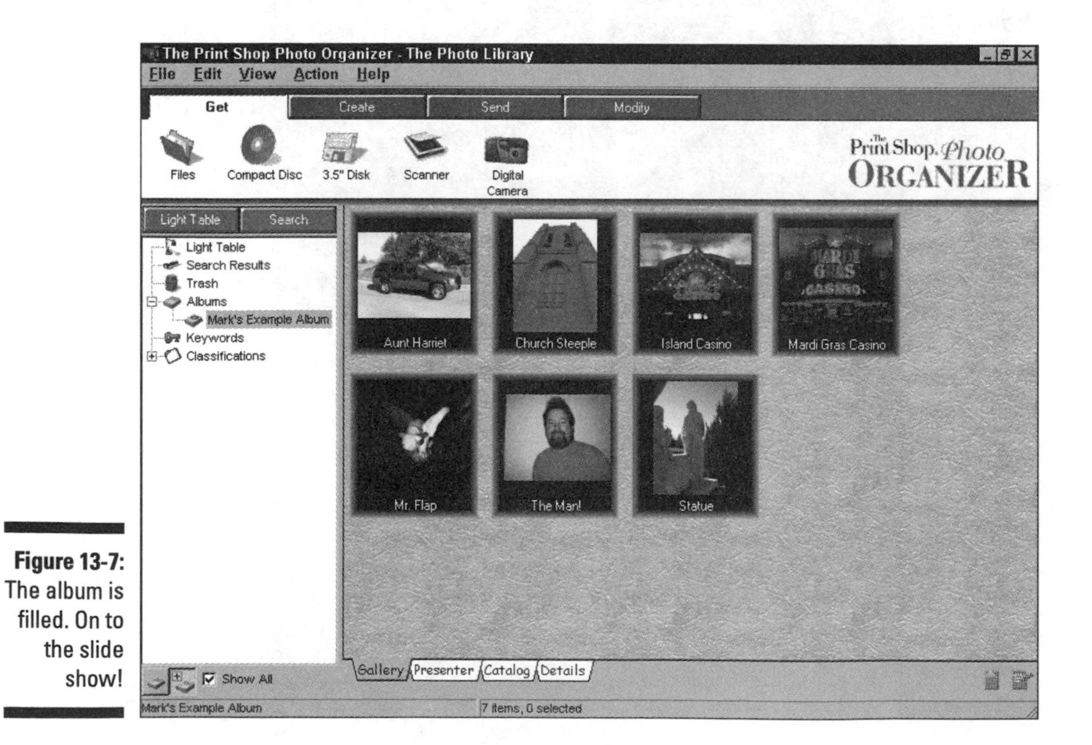

Figure 13-7: The album is filled. On to the slide show!

11. **Click Yes to confirm the creation of the new folder.**
12. **Choose the operating system the recipient will use, as shown in Figure 13-9. Click Next to continue.**
13. **Click Finish to create the slide show.**
14. **If you want to see the slide show before recording it, click Yes; otherwise, click No. To close the program, click the File menu and choose Exit.**

Now you can save your slide show to a CD-R or a Zip disk. If you're sending only a handful of images, you can probably even fit everything on a standard 1.44MB floppy!

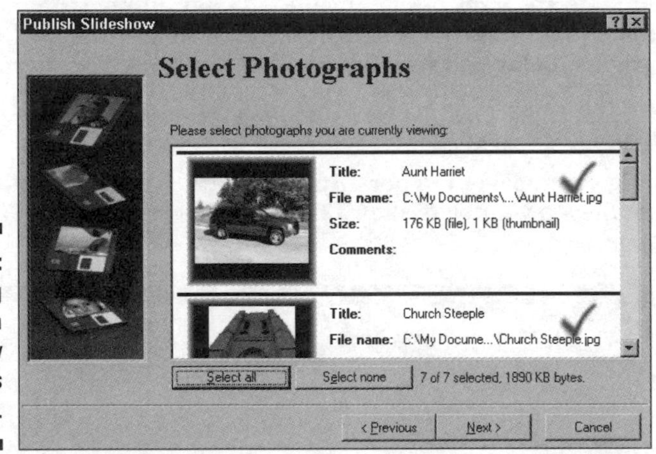

Figure 13-8: Selecting images for a slide show is child's play.

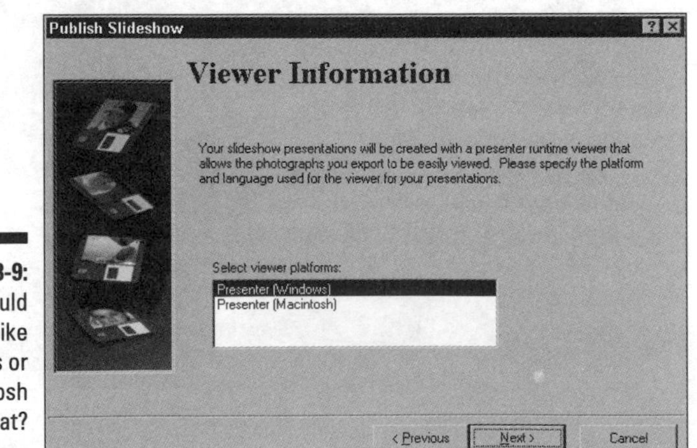

Figure 13-9: Would you like Windows or Macintosh with that?

Using an OCR Program

Earlier in this chapter, I talk about the wonders of OCR (optical character recognition). Now it's time to see for yourself how much time and trouble this technology can save you! In this example, I use the Macintosh version of OmniPage Pro to show you how to re-create a text document within Microsoft Word. After all the dust has settled, you have a Word document with the same text as your scanned original!

Follow these steps:

1. **Run OmniPage Pro by clicking the OmniPage icon on your desktop.**

   The program displays the main dialog box, as shown in Figure 13-10.

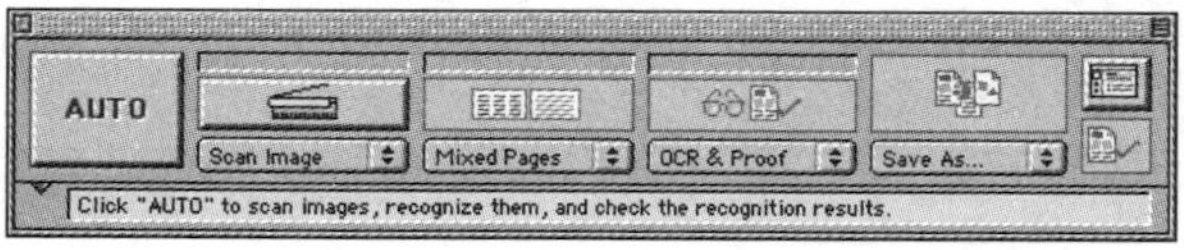

Figure 13-10: The OmniPage main dialog box may look simple, but plenty of power is on tap.

   I could simply say "Click the Auto button" (which automatically takes care of the next several steps for you), but instead I follow the manual route so that you can see what steps the program takes.

2. **Click Process and choose Scan Image to display the control program you installed with your scanner (in this case, ScanWizard) and scan the original as I demonstrate in Chapter 6.**

3. **After the document has been scanned into OmniPage Pro, click Process and choose Zone Image.**

   As you can see in Figure 13-11, the program draws borders around the major boundaries of text and graphics within the image (hence, the word *zones*), and assigns each zone a number. You can use these numbers to change the order in which the text and graphics are placed in the document, but you rarely have to do this. Typically, you want things read in the traditional order of up to down, left to right, so the default zone order is usually the best.

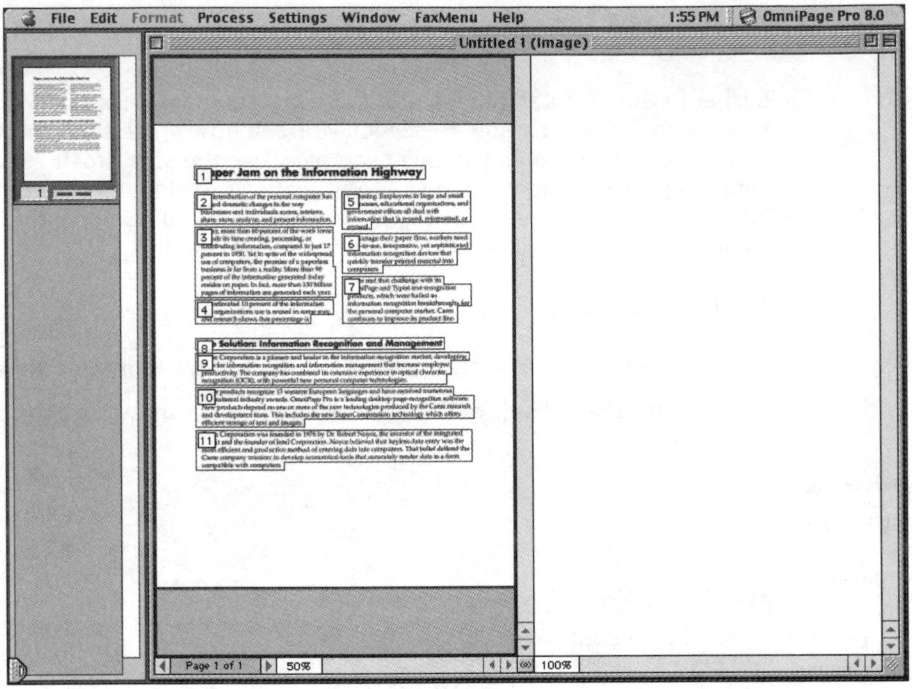

Figure 13-11: You're in the zone! (Sorry — I couldn't help that.)

4. **Now for the amazing part: Click Process and choose OCR & Check.**

   Sit back and watch OmniPage Pro zip through your document, paste the recognized text into the editing window, and then automatically check for recognition errors with its built-in proofreader! (Moments like these make me proud to be a first-generation computer nerd — you know — from the late 1970s and early 1980s, back when it wasn't cool.) Figure 13-12 illustrates the completed text document.

   Wait! I promised you a Word document, didn't I? No problem. If the formatting weren't important, I could simply have you select all the text and copy it into an empty Word document, but you want things to look exactly like the scanned image.

5. **Click File and choose Save As to display the Save dialog box, as shown in Figure 13-13. Click the Format drop-down list box and choose Microsoft Word 6.0, enter a filename in the Save Recognized Text as field, and click Save. There's your file!**

6. **Close OmniPage Pro by choosing Quit from the File menu.**

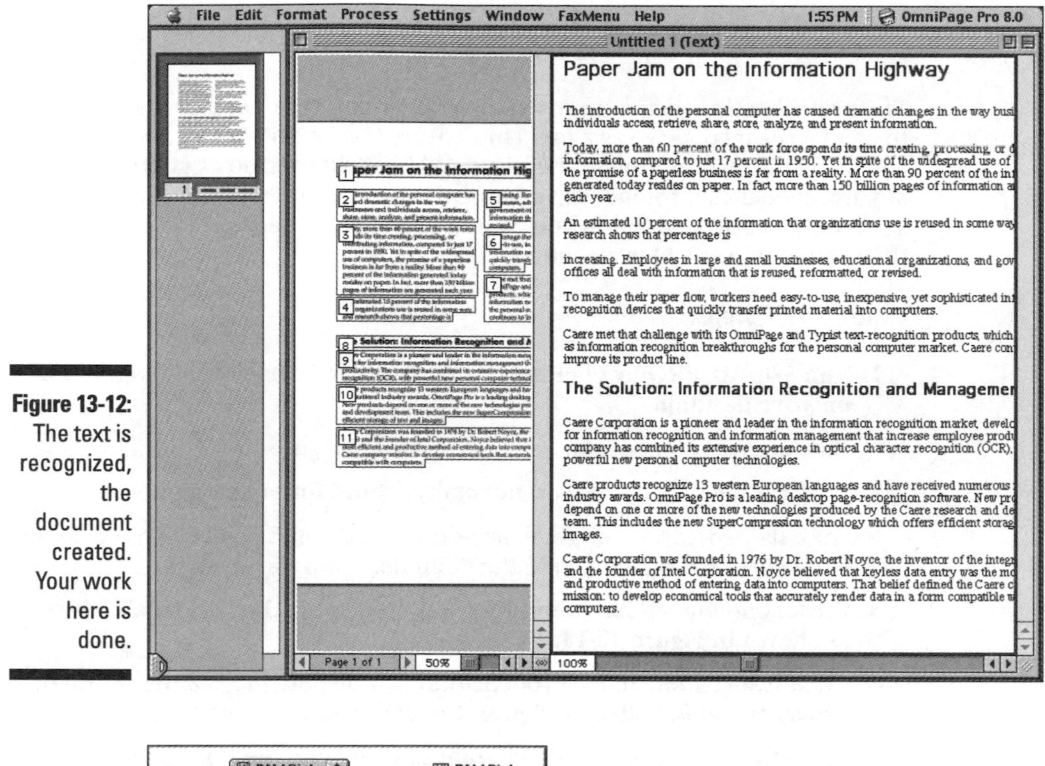

Figure 13-12: The text is recognized, the document created. Your work here is done.

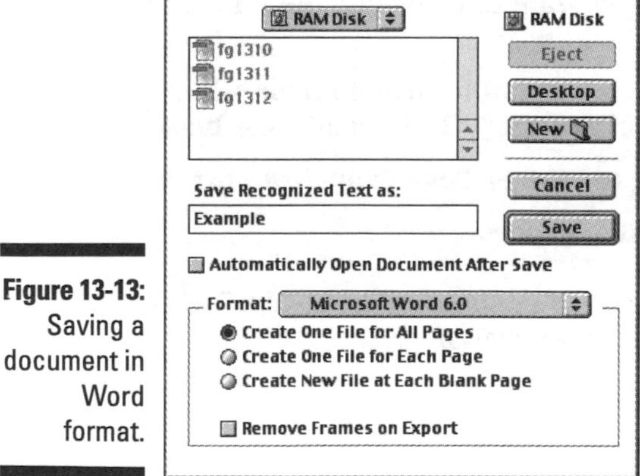

Figure 13-13: Saving a document in Word format.

Faxing a Scanned Image

The project in this section teams your scanner and your computer's modem to send a scanned image as a fax. This feature is a favorite with telecommuters and small businesses around the world. WinFax PRO can do as good a job as any traditional stand-alone fax. In fact, because the program can use a flatbed scanner, you can send things you couldn't send with the sheet-fed scanner that's built-in to most fax machines.

Follow these steps:

1. **Run WinFax PRO by clicking the WinFax PRO Message Manager icon on your desktop.**

   The Message Manager appears, as shown in Figure 13-14.

2. **Prepare the original as you normally would for your scanner.**

   For a flatbed, lay the original face-down on the glass and close the cover. For a sheet-fed scanner, load the document into the machine.

3. **Click Send and choose Send New Fax to display the Send dialog box, as shown in Figure 13-15.**
4. **Click Insert and choose From Scanner to display the scanner-control program you installed, and scan the original as you usually would.**
5. **Close the scanner-control program to redisplay the WinFax Send dialog box.**
6. **Enter the recipient's fax number and information, or select one from your WinFax phonebook or Microsoft Outlook address book.**
7. **Choose a cover page using the Cover Page drop-down list box.**
8. **Click Send to start the dialing process.**

In Chapter 14, I open the famous *...For Dummies* "Part of Tens" with a chapter on my top ten tips and tricks for better scanning.

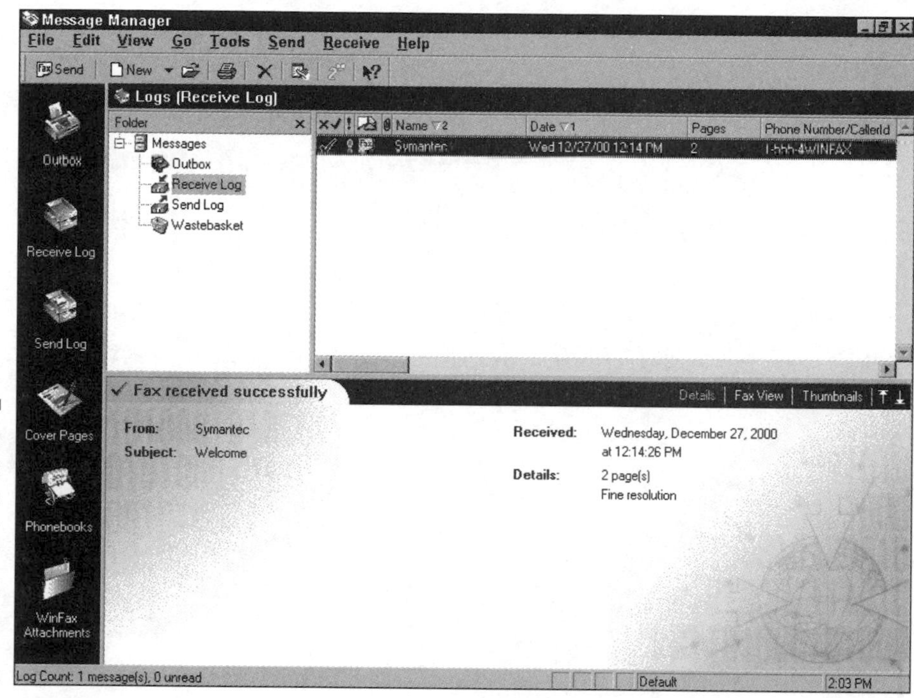

Figure 13-14: The WinFax Message Manager is your "virtual" fax control center.

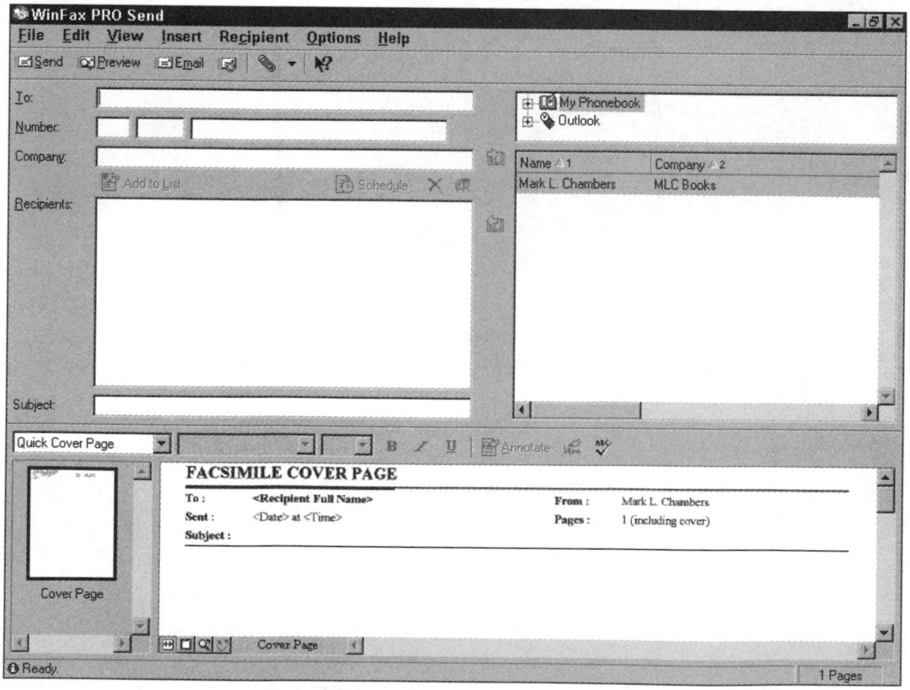

Figure 13-15: Setting up a new fax.

Part V
The Part of Tens

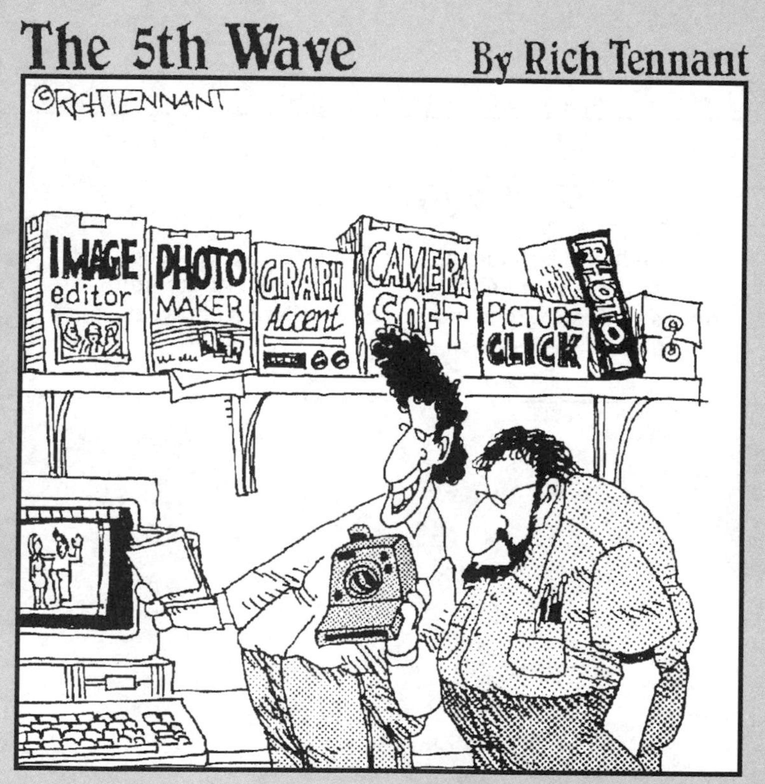

"...and here's me with Cindy Crawford.. And this is me with Madonna and Celine Dion..."

In this part . . .

You'll find tips and advice that will help you use your scanner more effectively and creatively, including things to avoid, signs of a good scan, and a showcase of image-editing effects.

Chapter 14

Ten Tips and Tricks for Better Scanning and Editing

In This Chapter

- Watch for new programs
- Experiment with your images
- Optimize your memory
- Keep things current
- Check your scanner's edges
- Trade in your mouse
- Reorganize your hard drive
- Become an expert on your software
- Defragment your hard drive
- Invest in a larger monitor

Almost all the tips and tricks I cover elsewhere in this book revolve around your scanner, its software, and your image editor — no big surprise there. Without a good working knowledge of your scanning hardware and the software you need to acquire and edit images, why go any further?

However, if you've read the rest of this book, you're now a seasoned scanning veteran and you're familiar with both your scanning hardware and software. In this chapter, I cover your entire system — not just tips and tricks to optimize your scanner and image software but also your hard drive, system RAM, and monitor. Even your rodent gets coverage.

Investigate New Software

I don't watch daytime drama (soap operas, to most of us), but I'm told by my friends who do that it's essential to watch every day or at least to stay current with the story line. Otherwise, how would you know who's doing what to whom and why?

The same is true in the software world. Well, not necessarily "who's doing what to whom," but rather the need to stay up-to-date with new scanning software. Scanners are a hot peripheral these days. With more and more computer owners investing in scanners, an explosion of both commercial and shareware image editors, scanning applications, and plug-ins has occurred. Although your scanning hardware may not change over the next few years, what you can *do* with that flatbed changes and expands!

How can you stay on top of new trends in software? Here's how I stay connected:

- **Online and print magazines:** Whether you choose the old-fashioned paper version or the Web, computer magazines are now your best bet for software reviews, product announcements, opinions, and rumors. My favorites are *Desktop Publisher's Journal* (`www.dtpjournal.com`), *PC* magazine (`www.zdnet.com/pcmag/`), *PC World* (`www.pcworld.com`), *MacWeek* (`www.macweek.com`), *Macworld* (`www.macworld.com`), and *Windows* magazine (`www.winmag.com`).
- **Web sites:** A number of great Web sites are well known for their coverage of hardware and software, including Tom's Hardware Guide (`www.tomshardware.com`), Ace's Hardware (`www.aceshardware.com`), and the PC Technology Guide (`www.pctechguide.com`). You can also browse online shareware sites, like CNET Shareware, at `shareware.cnet.com`, and Topsoft.com for scanning software.
- **Internet newsgroups:** Talk about opinions! Fire up your newsgroup reader and visit the following hotbeds of scanning and imaging discussion: `comp.periphs.scanners`, `alt.comp.periphs.scanners`, `alt.graphics.photoshop`, `comp.graphics.misc`, `comp.graphics.apps.photoshop`, and `comp.graphics.apps.paint-shop-pro`.

Experiment!

Your scanner is a fantastic piece of equipment. Throughout this book, I do my best to give you an overview of what it can do, what's available, and how you can use it.

However, no book can take the place of your own eyes — so use them! Take your image editor, OCR program, plug-ins, and image-manipulation software out for a drive and try a new filter, new effect, or new command every day. Unless you're looking for a specific appearance in your image, take your shoes off and experiment.

For example, whenever I'm trying to create an original piece of artwork for a publication, I generally try several different filters on the same scanned image. You see some of the results of this kind of work in Chapter 17, where I demonstrate the appearance of ten of my favorite filters and effects on the same image. Dark and frightening, light and fanciful, hi-tech or natural, antique or gleaming chrome — you can project all those moods and many more from the same image!

Before you utterly throw caution to the wind, however, keep three very important tips in mind:

- **Don't overwrite the original.** I make it a rule never to overwrite an original with an edited copy — no matter how happy I am with the results of my work — unless I'm sure that I will never need that image for another purpose. You would be surprised how often you turn to a favorite image for a new inspiration. (Naturally, this is yet another argument for archiving your image collection on a CD-R; it has plenty of room for all your experiments as well as all the originals.)
- **Don't forget the Undo command.** Oh, man! That was *not* the effect you were looking for. Luckily, virtually every image editor on the face of the planet has an Undo command. Some allow you multiple Undo steps, so you can back off of the last two commands rather than just one.
- **Don't degrade the image.** Applying an artistic filter or effect works fine; just don't obliterate the image in the process! Keep your subject recognizable (even if that subject is suddenly embossed, rendered in pastels, changed into glass, or covered with flames). Change the image too much and you lose the message you were trying to convey. Avoid enjoying too much of a good thing.

Thanks for the Memory

Memory. Your computer needs it to function; it stores data while your CPU performs calculations and then holds the results for you to examine or save to disk. You probably know how much memory your computer has, but did you also know that your computer's operating system creates more "on the fly?"

This pseudomemory, called *virtual memory,* is well hidden within both Windows and Mac OS. However, virtual memory is vitally important — without it, a computer with only 64MB of system RAM would find it very hard indeed to open a 40MB image file with a huge, memory-hungry application like Photoshop.

Why? When your computer runs out of physical RAM (for example, when all 64MB has been filled by the operating system, the application you're running, and the image itself), it uses space on your hard drive to temporarily store the excess data. Although this process is much less efficient and much slower than storing data in actual RAM, it gets the job done.

To enhance the memory usage (and therefore the performance) of your computer while editing images or using your OCR software, follow these guidelines:

- **Buy at least 128MB of system RAM.** The more physical memory you can afford, the less your computer has to rely on virtual memory, and the faster your entire system runs. This is the reason that power users demand at least 128MB of RAM when they're buying a computer; 256MB, of course, is even better.
- **Free up as much hard drive space as possible.** If you're running Windows, the virtual memory file (also called a *swap file*) is set to dynamically increase and decrease as your program requests and frees up more memory. To make sure that you have sufficient space for the swap file, I recommend that you try to keep at least 500MB of free space available on the hard drive that holds your Windows directory.
- **Defragment your hard drive.** I talk about this issue in more detail later in this chapter, in the section "Defragment Your Hard Drive." Defragmenting your drive helps the performance of your virtual memory.
- **Configure more virtual memory.** If you're running Mac OS 9 with less than 256MB of RAM, you can benefit from configuring additional virtual memory for programs like Photoshop and Super Goo. (If you have more than 256MB of system RAM, it's really a trade-off, and I recommend that you disable virtual memory; see the next set of steps.)

To disable virtual memory, follow these steps:

1. **Click the Apple menu and choose Control Panels.**
2. **Run the Memory Control Panel, which is shown in Figure 14-1.**

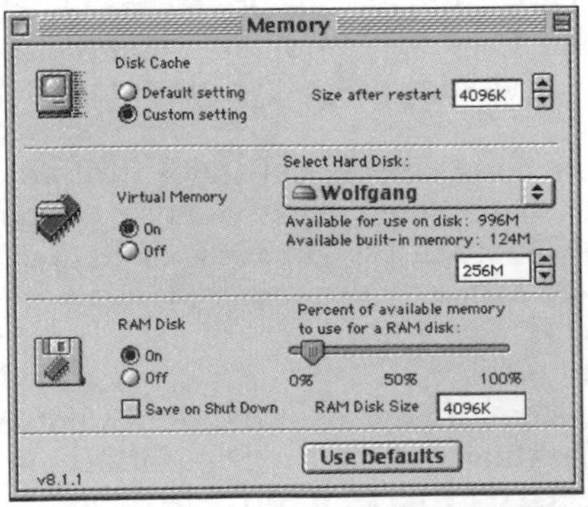

Figure 14-1: Configuring memory on a Mac.

3. **If Virtual Memory is turned off, click the On button in the Virtual Memory portion of the dialog box.**
4. **Click in the Virtual Memory field and enter a higher value (typically, I recommend around 128MB more than the amount of system RAM you have).**
5. **Click the Close box to close the dialog box and save your changes.**
6. **Restart your Mac.**

Update Everything

Although I've mentioned that it makes sense to monitor new commercial and shareware scanning applications, staying current on your scanner's drivers and scanner-control software is even more important. After all, these programs are responsible for keeping your scanner happily humming.

I recommend that you check your scanner manufacturer's Web site at least once a month to check for new updates and to apply them as soon as you've downloaded them. New updates can

- Add functionality to your scanning-control program
- Fix bugs in your scanner's driver
- Add compatibility with the latest operating system and applications

If you have to reinstall your scanner software because of a hard drive crash, don't forget to apply past updates. This is often the cause behind the oft-heard remark "This was working like a charm before I had to rebuild my system!"

Avoid the Edge

It's sad, but true: Because of age and normal wear, calibration problems, or rough handling, some flatbed scanners don't produce an even image quality across the entire area of the glass. If you notice that your scans are dark around the edges when you place an original flush against your scanner's home corner, try scanning the same original when it's placed smack-dab in the center of the scanner glass. After you have saved both images, open both of them side by side in your image editor and compare them. If the image produced from the centered original is better, it's time to avoid the edges of your scanner's glass.

"How can I fix this problem?" That depends on the manufacturer, the age of the unit, whether it's a single-pass or triple-pass model, and what type of handling the scanner has received. If your scanner-control program allows you to perform a calibration, that may take care of the problem. If not, just continue to center your originals.

Toss Your Mouse

I jettisoned my mouse many years ago, and now I use a Logitech Trackman Marble. It's a *trackball,* which is something like an upside-down mouse, as shown in Figure 14-2. Unlike a traditional mouse, the body of this pointing device stays stationary on your desk, and you move the ball with your thumb or forefinger.

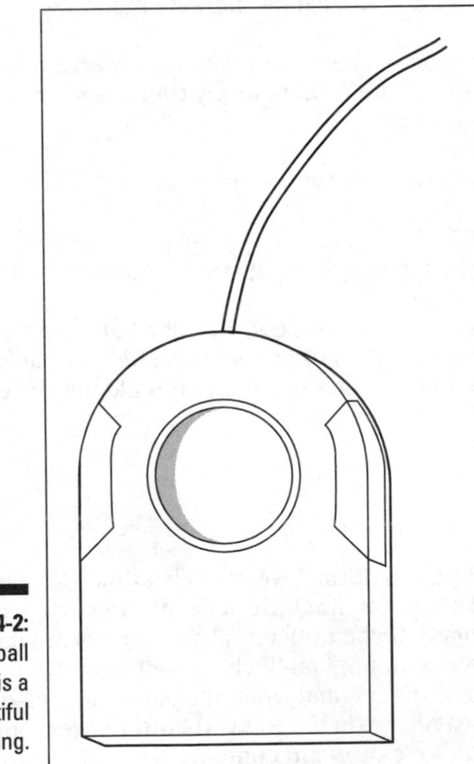

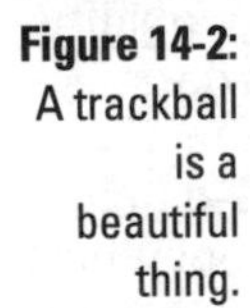

Figure 14-2: A trackball is a beautiful thing.

Since a mouse came standard with your computer, why choose another type of pointing device? After all, the mouse has been around since the early days of graphical user interfaces: Even before Windows 3.0, the Atari ST and the Commodore Amiga both used mice.

Here's the inside story on your typical standard equipment mouse:

- **It's less precise.** Most mice lack the precise control necessary for proper image editing. If you're serious about image applications, you need a high-resolution pointing device.
- **It places strain on your wrist.** With a trackball, your wrist and forearm barely move at all, reducing the strain.
- **It's harder to maintain.** Most standard equipment mice still use an antiquated ball and roller system. The rollers get covered with gunk and have to be cleaned regularly, and you probably need a mouse pad to get consistent tracking response. I strongly recommend an *optical* system, which eliminates the rollers (no maintenance) and doesn't need a mouse pad.
- **It takes up more of your desktop.** With a traditional mouse, you end up readjusting its position from time to time when you reach the edge of your desktop. A trackball doesn't move on your desktop, so it doesn't need position adjustments — and it takes up much less room than a mouse and mouse pad, which constantly drags that cord around behind itself.

A trackball typically costs anywhere from $40 to $80, depending on the features you get. However, if you want to stay with the basic design of a mouse but you want to eliminate some of these problems, consider a wireless mouse (which has no cord) or an optical mouse (which doesn't use a ball, so maintaining it is much easier) or a model that's a combination of both.

Hard Drive Tips and Tricks

Let me give you a quick prediction here. In Chapter 15, I talk about how quickly you use up drive space by trying to squeeze an entire family's worth of software and Windows 98 and your scanned images onto a single 4GB drive; therefore, I don't go into these things now.

After buying a scanner, though, you may not have enough spare pocket change to afford a new 30GB or 40GB drive. What then? How can you help make sure that you have the space you need for 100MB of scanned images when elbow room is tight on your system?

First, consider cleaning house! Delete as much unnecessary data as possible from your hard drive. Remember to *use caution!* I strongly recommend that you delete only those data files you *know* are scrap, like MP3 files you no longer want. If you decide to delete those game demos and forgotten shareware applications, use the application's uninstall program (or use the Add/Remove Programs option in the Control Panel, which you can reach by choosing Start⇨Settings⇨Control Panel).

You can usually also delete a number of files without fear of causing problems in Windows. They include

- **Trash/Recycle Bin files:** To regain the space from your deleted files, empty the Trash (in Mac OS) or the Recycle Bin (in Windows). Under Windows, right-click the Recycle Bin icon and choose Empty Recycle Bin. Under Mac OS, click the Special menu and choose Empty Trash.
- **Temporary Internet and Web browser files:** You can often reclaim an amazing amount of space by deleting the images and HTML pages stored in your Web browser's cache. Within Internet Explorer, for example, click Tools and choose Internet Options to display the dialog box shown in Figure 14-3 and click Delete Files to purge the cache directories. Click OK to return to Internet Explorer.
- **Windows temporary files:** Shut down any applications running on your PC, run Windows Explorer, and delete the contents of your \WINDOWS\TEMP directory. This action eliminates all the temporary files created by programs in Windows (at least those that aren't locked by a background application).

If you're running Windows 98 SE or Windows Me, you can also use the Disk Cleanup Wizard (shown in Figure 14-4) to automate the entire cleaning process. Choose Start⇨Programs⇨Accessories⇨System Tools⇨Disk Cleanup to run the Wizard.

Another good idea is to reserve a drive for your scanned images. This idea is a great one if you happen to have an old, scavenged 1GB drive lying around and gathering dust. By dedicating a drive just for your scanner, you gain a number of advantages:

- Locating your image files for editing is easier than searching all over your system.
- You know that the reserved space is always available.
- Using the Windows Find Files or Folders feature takes less time.
- Backing up an entire drive to CD-R, Zip disk, or tape with a backup application is easier. You're assured that all your images are located in one place.

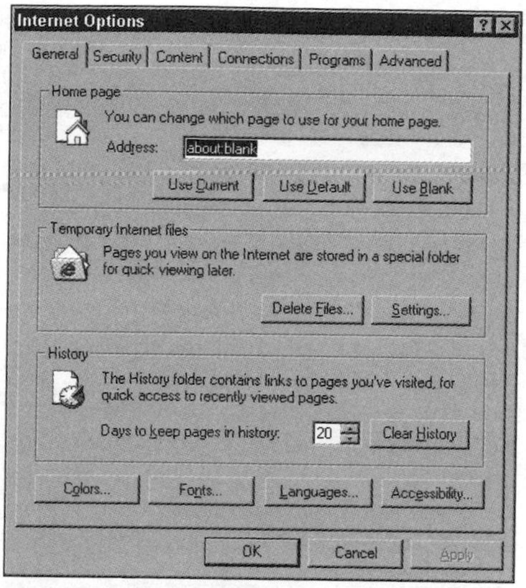

Figure 14-3: Time to nix all that temporary Web clutter.

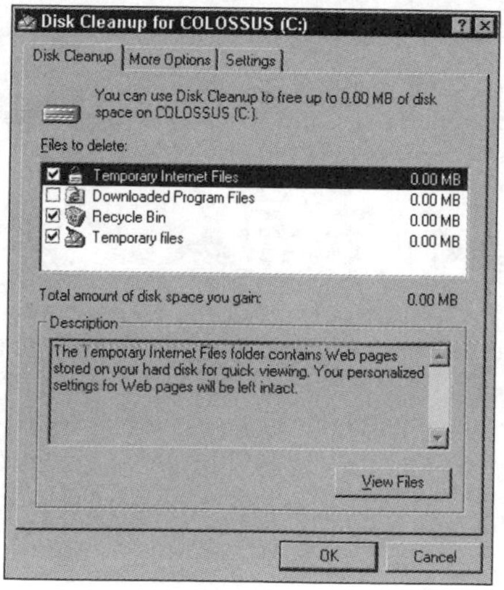

Figure 14-4: Cleaning your drive the Windows wizard way.

If you don't have a spare drive, you can still create one using a program like Partition Magic from PowerQuest. Figure 14-5 shows the main menu from this great utility. Even if you only have one physical drive, you can subdivide that drive into more than one logical drive, so your drive C can become both a drive C and a drive D! (Partition Magic also allows you to choose a smaller cluster size, which yields more efficient use of your existing drive.) With a dedicated partition, you have the advantages of a separate drive reserved for your images, which I mention in Chapter 5.

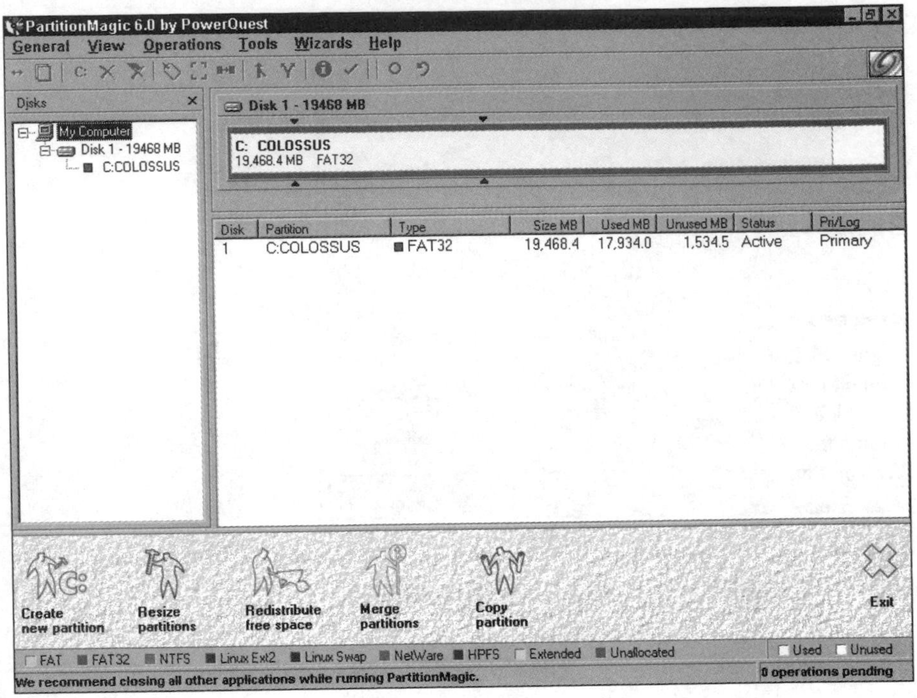

Figure 14-5: The Partition Magic main menu.

Know Thy Scanning Software

I know that it's not a particularly popular thing to say, but as a technical writer who has written many product manuals, I can honestly say that it pays to read the documentation! Sure, most programs for Windows and Mac OS that are now on the market are designed with ease of use in mind, and you can probably figure out — *eventually* — 60 percent of the commands in that new whiz-bang editor you bought without cracking open the manual. Any graphics professional can tell you, however, that those *other* 40 percent of the commands save you time and significantly improve your work.

Even if you have a phobia about reading software manuals, image applications now include a host of other methods you can use to teach yourself more than "just the basics," including

- **Tutorials:** I think that tutorials are the cat's meow. Nothing can help you learn like hands-on training. I highly recommend that you try out the tutorials that accompany all your applications.

- **Online Help files:** Why try to puzzle things out by yourself? Unless you like frustration and would rather spend your time scratching your head, use the online help system! Both Windows and Mac OS allow you to search for keywords, so it's usually even more convenient than checking the index in the manual.
- **Web site tips and tricks:** Take advantage of the extra content provided on the manufacturer's Web site. I've seen everything from program walk-throughs to additional filters and effects, free for the downloading!
- **Frequently Asked Question files:** FAQ files are pure gold in my book. Why? Because they address the most common questions about a program, with a minimum of fuss and formatting. Also, most FAQ files are written by customers for customers, so I get more of the information I'm likely to need.
- **Customer mailing lists and newsgroups:** Think of a customer mailing list and a topical newsgroup as ongoing FAQ discussions. Because you can join in, however, you can ask the specific questions you want, and other folks provide the answers.

Defragment Your Hard Drive

If you're not familiar with disk fragmentation, it's high time I introduced you! A fragmented hard drive can slow down your entire system.

As you delete files and copy new files into the free space on your hard drive, the files on the drive become *fragmented.* They're separated into dozens of smaller pieces, and your drive and computer have to work together to keep track of them and "reassemble" the smaller pieces into the original file whenever it's needed. This reassembly step takes time — only a few milliseconds or so — but those delays add up when your computer has more than one application open or when you're editing images while checking your mail and working on your word processor. The older the CPU and the slower the hard drive, the more noticeable this slowdown becomes, and, unfortunately, you can't prevent this ongoing fragmentation. Figure 14-6 illustrates the effects of fragmentation.

Luckily, you can reverse the effects of fragmentation with a defragmenter, which rewrites the files on your drive in contiguous form, as shown in Figure 14-7. This file now takes much less time to read, improving the performance of your hard drive and your computer. When you're working with larger scanned image files, you definitely can tell the difference.

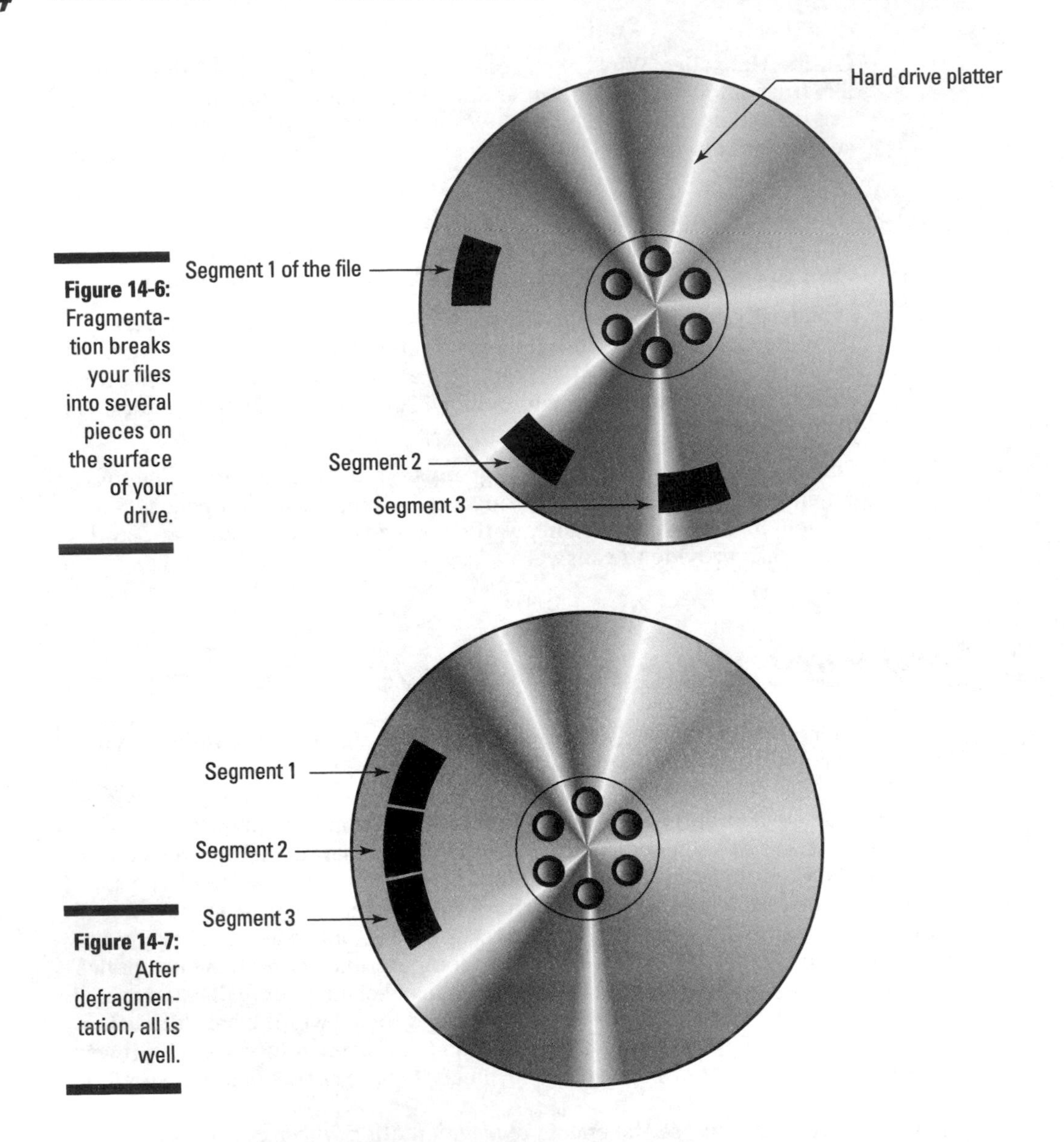

Figure 14-6: Fragmentation breaks your files into several pieces on the surface of your drive.

Figure 14-7: After defragmentation, all is well.

If you're running Windows 98 or Windows Me, I recommend running the Disk Defragmenter program at least once a month. Follow these steps:

1. **Click Start and choose Programs⇨Accessories⇨System Tools⇨ Disk Defragmenter to display the screen shown in Figure 14-8.**
2. **Click the hard drive you want to scan. If you have more than one drive, choose the drive that holds the files you're recording.**

3. **Click Settings and enable the Rearrange program files so my programs start faster check box. Click OK to exit the Settings dialog box.**
4. **Click OK.**

Although Mac OS 9 doesn't come with a defragmenter, you can choose from a number of utility programs to do the job. I recommend Norton Utilities for the Macintosh, which comes with the Speed Disk program (`www.symantec.com`), as shown in Figure 14-9, or PlusOptimizer, from Alsoft, Inc. (`www.alsoft.com`).

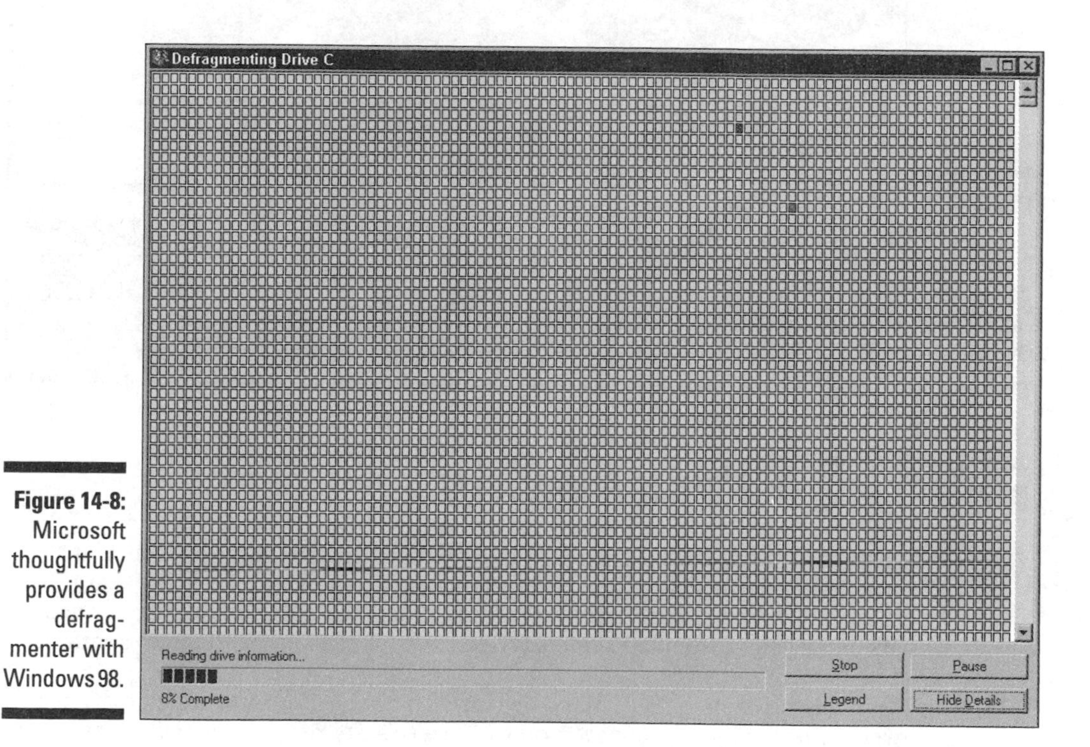

Figure 14-8: Microsoft thoughtfully provides a defragmenter with Windows 98.

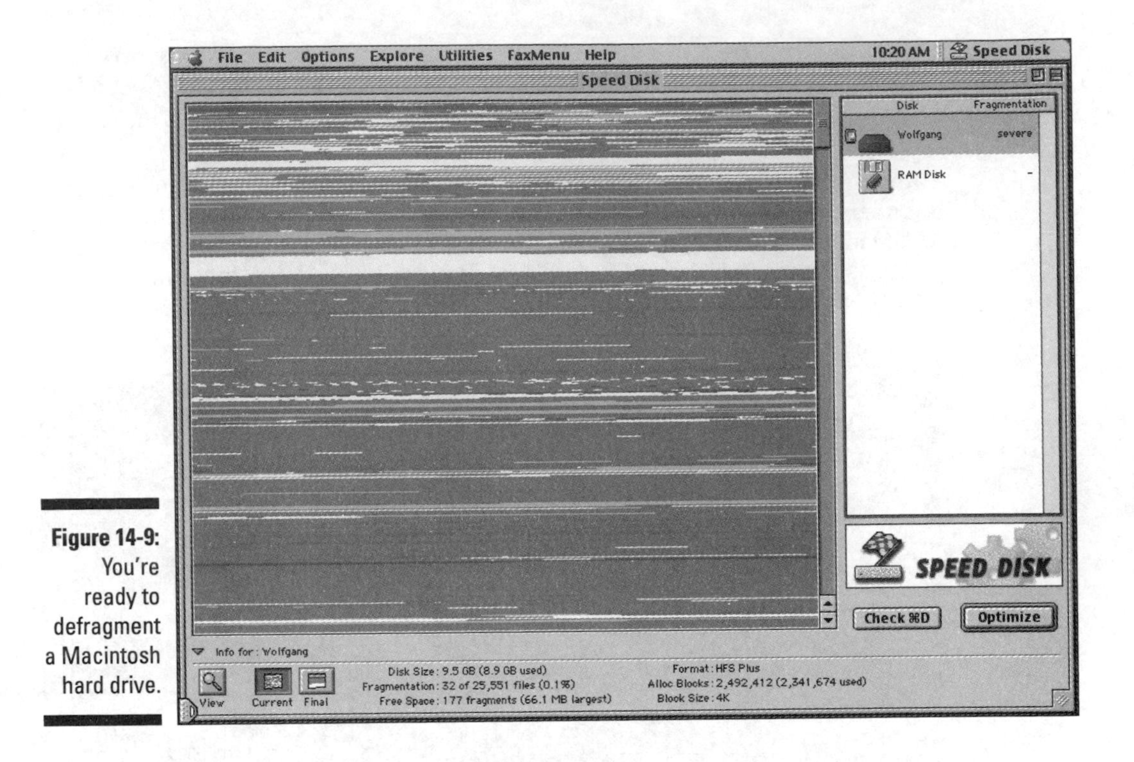

Figure 14-9: You're ready to defragment a Macintosh hard drive.

Splurge on Your Monitor

Ever end up tired after an hour or two of image editing, with red eyes and a headache? Perhaps it's that 15-inch monitor you're using. You know that this is the problem if you spend most of your time at your computer with your nose six inches away from the screen. (Watch out for the famous "techno-suntan".)

You may be saying, "Hey, Mark, I work with image files only once or twice a week. Do I really need a new monitor?" Here's my reply: Even if you use your scanner just twice a week, what about all those other computer activities? Do you play your fair share of computer games, use a word processor several times a week, or maintain a checkbook on your computer? If you're still using a 15-inch monitor, shouldn't you spend a little to improve your computing experience and ease the strain on at least one set of eyeballs?

Part of the reason I stress this concept so much is the rapid drop in prices for monitors over the past few years. Sure, a 17-inch monitor used to cost $400, although now you can pick a good one up for $200 at any Web store. That same $400 now buys you an excellent 19-inch screen (like the one I use). If you want to save energy and lower the radiation level of your system even further, you can invest in a crystal-clear LCD display. However, be prepared to pay well over $1,000 for a 17-inch LCD monitor.

You have to consider more than just your ocular health — as though that weren't enough. With a larger viewing surface (and, typically, a higher resolution), you can see more of an image on a 17-inch or 19-inch monitor, which means less scrolling. (I'm all for less scrolling!)

Chapter 15

Ten Things to Avoid Like the Plague

In This Chapter

- Antique processors
- Antique scanners
- Old printer cables
- Refurbished scanners
- Scanning copyrighted work
- Antique operating systems
- Strange image formats
- Tiny storage solutions
- Unreliable storage solutions
- Scanner glass damage

I love this chapter. I have a chapter with the same title and general direction in my other *...For Dummies* book, too. Why? Well, it's not every day that you can pull up a soapbox and launch word missiles at the things that have earned your wrath!

Naturally, I don't tear into things just to amuse myself. (Not in a book, anyway.) The idea behind this Part of Tens chapter is to save *you* the frustration and wasted time that these things represent. Consider these words as "distilled experience." In my consulting practice and my years as a hardware technician, I've been forced to put up with a number of the items in this chapter personally, and I wouldn't wish things like printer cartridge scanners on my worst enemy.

Evade these ten things as you pass them in life, and I can guarantee that you'll be a happier person.

The 486 and the 68030

I'm the first to admit that the Intel 80486 and the Motorola 68030 were great CPUs (short for *c*entral *p*rocessing *u*nit) in their time. Heck, I can remember when PCs and Macs based on these chips were cutting edge, and technowizards would fall asleep at night dreaming of them. You would spend $2,500 for one of these machines a mere five or six years ago.

My friends, those days are over. Boy, howdy, are they over. If you've just spent $200 on a new scanner, why connect it to a computer that most experienced computer owners would ignore if they saw it at a garage sale? Yes, I admit that — technically, anyway — a 486-based computer can power a scanner. However, keep the following concepts in mind:

- **You have less.** Unless someone has spent a fortune upgrading that old computer, you'll have a smaller hard drive — probably much less than a gigabyte (1,000 megabytes) — that can't hold more than a handful of high-resolution images after you've installed Windows. A machine that old also has an older video card that may not even be able to display the 24-bit color displayed by your scanner. And don't even mention the amount of RAM you have: Back then, 32MB was all you needed!
- **Ports? What ports?** Older PCs and Macs don't support USB (unless you spend more money than the computer's worth to upgrade them). On the PC side, you end up with a parallel port scanner, which is not my first choice; on the Macintosh side, you end up with SCSI, which is fast but significantly more expensive. You miss out on more peripherals than just a scanner, especially because more and more hardware will rely on USB in the future.
- **Performance is futile.** Running Windows 98 on a 486 is the equivalent of trying to pull a double-wide mobile home with a lawn tractor. Every application you run (not just your scanning software) acts like the silicon equivalent of a Galapagos turtle. How much is your time worth? Most people can't spend all day sitting in front of their computers, so a slow computer converts directly into lost productivity.

Upgrading a computer that's more than five years old isn't a cheap proposition — especially when you compare the amount you have to spend to the cost of a new machine. If $800 buys you a brand-new PC with an Athlon or Pentium III processor, why break yourself with technology used by the Pharaohs?

Here's my recommendation: If you're using a PC or Macintosh that has already reached its fifth or sixth birthday and you're serious about producing the best scans for home or business use, it's time to put that computer out to pasture. If someone tries to give you or sell you such a machine, smile quietly to yourself and pass on that "bargain."

Printer Cartridge Scanners

Every time I see a printer being used as a scanner, I start chuckling. I can't help it! The idea made sense back in the days when a typical flatbed cost well over $500: You bought an inkjet printer, and then you snapped in a scanning head that masqueraded as a printer cartridge. Because an inkjet printer's ink cartridge takes the same path across a sheet of paper as a scanning head — voilà — you had an instant inexpensive scanner.

Not quite. Oh, printer cartridge scanners work (after a fashion), although the caveats are ridiculous:

- They deliver a lower dpi than even the cheapest modern flatbed. (The maximum I've ever seen for this technology has been 360 dpi.)
- They scan significantly slower than a dedicated flatbed scanner.
- You can't use your printer at the same time as your pseudoscanner.
- You have to snap in the scanning cartridge every time you want to use it — and then replace it with the ink cartridge again to print.
- As with a sheet-fed scanner, you're restricted to standard-size paper documents; unlike with a sheet-fed scanner, however, you can't use a sleeve to scan smaller items.
- Your "scanner" uses a parallel port interface.

A printer cartridge scanner is basically half of a multifunction device — it prints and scans — but with none of the convenience of a genuine all-in-one unit. Leave your printer to do the job it was designed for, and — for $30 or $40 more — invest in the convenience and versatility of a flatbed scanner.

Serial Scanners

Another variety of scanner technology that should have faded into obscurity years ago, an older serial scanner may look very similar to a typical modern flatbed that uses a USB connection. So why do I dislike them? The issue is speed!

Let me explain — or, even better, look at Figure 15-1, which contrasts a parallel connection and a serial connection. Notice how the data bytes in a serial connection travel in a series, one after the other (hence the name *serial*), and the data bytes in a parallel connection travel simultaneously on separate wires (hence the name *parallel*).

A serial connection is therefore much slower than any type of connection in use with modern scanners. As you may recall, I'm not particularly a fan of parallel port scanners either, but even a parallel port model is a speed demon when compared to a clunky serial scanner.

Speed becomes more of an issue as the size and dpi of a scanned image increases. You may be able to wait while a 200 dpi JPEG image (with a file size of 256K) crawls across a serial connection, but what about a 600 dpi Windows bitmap image that may take up 30 or 40 megabytes? You could play a game of Monopoly while you're waiting!

Compared to a sweet and simple USB connection, serial ports are also finicky beasts to configure; if you're using an older PC with a serial mouse, adding a serial scanner could interfere with the mouse, causing it to lock up your computer.

Like the human appendix (and, in the world of computers, the antique Turbo button), the serial port itself is becoming more and more of an anachronism. Traditionally the port of choice for modems and digital cameras, the once lofty position held by the serial port has been superseded by the USB port, which is much faster, much easier to use, and much more versatile. With a serial port, you can attach only one device. With a USB port, you can attach more than 100 devices!

Steer clear of a serial scanner. You'll be much happier.

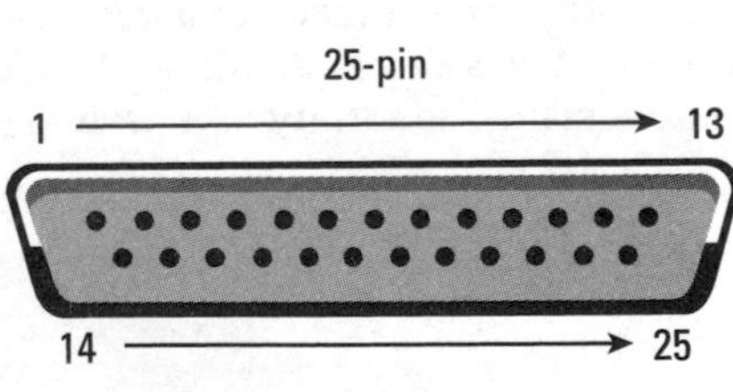

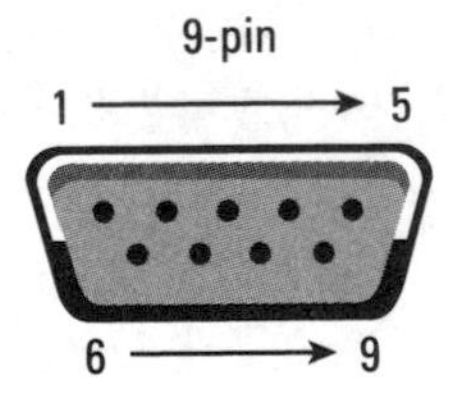

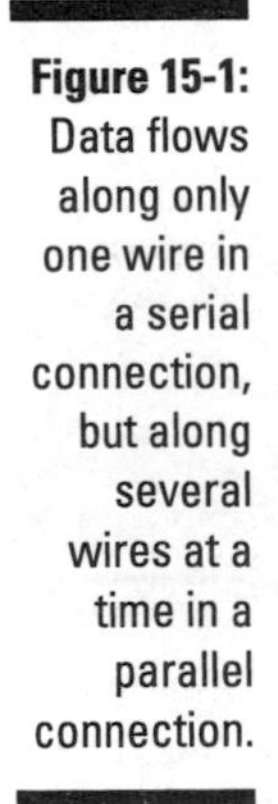

Figure 15-1: Data flows along only one wire in a serial connection, but along several wires at a time in a parallel connection.

Old Printer Cables

Sounds a little weird, doesn't it? Believe me, a 10-year-old printer cable can cause you more headaches than you would think possible because it can prevent your parallel port scanner from working, and it's practically impossible to track the problem down!

Here are the facts: Suppose that I pick up a used printer cable at a garage sale. Figuring that all printer cables are created equal (and I would *almost* be right), I decide to use it to connect my new parallel port scanner to my computer. (The same problem also crops up for parallel port Zip drives, CD-ROM drives, and tape backup units.)

The problem lies in the cable's design. It doesn't conform to the IEEE-1284 standard, which is an international cable specification that's required for bidirectional devices. Whoa — sorry about that — the technonerd in me took over. In terms that a normal human being can understand, your scanner needs to be able to communicate with your computer through the cable (hence the term bidirectional). However, that antique cable was made back in the Dark Ages of computing, when printers only received data from a computer and didn't talk back.

Therefore, even if you have everything set correctly on your scanner and your computer (including your parallel port mode, which I cover in Chapter 12), the connection still doesn't work. Essentially, your scanner can understand your computer, but your computer can't receive data from your scanner.

Fixing this problem is refreshingly simple: Check the cable you intend to use with your scanner and see whether the words *IEEE-1284 Compatible* are stamped on it. If so (or if your cable came with your scanner, naturally), you should have no problem with bidirectional communications between your scanner and your computer.

Refurbished Hardware

I know that I'll catch some flak from some readers when I list refurbished scanners as something to avoid. If you're not familiar with the refurbishing process, here's the tale:

1. A scanner returns to the manufacturer from the original owner. Typically, the reason is that because the scanner was broken "out of the box" or broke soon after it was opened.
2. The manufacturer takes the scanner back to the factory, repairs it, and then tests it — or at least tests the part that broke. (This step is also called remanufacturing, which I find very amusing.)
3. The newer, even-fresher-smelling scanner is sold for pennies on the dollar to an eager discount chain (or, increasingly, to an online clearinghouse).
4. The scanner is sold again to another person.

By law, a refurbished scanner must be clearly marked as refurbished or remanufactured, although you usually have no other way to tell other than the bargain-basement price.

Some of my friends point out that refurbished hardware is repaired and tested by the manufacturer. You definitely can't beat the price. For example, I recently saw a $120 flatbed scanner selling in refurbished form for $50. You may even receive a short warranty from the manufacturer.

So why do I dislike refurbished stuff so intensely? Here's an *abbreviated* list of my grievances:

- **I'll bet you that all sales are final.** Most of these companies cut you off from returning that refurbished scanner. If it breaks again, you're stuck.
- **It's a traveling thing.** When that refurbished scanner finally arrives at your door, it has likely been shipped to Timbuktu and back — and it may have picked scratches, dings, and nicks to prove it. Call me picky, but I take good care of my equipment, and cosmetic damage isn't pretty.
- **You're in the dark.** *Something* was wrong. You don't know what, but this scanner has already broken once. If you're a Vegas gambler, consider the odds: I would rather pay full price for something brand-new from the factory than a secondhand piece of repair work.
- **How well do you trust the manufacturer?** Did the entire scanner get tested or just the broken components? How thorough was the examination?
- **You call that a warranty?** Personally, a 90-day warranty from the manufacturer just isn't enough for me (especially when all sales are final). Buy a brand-new scanner, and you're protected by a full year of warranty coverage. In fact, some stores even have the shameless urge to sell you an extended warranty on a refurbished scanner. What a deal! You get a used piece of hardware (previously broken, mind you) with a very expensive extended warranty for about the cost of a new printer and an equivalent standard warranty!

If you do decide to take the plunge and save the money up front on a refurbished scanner, promise me that you'll read the fine print before you click the Buy Now button. As that sharp Mr. Barnum once said — well, you know that one, along with "If it seems too good to be true, then it probably is."

Scanning Copyrighted Work

This one is just common sense. Why risk it? If you're scanning a photograph from a book or some text from a magazine article for your own personal use, I can understand it — but scanning copyrighted work and distributing it? Entire Internet newsgroups and Web sites are devoted to the "anonymous" posting of scanned images, but I avoid them.

What's even worse, however, is representing someone else's copyrighted work as your own and trying to profit from it. I'm told that lawyers are tenacious. Luckily, I don't know from personal experience, and I'm going to try my hardest to keep things that way. Sure, someone is probably scanning an 8 x 10 publicity photo of Slim Whitman at this very moment, planning to sell copies on eBay — but not me.

Call me old-fashioned and narrow-minded, but *copyright infringement is against the law.* Chalk it up to my profession: As an author, I'm very sensitive to copyrighted work.

Windows 95 and System 7

You may remember my tirade on tired processors at the beginning of this chapter. Well, the same argument also holds true for antique operating systems — and, believe it or not, that includes the venerable Windows 95 (and, on the Mac side, the august System 7).

Why upgrade your operating system just for your scanner? Good question, and I have plenty of reasons:

- **That acronym again:** I know that I keep harping about USB (and, to a lesser extent, FireWire), but they really are that easy to use and that simple to set up. Both the original version of Windows 95 and System 7 were released in the halcyon days before USB, and neither supports it. (Later versions of Windows 95 do support USB, although not as well as Windows 98 and Windows Me.)
- **Support for more image formats:** More info about this topic is coming up soon in this chapter. Let me just say that the more support in your operating system for built-in image formats, the better! Although you can install image-display or -editing software, Windows 95 by itself typically recognizes only the Windows bitmap format.
- **Better performance:** Windows 98, Windows Me, Mac OS 9, and Mac OS X all provide significant improvements in disk access and virtual memory usage, which translates into faster scanning times and faster image editing.
- **Updated software requirements:** Naturally, you want to run your scanner for several years to come. Unfortunately, however, both Windows 95 and System 7 have reached the end of their operational careers. Software developers know this, and they'll soon be writing image software (and updated scanning-control software) that requires Windows 98 or

Windows Me. I'm a procrastinator by nature — except when it comes to drivers, application software, games, and operating systems, which I like to keep updated whenever possible.

- **Cutting-edge operating systems are the cat's meow:** Am I right? (Or am I just a big-time technonerd? Don't answer that.)

You have to upgrade your operating system sooner or later; if upgrading helps improve your efficiency and productivity with your scanner (as well as all your other programs and devices), why wait?

Obscure Image Formats

"Oh, I've got just the document you need. I'll send it as a WIF file. You *can* read WIF images, right?"

What exactly is a "WIF" file? That's a scanned image that's saved in what I call *w*eird *i*mage *f*ormat. No one else on earth *ever* uses WIF files — but, for some unknown reason, you're sure to run into some poor soul who sends a WIF file to you as an e-mail attachment. Of course, *everyone* has an image editor that can display it. Right?

Don't get me wrong here: I use several obscure image formats myself, and I know that proprietary formats are a way of life for professions like computer-aided drafting (CAD). I use images in Targa (TGA) when I'm rendering three-dimensional graphics — and the Macintosh still produces PICT images (PCT) whenever you snap a screenshot.

What I don't understand, however, is why some otherwise wonderful folks insist on using murky formats to send images to their innocent friends, family, and fellow employees! For example, in just this past year, I've received images in the following well-known formats on disk or through e-mail:

- **MAC:** MacPaint, the program that reads this file type, uses a Macintosh format so antiquated that it creaks when you use it.
- **FPX:** FlashPix is a recent format developed for digital camera owners and used by virtually no one else on the planet.
- **IFF:** This format was used on the Amiga — which (until very recently, when the brand was revived) no longer even existed!

Luckily, I have an entire shelf full of different image editors, and I had no problem converting these things — but what about Aunt Harriet? She's running her original copy of Windows 95, and she knows about as much about displaying a digital image as she does about nuclear physics. Send her a WIF file and you're wasting both your time and hers, especially when you end up sending two or three e-mails to lead her through the process of downloading and installing the trial version of Paint Shop Pro.

Follow my recommendations in Chapter 10 and you'll never be accused of wasting someone's time with an incomprehensible image on a Web page or in an e-mail message.

Small-Capacity Hard Drives and Floppy Disks

I enjoy scale modeling. Creating a detailed miniature of something in a smaller scale gives you some idea of how the real McCoy works and how it was constructed.

On the other hand, I do *not* enjoy working with a "miniature" hard drive, especially when I'm trying to prepare high-resolution scanned images. A 2GB hard drive just doesn't do the trick, unless you've dedicated the entire drive to scanning and you run Windows from another drive. To illustrate, suppose that your family's computer system has a single 4GB drive (which used to be the norm just two or three short years ago). These days, it's safe to assume the numbers shown in Table 15-1.

Table 15-1 Where All Your Disk Space Goes

Software	*Typical Size*	*Remaining*
Windows 98	1.2GB	2.8GB
Four of the latest 3-D games	400MB each	1.2GB
Microsoft Office	200MB	1GB
A collection of 200 MP3 songs	4MB each	200MB

That hard drive territory vanishes pretty quickly, doesn't it? And note that I haven't added any other applications, either. (I'm assuming that you probably do something else than use Word, play games, and visit Napster.) Now factor in the space you need to store your scanned images, edit them, and store a few experimental images before you print them. Do you remember saying to yourself just a few years ago, "Who could ever fill up all that space?"

Let me be blunt: *Don't short-change yourself on hard drive space!* At the time this book was written, a 30GB drive cost only about $125 on the Web. Don't forget that you can add a second or even a third hard drive to today's PCs. If you would rather not crack open your computer's case, both PC and Macintosh owners can choose an external hard drive that uses a USB or FireWire connection.

Now that I've held forth with my opinions on small-capacity hard drives, I want to turn my scathing attention to an icon of PC computing: floppy disks. You may be wondering why — after all, I just finished talking about the need for a high-capacity drive on system with a scanner. JPEG and GIF images are small enough, however, to store on floppies, and many computer owners store their only copies of their priceless scanned images on a floppy rather than on a CD-R or a Zip disk. I can understand this logic: Floppies are cheap and plentiful, and every PC has a floppy drive. Not a bad solution, right?

Wrong. I mean dead wrong. In fact, floppies are about the most unreliable storage media on the face of the planet! Here are the facts that every PC owner should know — unless, of course, you've already fallen victim to floppy disaster, in which case you already know this stuff:

- **They're unreliable.** Floppy disks have the shortest shelf life of any common media. In English, that means that you can't use them for long and be 100 percent sure that your computer can reliably read that data, primarily because of wear and tear on the disk's spindle mechanism and magnetic fields. (If you must use floppies, *never* store them near a magnetic source, like a set of stereo speakers.)
- **They're not error-free.** Floppies from one computer may not be readable on another, even *immediately* after you've copied files, because of the minute discrepancy between the magnetic read-write heads on the two drives. (You should still be able to read that disk on the source drive, but for how long?)
- **They can carry viruses.** Floppies are a prime transmission method for viruses. Keep your antivirus program running in the background, and check any floppy you receive from someone else. Also, write-protect a floppy as soon as you've copied files to it to prevent catching a nasty digital something.

So what *are* floppies good for? Temporary storage, that's what — carrying an image home from school or work or sending it through the mail, but definitely not for storing your only copy of an important document. They're simply not the right choice for permanent storage.

As you probably have guessed, I recommend a CD-R or CD-RW for storing those images permanently — without worry about data loss, viruses, errors, or compatibility between drives! Chapter 5 tells you more.

Materials That Should Never be Scanned

In Chapter 12, I caution you about cleaning your flatbed scanner's glass with solvents or abrasive cleansers. A host of other damaging items can make contact with your glass, and many folks don't think about them until they end up with a scratch or stain. Remember that even the smallest shallow scratch can interfere with a high-resolution, high-dpi scan.

For example, some of these materials include

- Fabrics with a coarse, heavy weave, like canvas or leather
- Metallic items, like coins, jewelry, rings or keys
- CD-ROMs
- Originals that carry oil, fresh ink, paint, or other liquids that could stain your scanner's glass
- Items that carry adhesives
- Exceptionally heavy items that could break your scanner's glass

My point? *Think before you scan!* Before you place an original on your scanner's glass, consider whether it fits into this category of Materials That Should Never Be Scanned. No matter what materials you scan, take care in placing and removing them.

Consider this chapter as a series of ten signposts to help you out of ten potential minefields. It's my sincere wish that you never encounter any of these. If you do, however, remember that Chapter 12 has troubleshooting information and that you can always obtain technical support from your scanner manufacturer.

Chapter 16

Ten Signs of a Good Scan

In This Chapter

- Straightening your scans
- Cropping to improve an image
- Sharpening a scanned image
- Adjusting and closing the scanner cover
- Solving transparency problems
- Preparing your original
- Using first-generation originals
- Selecting the right-size original
- Balancing color
- Choosing the correct format

In other chapters in this book, I trundle on and on about specifics: what to do in certain situations, when to edit your images, what steps you need to take to accomplish something. Don't get me wrong: I'm not saying that that's a bad thing! Specific instruction is the bread and butter of any title in the . . .*For Dummies* series, and it's what I would want to read if I had bought this book.

However, I want to take a chapter from "the other direction" and examine the process by presenting the top ten general characteristics of a good scanned image. I don't go into any great detail here, although I list the hallmarks that every image should have — no matter what the subject and no matter what application uses the image.

(By the way, thanks for buying this book! I like to say that at least once in every dusty tome I write.)

Keeping Things Straight

Naturally, a scanned image doesn't look its best when tilted. Believe me: Your eye can tell when things aren't straight! As I mention in Chapter 6, aligning the original correctly with the sides of your scanner's glass is essential to a good scan; you can also save yourself a session of image editing by marking which edge of the scanner glass is "up" (according to your scanning software's preview display), or by changing the orientation before you scan.

Even if the original is aligned and facing in the right direction, you may still have an alignment problem if you're capturing just a portion. For example, if I were scanning just the title text from the book cover shown in Figure 16-1, I would still have to use the Rotate feature in Paint Shop Pro (which I show you in Chapter 8) to make those words level, as shown in Figure 16-2. Because the edges of the image were tilted after the rotation, I further cropped the scanned cover, which both straightened the edges of the image and focused the viewer's interest on the words. Always be prepared to crop after rotating an image.

Figure 16-1: A *...For Dummies* book cover I chose *completely* at random from the hundreds of titles in the series.

Figure 16-2: By rotating and cropping the scanned image, I can bring the title in line.

Crop 'Til You Drop

Speaking of cropping, you can't consider your scan complete if it contains extraneous details or text. That extra area not only detracts from the image but also adds to the file size. Even if you caught only an elbow at the corner of the sofa or an unnecessary paragraph heading at the bottom of a document, taking a moment to crop an image to improve it is worthwhile.

For example, Figure 16-3 may look fine as it is — after all, this photo is centered, the subject fills most of the frame, and nothing appears particularly out of place. To my photographer's eye, however, too much free space is surrounding the baby, and she's "floating" in the open expanse of white that fills the foreground. Figure 16-4 illustrates one possible crop that maintains the centered approach, but loses a portion of the baby's arm. The second crop in Figure 16-5 keeps the baby's arm in view, although she's somewhat off-center in the frame. Which is the "right" choice? It's up to you and your personal tastes when you're cropping your scanned images.

Figure 16-3: An innocent piece of chocolate cake is consumed.

Figure 16-4: One possible crop, keeping everything centered.

Figure 16-5: This cropped image keeps the baby intact.

You're Looking Sharp

I'm a dyed-in-the-wool fan of the Sharpening filter available in image editors and many scanner-control programs. A certain amount of sharpening is suitable for just about every photograph — even text documents can benefit from sharpening. It helps enhance details and helps your subjects stand out, particularly when little contrast exists between the light and dark areas in the original.

Take Figure 16-6, for example — because of the distance from the camera and the shadow cast by the sun, the features in this stone statue are less distinctive than they should be.

By applying the Sharpen More filter within Paint Shop Pro, the curves of the face are now cleaner and easier to see, as shown in Figure 16-7.

As I point out in Chapter 8, however, you can easily get carried away with sharpening! I strongly recommend that you never apply more than one level of Sharpen or Sharpen More to a scanned image. Remember that this technique can't add detail that doesn't exist. For example, apply the Sharpen More filter again to the statue and see what happens (see Figure 16-8).

Figure 16-6: The face of this statue needs a good sharpening.

Figure 16-7: A level of Sharpen More adds stronger lines and improves the image.

Figure 16-8: Whoa! Too much sharpening is not a good thing!

That second level of Sharpen More has turned the fine marble into what looks like coarse concrete. The program has enhanced the already enhanced pixels a second time, so they end up looking like something drawn on bubble wrap with a felt-tip permanent marker.

Flat Is Nice

In Chapter 6, I recommend that you always close the cover on your scanner because many types of originals can be completely scanned only if they're perfectly flat (or as flat as possible). Of course, if you're using a sheet-fed scanner, you can scan only flat originals.

For example, Figure 16-9 illustrates a scanned image I made of a hardbound book — with my scanner's cover raised. Figure 16-10 shows the same material with the cover adjusted and down. As you can see, a dramatic difference exists in the amount of text you can see, as well as the quality of the image overall. If you were planning to use the scanned image shown in Figure 16-9 with your OCR software, I would have to confiscate your mouse — you would be wasting your time because many characters are unreadable.

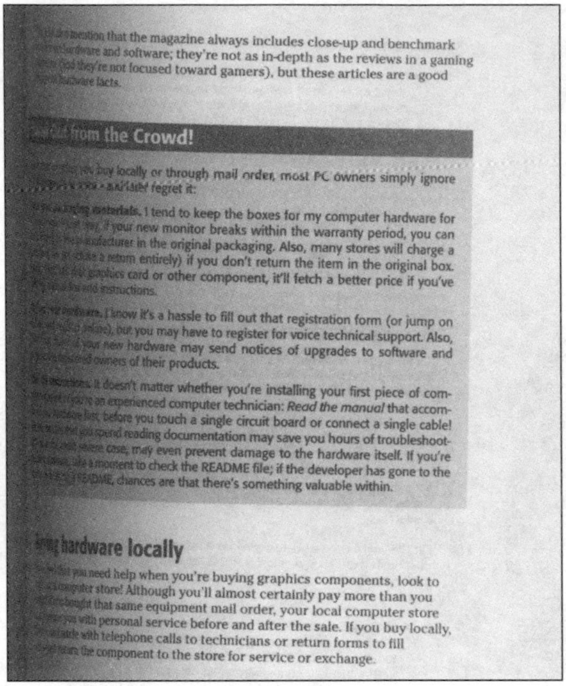

Figure 16-9: With the cover up (or not properly adjusted), a book's spine is likely to give you trouble.

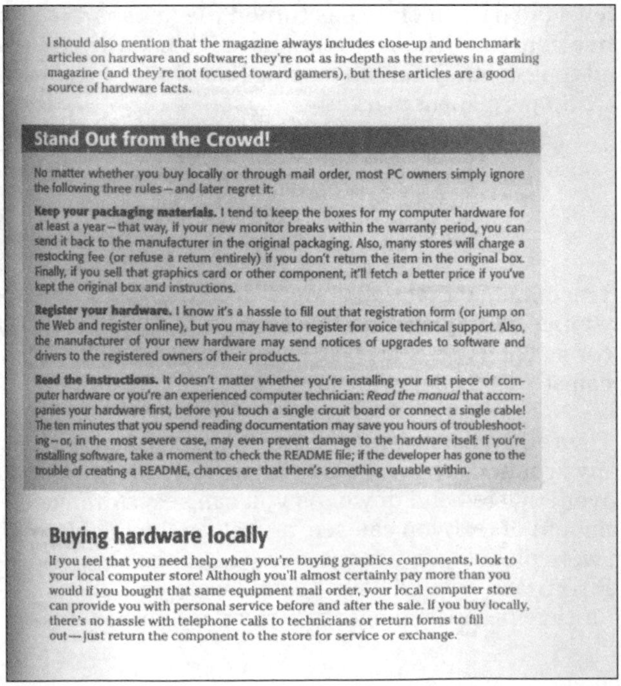

I should also mention that the magazine always includes close-up and benchmark articles on hardware and software; they're not as in-depth as the reviews in a gaming magazine (and they're not focused toward gamers), but these articles are a good source of hardware facts.

Stand Out from the Crowd!

No matter whether you buy locally or through mail order, most PC owners simply ignore the following three rules—and later regret it:

Keep your packaging materials. I tend to keep the boxes for my computer hardware for at least a year—that way, if your new monitor breaks within the warranty period, you can send it back to the manufacturer in the original packaging. Also, many stores will charge a restocking fee (or refuse a return entirely) if you don't return the item in the original box. Finally, if you sell that graphics card or other component, it'll fetch a better price if you've kept the original box and instructions.

Register your hardware. I know it's a hassle to fill out that registration form (or jump on the Web and register online), but you may have to register for voice technical support. Also, the manufacturer of your new hardware may send notices of upgrades to software and drivers to the registered owners of their products.

Read the instructions. It doesn't matter whether you're installing your first piece of computer hardware or you're an experienced computer technician: *Read the manual* that accompanies your hardware first, before you touch a single circuit board or connect a single cable! The ten minutes that you spend reading documentation may save you hours of troubleshooting—or, in the most severe case, may even prevent damage to the hardware itself. If you're installing software, take a moment to check the README file; if the developer has gone to the trouble of creating a README, chances are that there's something valuable within.

Buying hardware locally

If you feel that you need help when you're buying graphics components, look to your local computer store! Although you'll almost certainly pay more than you would if you bought that same equipment mail order, your local computer store can provide you with personal service before and after the sale. If you buy locally, there's no hassle with telephone calls to technicians or return forms to fill out—just return the component to the store for service or exchange.

Figure 16-10: By adjusting the cover and lowering the cover, you get better results.

That's, Like, So. . .Transparent

Creating a good scan from a transparent original may seem like holding a wriggling fish in your bare hands: It takes practice to get a handle on things. Why?

- Most scanners use a black foam backing on the underside of the cover. This is great when your original has an opaque background (it helps differentiate the edges of your original). However, if the original has a transparent background, like an overhead transparency or an animation cel, the text or images on the original are surrounded in a sea of black.
- A transparent original often reflects the light from the scanner head, which can produce "hot spots" in your scanned image.
- Inkjet printers and colored markers can both create semitransparent colors themselves, which just don't have the necessary contrast to show up well in the scanned image.

Check out Figure 16-11, and you can see what I mean — the original is a transparent overhead line drawing printed by a laser printer. As you can see, the text is virtually impossible to distinguish; in effect, it's a solid black page.

Figure 16-11: Don't expect to see much detail here — the original is transparent.

On the other hand, Figure 16-12 looks fine! That's because I added a simple, blank white piece of paper between the transparency and my scanner's cover. The white background helps to add depth and clarity to the transparency.

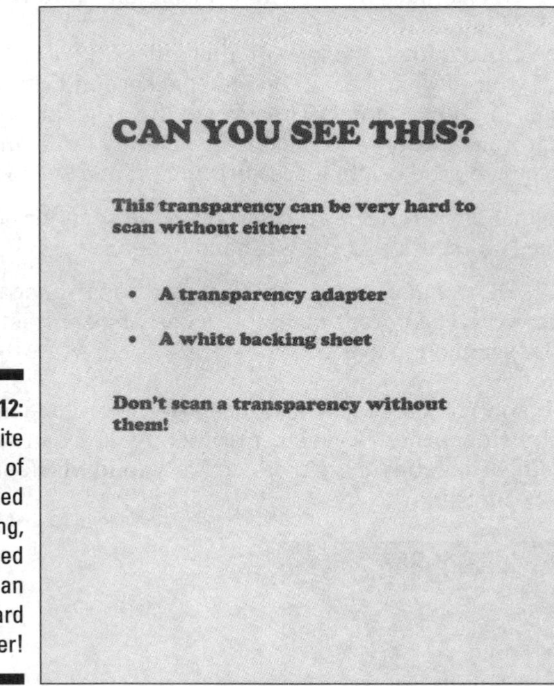

Figure 16-12: With a white piece of paper added as backing, the scanned image is an award winner!

As I mention in Chapter 2, the manufacturer of your scanner may also offer a transparency adapter for your scanner, which eliminates the need for a background (and also allows you to easily scan photograph negatives). Visit the company's Web site and check out your scanner's description to see whether you can buy an optional transparency adapter.

Your Original Is Your Friend

In the end, the quality of your scan depends on the quality of your original, and the next three signs of a good scan all concern the condition and quality of your original.

I realize that not every scanned document is in pristine condition: Old family photographs, for example, present more of a scanning challenge than a document that has just arrived on your laser printer. However, you can take action to ensure the best possible scan from an original that has seen better days:

- **Remove staples and paper clips before you scan.** These items are double trouble. They show up in your scanned image, so you have to remove them using your image editor, and you face the danger that they can scratch your scanner's glass.
- **Fix creases whenever possible.** In most cases, you can bend a crease back to straighten it. If the original is brittle or the crease is a different color, however, you have to load the image into your editor and do your best to remove the crease by matching pixel colors with the surrounding area.
- **Roll crumpled documents.** If your original is a paper document that has been crumpled up, roll it into a tube (if possible) and then roll it in reverse. This trick helps flatten the original, reducing the number of "hills and valleys" and producing a better scan. (Don't forget to close the cover on your scanner, which also helps to even out those wrinkles.)

Favor the First Generation

Here's a rule of thumb that comes in handy when you're shooting for The Perfect Scan — avoid these types of originals whenever you can:

- **Photocopies:** The copy machine is a modern miracle — just ask any hard-working medieval monk or Egyptian scribe. Using a photocopy as an original, however, is likely to produce a scanned image of much lower quality than scanning the original document itself. If you're sending that image with a fax/modem to a fax machine, on the other hand, the quality of the image is less important, so feel free to give away the original document in that case.
- **Photographs printed on older inkjet printers:** If your printer provides less than 600 x 600 dpi in either black and white or color, consider finding a laser printer or a newer inkjet that can produce higher resolutions. A high-resolution scan of a photograph printed on an inkjet at 300 x 300 dpi probably doesn't provide the results you're looking for. That photograph is likely to look like a halftone even to the naked eye, which is always a bad sign!
- **Faxes sent in Standard mode:** Whenever possible, ask those who send you faxes to send them in Fine or Superfine mode; the former delivers 203 x196 dpi, and the latter provides 300 x 300 dpi. (Unlike the color photograph produced on an inkjet printer that I mention in the preceding paragraph, 300 x 300 dpi is pretty doggone good for a fax transmission.) A fax sent in Standard mode may be okay for the human eye, but at 203 x 98, it's dismal for scanning, especially when you want to use that image with your OCR software.

Size Does Matter

When it comes to an original you want to scan, less is *not* more. Although you can certainly resize your scanned image with an image editor, you can stretch pixels only so far. Resizing doesn't add detail — it simply expands the image by "inflating" the elements within the image. Speaking of inflating, that's a good analogy. Think of a balloon with a printed logo on the side: If you blow up the balloon, the logo grows in size; when the balloon is full of air, however, the logo doesn't look as good as it did before the surface was stretched.

Naturally, if you need to use an original at its actual size in another document, you don't have this problem because you don't have to resize the image; simply scale the image at 100 percent and forget it.

Translated to scanners, the rule is simple: Always try to use an original that's at least the size of a typical 35mm print. For example, Figure 16-13 illustrates an image the size of a postage stamp blown up to 1024 x 768. Not the best quality, is it? The image just didn't have enough pixels to allow that kind of expansion without introducing jagged edges and a loss of focus.

Figure 16-13: Resizing a scanned image from a tiny original usually leaves much to be desired.

Figure 16-14, though, was scanned from a standard-size 35mm photograph print. Notice that resizing the image to 1024 x 768 had no adverse effect. In fact, I could have probably jacked this image up to a whopping 5000 pixels horizontally before you would see any significant problem.

Figure 16-14: With a larger original, the scan works much better.

"What if I *have* to use a small original?" Well, I can give you one tip: When an original is particularly small, increase the dpi rating by 100 to 200 dpi. This increase allows your image editor to do a better job of resizing (but results in a much larger file size).

Colors That Balance

I discuss color balance and how you can take care of it through either your scanner software or your favorite image editor in other chapters, so I don't go into great detail here.

However, I want to remind you to take a moment before scanning any original to check for the symptoms of a color balance problem. (Professional printing shops do the same thing as soon as copies of a color publication begin to emerge from an offset press.) You can look for

- Washed-out or over-saturated flesh tones
- Sections of your image that should be a "pure" color (like a red stop sign) that are a diluted hue
- An overall "tinge" to the lighted areas of the original, usually caused by harsh fluorescent lighting or colored lights

By the way, an exception to those colored lights exists: I would never (and I mean *never*) correct the color balance for photographs taken at a concert or play! Such "mood lighting" is there for a reason, and unless you want to diminish the impact of *Romeo and Juliet* (or Mozart or Devo or the Violent Femmes), I suggest that you leave them as is.

A Finely Tuned Format

Here's one other sign of a superb scan that's destined to become royalty (or the head of a democracy, if you will): It *must* be saved in the proper format for the application you're using! I don't care whether your scanned image proves the existence of a dinosaur that looked like Elvis — an image stored in the wrong format causes problems for owners of other computers, as well as most of your e-mail recipients and Web site visitors. (To be honest, I would want to see that particular image no matter *what* format it was in, and I would see it faster if it were a JPEG!)

Although I cover this subject in greater detail elsewhere in this book, mentioning the highlights is worthwhile:

- **Word processing and importing:** If you're going to import your scanned image into a word processing document, spreadsheet, or presentation, I recommend saving the image in either the TIFF or Windows bitmap formats.
- **Printing or display:** For scanned images that are destined to be printed or displayed on a computer monitor, choose TIFF (for all computers) or Windows bitmap (for computers running any breed of Windows). Although they take up more space, quality is the name of the game.
- **OCR or faxing:** Scanning for OCR or faxing use? A JPEG works well for these applications. However, the documentation for the program may recommend a specific format, so check the manual too.

- **Web or e-mail use:** Choose GIF or JPEG for Web image scans (depending on the color depth and file size you need), and using JPEG format for scanned images you're sending through e-mail is always a good idea.
- **Archival storage:** I typically use the Windows bitmap format for images I'm saving on CD-R or Zip disks; if you're using a Mac or a Linux machine, though, TIFF is likely a better choice.

As a general rule, use a format that offers compression whenever you're sending images through any medium on the Internet, and avoid compression where space is not a problem or image quality must be the best.

Chapter 17

Ten Favorite Effects

In This Chapter

- Introducing a sample scanned image
- Applying effects using Paint Shop Pro

This last chapter is pure, unadulterated fun. (Or, I should say, it's even more fun than the other chapters in this book.) Because I talk about filters and effects everywhere after Chapter 11, now you can take the time to see how ten of my favorite Paint Shop Pro effects look when they're applied to a sample image. No, I do *not* ask you to apply all ten at one time. Remember that you want the subject to resemble something more coherent than a random pattern of colored pixels.

I've also selected the ten effects in this chapter because of their universal nature. You find these same filters in Photoshop and PhotoImpact, for example, and in most of the other image editors on the market. Therefore, no matter what editing program you're using, you should be able to achieve results like these at home. I can't go into every control in every dialog box — at least, not if I want to keep this book at less than 600 pages. I can, however, point out the settings I use most often to control these effects and tell you what they do to your image.

So, go ahead: Fire up your image editor, select a favorite scanned photograph or drawing, and exercise the artist in you!

Introducing the Sample Scan

I've chosen the scanned image shown in Figure 17-1 as a sample image. It shows the business end of a WWII Curtiss P-40 Warhawk fighter plane I shot with my trusty 35mm film camera at a local air show. The image has plenty of detail and bold contrast as well as a number of recognizable elements that should show up after you apply any effect to it, including the signature shark-mouth used by the Flying Tigers. The image was scanned at 300 dpi using 24-bit color.

Figure 17-1: *That,* ladies and gentlemen, is a distinctive grin.

Without further ado, start applying yourself!

The effects in this chapter can be applied only to 24-bit color and grayscale images; if you have to increase the number of colors in your image, click Colors and choose Increase Color Depth.

Fur

The first effect, Fur, may not produce exactly the effect you may have thought. It does produce feathered or spiky borders along the edges of strong contrast lines in your image, as shown in Figure 17-2. The default settings, though, create an effect that I would liken to a bristle brush or a hedgehog.

Most effects in this chapter can be configured before you apply them — usually with a preview dialog box like the one shown in Figure 17-3. I encourage you, therefore, to tweak settings and see the result on the thumbnail on the right before applying the filter. Remember that experimentation is the key to discovering the perfect effect.

Important settings to try with Fur include

- **Density:** Controls the thickness of your fur
- **Length:** Determines the length of the fur

Figure 17-2: Spiky! The effects of the Fur effect.

Figure 17-3: The Fur effect dialog box is a typical preview dialog box from Paint Shop Pro.

Texture

The Texture effect is a Pandora's box of nifty fun — you may find yourself lost in this one for some time. In general, the effect makes your scanned image appear as though it had been painted on top of a specific surface. You can choose from 66 different grayscale textures to be used as the surface, and you can control the lighting. In Figure 17-4, I've used one of the presets to give the illusion of a plaster surface.

Figure 17-4: Now how did I paint that image on a plaster wall?

Settings to experiment within the Texture dialog box include

- **The Texture drop-down list box:** Lets you pick out a texture on your own
- **The Presets drop-down list box:** Provides a number of common settings combinations
- **Light Elevation:** Can cast dramatic shadows on your textures
- **Image Depth:** Determines the height of the texture

Buttonize

Web developers are well-familiar with the Buttonize effect, used to create those cool thumbnail buttons with the three-dimensional edges. Figure 17-5 illustrates the sample image made into a huge button.

Important settings to try with Buttonize include

- **Solid/Transparent edge:** Specifies whether you want a colored edge or a semitransparent edge to your button
- **Width:** Determines the width of the edge in pixels

Figure 17-5: After buttonizing, you're ready to click the image.

Page Curl

Another great effect that's very popular among both graphic artists and Web developers is the Page Curl effect, which makes it look like a corner of your image is curling up. I've also seen this effect used often on the first page of an interactive demo or tutorial. Figure 17-6 shows a modest curl on the image.

Figure 17-6: Now the image is curling at the corner.

With the Page Curl effect, you can move the two "handles" at the corners of the edge to determine how deep the curl should extend. Other settings you should try include

- **Corner:** Determines which corner of the image is curled
- **Back color and color:** Specifies the background and foreground color for the curled section

Ripple

Rippling an image turns its surface into water — and then drops a pebble directly in the center! This dramatic effect looks great in grayscale as well. Figure 17-7 shows the fighter plane underwater.

When you use the Ripple effect, try adjusting these settings:

- **Amplitude:** Controls the width of each ripple
- **Wavelength:** Controls the distance between ripples

Figure 17-7: With a Ripple effect, anything can be put in a pond.

Sunburst

Because the sample scanned image was originally taken outside on a sunny day, why not add an artificial sunburst? This great effect simulates the glare from the sun on a camera lens, as you can see in Figure 17-8. Note how realistically the sunburst "emerges" from the propeller of the plane. If I hadn't taken this picture myself, I would certainly be fooled. I like to use this effect to add a dramatic quality to shots of towers, churches, and scenic photographs.

Figure 17-8: With the application of the Sunburst effect, a glare spot is added to the image.

Note that you can move the handle within the left preview thumbnail to specify the origin of the light source. The presets for the Sunburst effect can place the glare spot wherever you like, although I recommend that you try experimenting with these settings as well:

- **Rays:** Determines how many rays of light radiate from the lighted spot
- **Circle Brightness:** Determines the brightness of the "halos" cast by the spot

Glowing Edges

Boy, do I love this effect! Essentially, Glowing Edges creates a negative of your image and then applies a neon look to all the edges. As you can see in Figure 17-9, the effect is beautiful and the subject remains recognizable. No wonder you see this effect used in magazines all the time. That sharkmouth looks really good here.

Glowing Edges has only two settings you can change:

- **Detail:** Specifies the number of strokes (and hence the amount of detail) used to apply the effect
- **Opacity:** Specifies the strength of the glow

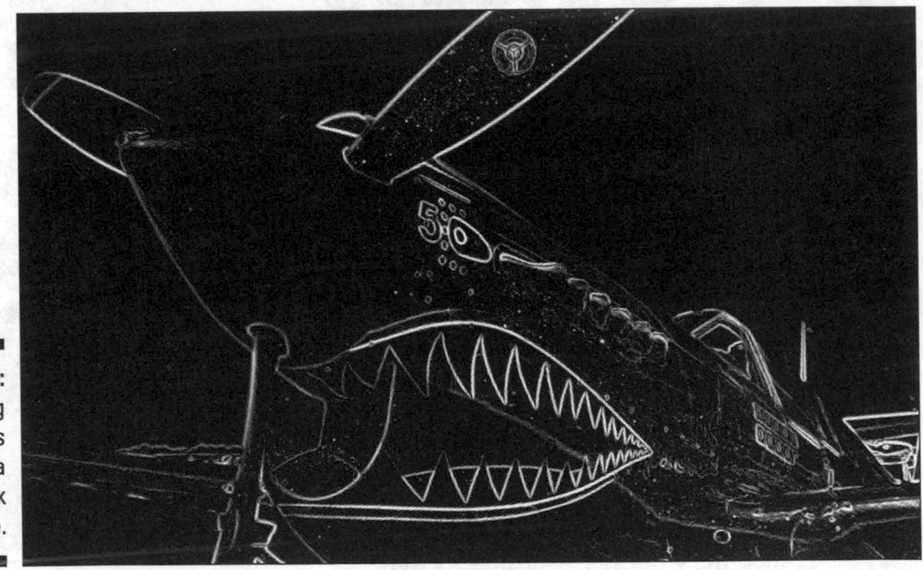

Figure 17-9: Glowing Edges creates a surreal look to an image.

Rotating Mirror

This one's self explanatory, as shown by the results in Figure 17-10! This great "funhouse" effect projects a somewhat crazy feel. Now the entire sharkmouth is in one image!

Try changing the Rotation control, which sets the angle of the rotation around the center of the image.

Figure 17-10: Mirror, mirror on the plane. . . .

Punch

Here's another effect I group in the "funhouse" category. Punch "pushes" the center of your image out toward the edges of the image, resulting in the neat distortion you see in Figure 17-11.

Figure 17-11: This effect packs a lot of punch.

Punch has only one control: You can use the Effect control to determine how much of the image is pushed outward.

Brush Strokes

The final favorite effect I describe in this chapter of tens is a true classic: Brush Strokes, shown applied to the image shown in Figure 17-12. I wish that I had a dime for every time I've seen this great effect used in all sorts of print media (including business cards and menus). I've even seen it used on stills within video presentations! Brush Strokes is an easy way of turning an image into an instant oil painting or watercolor.

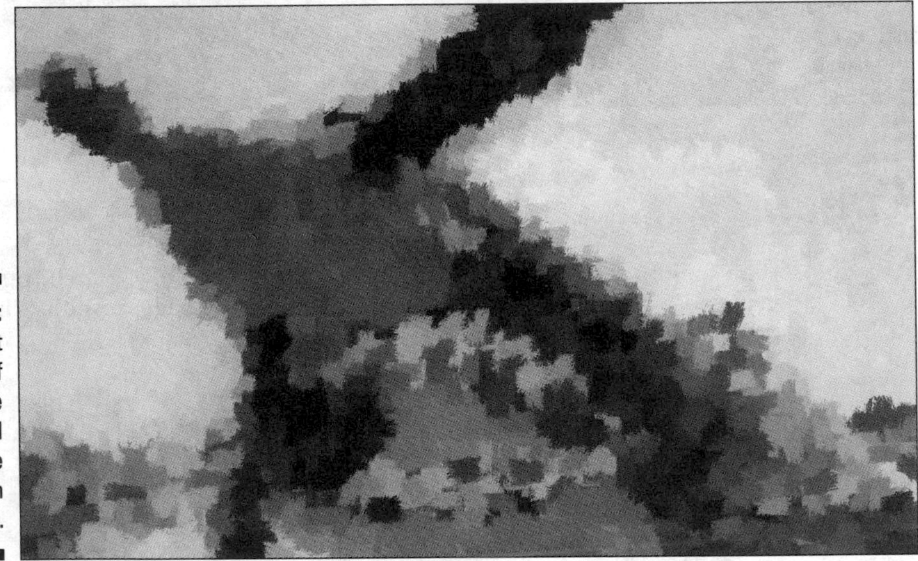

Figure 17-12: Rembrandt himself would have been proud of these brush strokes.

This effect comes with a number of presets, like Impasto, Large Drybrush, and Watercolor, and you can create your own look by changing these settings:

- **Strokes:** Controls the length of the brush strokes
- **Density:** Determines how many strokes appear in the image
- **Bristles:** Specifies how many bristles are used in your brush
- **Width:** Controls the width of the brush

Part VI
Appendixes

In this part . . .

The appendixes feature a wealth of information, including a scanner hardware and software manufacturers list, a glossary to familiarize you with those pesky terms and acronyms, and all the details on the programs you'll find on this book's companion CD-ROM.

Appendix A

Scanner Hardware and Software Manufacturers

In This Appendix

- Contact information for manufacturers of scanner hardware
- Contact information for developers of scanner software

In this appendix, you find contact information for manufacturers of scanner hardware and developers of scanner software of all kinds. Whenever possible, I list both the Web site and fax number for each entry.

Please note that many companies listed in the first section that manufacture hardware also produce their own scanning software. For example, I use Microtek ScanWizard with my Microtek scanner. On the other hand, the software in the "Software Developers" section is produced by independent companies, and these programs usually run on any scanner under one or more specific operating systems.

Hardware Manufacturers

Acer America
Phone: (888) 723-2238
`www.acer.com`

Agfa America
Phone: (201) 440-2500
Fax: (201) 342-4742
`www.agfa.com`

Brother USA
Phone: (908) 704-1700
Fax: (908) 704-8235
`www.brother.com`

Canon Computer Systems, Inc.
Phone: (800) OK-CANON
`www.ccsi.canon.com`

Corex Technologies
Phone: (617) 492-4200
Fax: (617) 492-6659
`www.cardscan.com`

Epson America
Phone: (800) GO-EPSON
`www.epson.com`

Fujitsu
Phone: (212) 599-9800
Fax: (212) 599-4129
us.fujitsu.com

Hewlett-Packard Company
Phone: (800) 222-5547
Fax: (650) 857-5518
www.hp.com

Howtek
Phone: (800) 444-6983
Fax: (603) 880-3843
www.howtek.com

Kodak
Phone: (800) 235-6325
www.kodak.com

Lexmark International, Inc.
Phone: (888) 539-6275
www.lexmark.com

Microtek
Phone: (800) 654-4160
www.microtekusa.com

Mustek
Phone: (949) 788-3600
www.mustek.com

NEC USA
Phone: (800) 632-4636
www.nec.com

Nikon USA
Phone: (800) 645-6689
www.nikonusa.com

Ricoh Corporation
Phone: (800) 63-RICOH
www.ricoh-usa.com

Umax
Phone: (510) 651-4000
Fax: (510) 651-8834
www.umax.com

Visioneer US
Phone: (888) 229-4172
Fax: (888) 887-0092
www.visioneer.com

Xerox Corporation
Phone: (800) ASK-XEROX
www.xerox.com

Software Developers

Captiva Software Corporation
Phone: (858) 320-1000
Fax: (858) 320-1010
www.captivasoftware.com

Corex Technologies
Phone: (617) 492-4200
Fax: (617) 492-6659
www.cardscan.com

Jetsoft Development Company
www.jetsoftdev.com

ScanSoft
Phone: (978) 977-2000
www.scansoft.com

Stalker Software
Phone: (800) 262-4722
www.stalker.com

Westtek
Phone: (425) 861-8271
Fax: (425) 861-7926
www.westtek.com

Appendix B
Glossary

adapter card: An expansion board that plugs into your computer's motherboard and adds functionality, like a SCSI card you add to your motherboard to provide support for devices like SCSI scanners.

application: A program that allows you to complete a task. Your scanning application, for example, controls your scanner and allows you to digitize images and save them to disk.

aspect ratio: The ratio of height to width in an image. If the aspect ratio isn't maintained when resizing an image, it becomes distorted.

binary: The common language used by computers to store information and communicate with each other, composed of just two values: 0 and 1.

BIOS: Short for *Basic Input Output System,* used to change the low-level functionality of a PC, like configuring your parallel port.

bit: The smallest unit of data that can be stored or used by a computer, with a value of either 1 or 0.

bitmap: An uncompressed image format used within the Windows operating system. Although bitmaps deliver great image quality, they're uncompressed and use a large amount of space.

bps: Short for *bits per second.* Modem speeds are measured in Kbps, or kilobytes per second.

bus: A slot on your motherboard that holds adapter cards. Most slots are now 32-bit PCI or 16-bit ISA slots. Video cards also have a special slot, called an AGP slot, reserved for them.

byte: A group of 8 bits that represents a single character of text. Your computer's programs store and read data as bytes in your computer's RAM.

calibration: The process of correcting the misalignment of a scanner's moving parts and scanning head. Most modern flatbed scanners don't require calibration, although sheet-fed scanners should be calibrated regularly.

case: The metal enclosure that surrounds your computer, usually fastened with screws or thumbwheels.

CD-R: Also called a *CD recorder*, a drive that acts as both a CD recorder and a regular CD-ROM drive. Recorded discs can store computer data, and you can record standard audio CDs. Although discs made with a CD-R can be read on any CD-ROM drive, they can be recorded only once.

CD-ROM drive: A drive that reads both CD-ROM discs and standard audio CDs.

CD-RW: A drive that can record and re-record CDs. Older CD-ROM drives and audio CD players cannot read discs made with a CD-RW drive.

CECSAUB: Short for *confusing everything with a collection of silly acronyms used as buzzwords.* (I don't like acronyms used just to muddle things up.)

color depth: The measurement used to indicate the number of colors in a scanned image. Popular color depths are 16 colors, 256 colors, 64,000 colors, and 16.7 million colors (commonly referred to as 24-bit color).

color-matching system: A software standard designed to ensure correct colors on all output and display devices within a computer system. With a monitor and printer that are color matched, for example, you can be sure that the colors you see on your display are as close as possible to the colors produced by your printer.

component: A piece of computer hardware — usually used to indicate an internal piece of hardware, like a hard drive or a SCSI card.

compression: The use of a mathematical formula to reduce the amount of disk space taken up by a file. In the case of scanned images, the most popular compressed formats are JPEG and GIF. A lossless compression scheme loses no detail; a lossy compression scheme loses detail as the degree of compression is increased.

cropping: Removing a portion of the background from a digital image, usually to remove unneeded objects or extra "white space."

CPU: Short for *central processing unit,* the "brain" in your computer that performs the commands within the programs you run. Popular CPUs on personal computers are manufactured by Intel, AMD, and Motorola.

digital camera: A type of camera that saves images as digital data (for uploading directly to a computer). Unlike with a traditional camera, no film and no development are necessary.

DIP switch: One of a bank of tiny switches that allow you to configure hardware devices and your computer's motherboard. You use the tip of a pen to set the switches in the proper sequence.

dpi: Short for d*ots per inch*, a measurement of the number of dots per linear inch of an image. This measurement is commonly used with scanners, although technically a scanner uses spi (samples per inch). No matter the terminology squabble, they're basically the same thing.

driver: One or more programs written by a hardware manufacturer that allow your operating system to recognize and use a device.

effect: A mathematical formula applied to a digital image to modify either individual pixel colors or the entire image. Most image editors include a number of effects that can change the appearance of an image.

external: A peripheral that's connected outside your computer's case, like a scanner.

FAQ: Short for *Frequently Asked Questions,* a document containing the answers to the most common questions asked within a group. A scanner manufacturer's technical support department usually creates a FAQ file for downloading by customers who are encountering problems.

FireWire: The common name for the Apple IEEE 1394 High Performance Serial Bus connection standard. Like a USB connection, a FireWire device can be added or removed without rebooting. As many as 63 FireWire devices can be connected to a single port. The FireWire scanner is the fastest on the market because of the connection's high data-transfer rate of 100 megabits per second.

flatbed scanner: A scanner that resembles a copy machine, featuring a long glass and a cover. Originals remain motionless while the scanning head moves across the scanner bed. A flatbed scanner is now the preferred scanner type because you can scan items like books and other objects that can't be scanned with a sheet-fed scanner.

flat-panel monitor: A monitor that uses liquid crystal display technology rather than a traditional tube. Most folks think of these monitors as displays for laptop computers. However, flat panels are much thinner than traditional tube monitors and use less electricity. They're now much more expensive than tube monitors.

floppy drive: Computers now use 3½-inch floppy disks that can store as much as 1.44MB of files and data on a single disk. Although this type of disk is cheap and practically every computer has one, it shouldn't be used for long-term storage.

format: A standard file layout used to store the data that makes up an image. Popular image formats now in use include GIF, JPEG, and TIFF.

GIF: Short for *Graphics Interchange Format,* a compressed image format that's popular on the Web. GIF, which supports only 256 colors, was the first major image format.

gigabyte: A measurement of data equal to 1,024MB (megabytes).

grayscale: Images with continuous tones in 256 shades of gray rather than color.

halftone: An image that represents tones with patterns of dots rather than continuous shades — most illustrations in books and newspapers are halftones.

handheld scanner: An external scanner you pass across the surface of an original. Handheld scanners can read anywhere from a single line to about a 4-inch strip of an original. This type of scanner is generally useful only for people traveling with laptop computers.

hard drive: Also called *hard disk.* Most hard drives are internal — the drive stores your data while the computer is turned off. All standard laptop and desktop computers use hard drives. Most hard drives available these days store anywhere from 4 to 60 gigabytes of files and data.

home corner: The corner of a flatbed scanner's glass that is marked. Your document normally should be positioned close to this corner.

image editor: A program that allows you to edit and modify digital images. Popular image editors like Photoshop and Paint Shop Pro are standard tools for people who scan photographs.

inkjet: An inexpensive printer that injects ink from a cartridge to paper.

interface: A method of connecting a peripheral to a computer. For example, a scanner can use a parallel port interface or a USB interface (which needs only the proper port and a cable); others use a SCSI interface (which typically requires an adapter card and a cable).

internal: A component installed inside your computer's case.

Jaz drive: A removable cartridge hard drive that can store as much as 2 gigabytes of data. Jaz drives require a SCSI interface.

JPEG: Short for *Joint Photographic Experts Group,* the most common image format used on the Web and the default format produced by most scanner control programs. JPEGs, because of their compression and small size, are often used as Web images and e-mail attachments.

jumper: A set of two or more pins that can be used to configure devices and adapter cards — you select a setting by moving a plastic-and-metal crossover on (or off) certain pins.

kilobyte: A measurement of data equal to 1,024 bytes.

laser: A printer that bonds toner powder to paper. Laser printers are fast and produce excellent print quality, and they're significantly more expensive than typical inkjet printers.

line art: A drawing produced in black and white (or two other colors) with no shading or tones.

megabyte: A measurement of data equal to 1,024 kilobytes.

modem: A computer device that converts digital data to and from an analog signal so that computers can communicate over standard telephone lines. Modems are used to access the Internet, online services, and computer bulletin-board systems.

monitor: An external component that looks like a TV screen and displays all the graphics produced by your programs.

motherboard: The main circuit board inside your computer that holds the CPU and RAM chips and any adapter cards you've installed.

mouse: A standard computer pointing device used in Windows and the Mac OS. You control programs by moving the mouse and pressing buttons to select items.

multifunction device: Also called an *all-in-one unit*, an external computer peripheral that can scan, print, fax, and copy documents. Multifunction devices are popular in home offices, where space is at a premium.

negative scanner: A scanner specially designed to scan photograph negatives, yielding a much higher-quality scan than a typical flatbed scanner can. A negative scanner is much more expensive than a typical home flatbed scanner.

newsgroup: An Internet message area dedicated to a special interest. Anyone can read or post messages in a newsgroup.

OCR: Short for *optical character recognition,* a type of software that can, using your scanner, "read" images and text from physical documents and place the material into a word-processing program.

one-button scanning: A feature offered by many scanners that allows you to push a button on the scanner to copy, scan, or fax automatically, without having to run any programs manually on the computer.

original: The document, object, or material you're scanning.

parallel port: A standard connector on every PC. Although initially used only to connect printers, other devices — like scanners and Zip drives — now also use this connection.

PC card: Also called a *PCMCIA* card; a thin device that plugs directly into most laptops and provides most of the functions of a full-size adapter card — including modems, SCSI adapters, and network connections.

photo paper: A heavy inkjet printer paper with a glossy finish that's specifically made for producing high-resolution color prints.

photo scanner: An internal scanner specially designed to read film prints, business cards, and smaller paper documents.

pixel: A single dot in an image. Text and graphics displayed by a computer monitor (or created by a scanner) are made up of pixels.

Plug and Play: A type of hardware that can automatically be configured by computers that support the Plug and Play standard, possibly eliminating the need for you to configure the hardware manually.

plug-in: An extension program that can be installed in your image editor to provide additional effects.

PNG: Short for *Portable Network Graphics,* a compressed image format developed recently to replace the older GIF format used on Web pages. This format can store 24-bit color images with lossless compression.

port: A connector on your computer or an external device you plug something into. A scanner, for example, may plug into your USB or your parallel port.

printer: An external device that can produce documents on paper with text and graphics from your computer.

RAM: Short for *Random Access Memory;* memory modules that hold programs and data until you turn off your computer.

red-eye: A reflective red shine produced by human and animal eyes that are illuminated by a camera's flash.

refurbished: A piece of broken computer hardware that has been "remanufactured" (read that as "fixed") by the manufacturer and typically sold again at a greatly reduced price.

resizing: Changing the dimensions of an image to make it larger or smaller.

resolution (dimensions): A common method of measuring the number of pixels displayed on a screen or within an image, expressed as horizontal by vertical; for example, a resolution of 640 x 480 means that you see 640 pixels across your screen and 480 lines down the side of the monitor.

resolution (image): The number of pixels in an inch within an image. Scanner resolution is usually referred to as dpi, although this reference is technically incorrect.

rotation: The turning of an image to the left or right.

scanner: A device that digitizes (or converts) text or graphics from a printed page or object into a digital image that's stored on your hard drive. Scanners are often used to create images for documents, for display on your computer monitor, or for use on a Web page.

scanner sensor: An array of photosensitive cells that return variable electrical currents, depending on the amount of reflected light each cell receives. Every scanner has a sensor array.

SCSI: Short for *Small Computer Systems Interface,* an older interface technology that supports the connection of anywhere from 8 to 15 devices, including hard drives, CD-ROM drives, and scanners.

SCSI ID: A unique numeric identifier assigned to each device in a SCSI chain.

SCSI port: A connector included with a SCSI adapter card to connect an external device, like a scanner, to your SCSI device chain.

secure connection: A web server that creates an encrypted session between itself and your computer, allowing you to send your personal information and credit card information to Web sites without fear of being monitored. Whenever you order hardware or software from a Web store, make sure that you have a secure connection before sending any information.

selection box: An area of an image you choose with your mouse when you're using a scanner control program or image editor. The selection box is the target of your next command, like scanning that particular area of an original or cropping an image to just the selected area.

serial port: A standard connector on every PC. Serial ports are typically used to connect mice, joysticks, and external modems.

sharpening: An image editor effect that's often used to enhance a scanned image. Sharpening increases the contrast at all the edges within an image.

sheet-fed scanner: A scanner that resembles a fax machine, where documents are loaded through a slot. In a sheet-fed scanner, the scanning head remains motionless and the original moves past it. Although sheet-fed scanners take up much less room than flatbeds (making them popular in all-in-one and multifunction devices), they're limited in the type of materials that can be scanned.

single-pass scanner: A scanner that requires only one pass with the scanning head to capture an image. Most scanners now available are single-pass models.

terminator: A switch found on every SCSI device. Each end of a device chain must be terminated properly.

thumbnail: A small version of a full-size digital image. Because many thumbnails can fit on a single screen, selecting an image from a group of thumbnails is much faster than loading the full-size images — making thumbnails a typical feature in image catalogs and Web pages that offer images for downloading.

TIFF: Short for *Tagged Image File Format*, an image format favored by Macintosh owners, graphic artists, and the publishing industry.

trackball: A pointing device that looks like an upside-down mouse. You control the device by rolling the ball with your finger or thumb and clicking buttons with your other fingers.

transparency adapter: A device used with a standard flatbed scanner that allows you to scan transparent originals, like photograph negatives and overhead transparencies. Many manufacturers of flatbed scanners offer transparency adapters as optional extras.

triple-pass scanner: A scanner that requires three passes with the scanning head to capture an image. Most older scanners are triple-pass models.

TWAIN: Short for t*echnology* w*ithout* a*n* i*nteresting* n*ame,* a standard which ensures that TWAIN-compatible image hardware (like scanners) and software (like image editors and scanning control programs) all understand each other and work together properly.

USB: Short for *Universal Serial Bus,* a standard connector that enables you to connect as many as 127 devices at data transfers of as much as 12 megabits per second. USB connectors are common for all sorts of computer peripherals, including digital cameras, scanners, speakers, joysticks, external CD-ROMs, and hard drives. You get the picture.

USB hub: An external switch that allows you to plug additional USB devices into a single USB port.

Windows 98: The most popular 32-bit graphical operating system for the PC, which you control with a mouse and keyboard.

Windows 2000: The latest business and professional version of the Windows operating system, designed as a network or Internet server. It's much more expensive than Windows 98 or Windows Me.

Windows Me: Short for *Millenium Edition;* the latest version of the Windows operating system, designed especially for home computer use.

wireless mouse: A battery-powered mouse that doesn't require a cord to connect it to the computer.

Zip drive: A removable cartridge drive that stores anywhere from 100MB to 250MB of data. Zip drives are available with parallel port and USB connections.

Appendix C

About the CD

On the CD-ROM

- **Paint Shop Pro:** A powerful and inexpensive image-editing program
- **Snappy Fax 2000:** A popular program that turns your system into a fax and copy machine

System Requirements

The programs on the companion CD-ROM have a minimum set of system requirements, as shown in the following list (if your computer doesn't meet most of these requirements, you may have problems using the software):

- A PC with a Pentium or faster processor or a Mac OS computer with a 68040 or faster processor.
- Microsoft Windows 95 or later or Mac System 7.5 or later.
- At least 32MB of total RAM installed on your computer. For best performance, I recommend at least 64MB of RAM.
- At least 600MB of hard drive space available to install all the software from this CD. (You need less space if you don't install every program.)
- A scanner.
- A mouse or other pointing thing.
- A CD-ROM drive — double-speed (2x) or faster.
- A monitor capable of displaying 24-bit color or grayscale.
- A modem with a speed of at least 14,400 bps.

If you need more information on the basics, check out *PCs For Dummies,* 7th Edition, by Dan Gookin; *Macs For Dummies,* 6th Edition, by David Pogue; *iMac For Dummies,* by David Pogue; or *Windows 98 For Dummies* or *Windows 95 For Dummies,* 2nd Edition, both by Andy Rathbone (and all published by Hungry Minds, Inc.).

Using the CD with Microsoft Windows

To install the items from the CD to your hard drive, follow these steps:

1. **Insert the CD into your computer's CD-ROM drive.**
2. **Click Start⇨Run.**
3. **In the dialog box that appears, type** D:\HM.EXE.

   Replace *D* with the proper drive letter if your CD-ROM drive uses a different letter. (If you don't know the letter, see how your CD-ROM drive is listed under My Computer.)
4. **Click OK.**

   A license agreement window appears.
5. **Read through the license agreement, nod your head, and then click the Accept button if you want to use the CD. After you click Accept, you're never bothered by the License Agreement window again.**

   The CD interface Welcome screen appears. The interface is a little program that shows you what's on the CD and coordinates installing the programs and running the demos. The interface basically enables you to click a button or two to make things happen.
6. **Click anywhere on the Welcome screen to enter the interface.**

   Now you're getting to the action. The next screen lists categories for the software on the CD.
7. **To view the items within a category, just click the category's name.**

   A list of programs in the category appears.
8. **For more information about a program, click the program's name.**

   Be sure to read the information that appears. Sometimes a program has its own system requirements or requires you to do a few tricks on your computer before you can install or run the program, and this screen tells you what you might need to do, if necessary.
9. **If you don't want to install the program, click the Back button to return to the preceding screen.**

   You can always return to the preceding screen by clicking the Back button. This feature allows you to browse the different categories and products and decide what you want to install.
10. **To install a program, click the appropriate Install button.**

    The CD interface drops to the background while the CD installs the program you chose.
11. **To install other items, repeat Steps 7–10.**

12. **When you've finished installing programs, click the Quit button to close the interface.**

    You can eject the CD now. Carefully place it back in the plastic jacket of the book for safekeeping.

To run some of the programs on the *Scanners For Dummies* CD-ROM, you may need to keep the CD inside your CD-ROM drive. This is a Good Thing. Otherwise, the installed program would have required you to install a very large chunk of the program to your hard drive, which may have kept you from installing other software.

Using the CD with Mac OS

To install the items from the CD to your hard drive, follow these steps:

1. **Insert the CD into your computer's CD-ROM drive.**

   In a moment, an icon representing the CD you just inserted appears on your Mac desktop. Chances are, the icon looks like a CD-ROM.

2. **Double-click the CD icon to show the CD's contents.**
3. **Double-click the License Agreement icon.**

   This is the license that you are agreeing to by using the CD. You can close this window after you've looked over the agreement.

4. **Double-click the Read Me First icon.**

   The Read Me First text file contains information about the CD's programs and any last-minute instructions you may need in order to install them correctly.

5. **To install most programs, open the program folder and double-click the icon named Install or Installer.**

   Sometimes the installers are actually self-extracting archives, which just means that the program files have been bundled up into an archive, and this self extractor unbundles the files and places them on your hard drive. This kind of program is often called an *.sea.* Double-click anything with .sea in the title, and it runs just like an installer.

6. **Some programs don't come with installers. For those, just drag the program's folder from the CD window and drop it on your hard drive icon.**

After you have installed the programs you want, you can eject the CD. Carefully place it back in the plastic jacket of the book for safekeeping.

What You'll Find

There's nothing like a CD-ROM chock-full of good software toys, and this one has enough software to keep any scanner owner happy for quite a while!

Shareware programs are fully functional, free trial versions of copyrighted programs. If you like particular programs, register with their authors for a nominal fee and receive licenses, enhanced versions, and technical support. Freeware programs are free, copyrighted games, applications, and utilities. You can copy them to as many PCs as you like — free — but they have no technical support. GNU software is governed by its own license, which is included inside the folder of the GNU software. There are no restrictions on the distribution of this software. See the GNU license for more details. Trial, demo, or evaluation versions are usually limited either by time or functionality (such as being unable to save projects).

Here's a summary of the software on the companion CD-ROM, conveniently arranged by category. If you use Windows, the CD interface helps you install software easily. (If you have no idea what I'm talking about when I say "CD interface," flip back a page or two to find the section, "Using the CD with Microsoft Windows.")

If you use a Mac OS computer, you can take advantage of the easy Mac interface to quickly install the programs.

Hard-working image-editing software

Paint Shop Pro, from Jasc Software

For Windows 95, Windows 98, Windows Me, Windows NT. Evaluation version. Paint Shop Pro provides most of the features found on image-editing packages that cost several hundred dollars more, and I use it extensively throughout this book. This fully functional 30-day evaluation lets you take it on a test drive. *Nice!*

For additional information on the latest version of this great program, visit the Jasc site: `www.jasc.com`.

Photo Express, from Ulead Systems

For Windows 95, Windows 98, Windows Me, Windows NT. Trial version. Although Photo Express doesn't provide the creative power of PhotoImpact, Photo Express is designed especially with digital images in mind. It offers an easy-to-use interface that's perfect for the editing novice and has a basic feature set you'll use every day.

You can find more details at the Ulead Systems site: www.ulead.com.

PhotoImpact, from Ulead Systems

For Windows 95, Windows 98, Windows Me, Windows NT. Trial version. Another great inexpensive image editor that delivers the power of the big boys, PhotoImpact includes features that will appeal if you're editing images that you've scanned for use on the Web.

For the whole story, visit the Ulead Systems site: www.ulead.com.

SmartSaver Pro, from Ulead Systems

For Windows 95, Windows 98, Windows Me, Windows NT. Trial version. Are you a Web designer? If you've been itching to use your scanned images on your Web site, this 15-day trial version of SmartSaver Pro will have you creating animations, optimizing graphics, designing custom color palettes for your Web site, and building interactive "rollover" graphics with JavaScript!

For more information, check out the Ulead Systems site: www.ulead.com.

Trustworthy image-display software

ACDSee, from ACD Systems

For Windows 95, Windows 98, Windows Me, Windows NT. Trial version. ACDSee has been a favorite of the digital crowd for many years now. It's the fastest program available for displaying your scanned images, and it can handle more than 40 different image formats.

For additional information on the latest version, visit the ACD Systems site: www.acdsystems.com.

Photo Explorer, from Ulead Systems

For Windows 95, Windows 98, Windows Me, Windows NT. Trial version. Photo Explorer is a great "Swiss Army knife" for scanner owners. It can acquire images directly from your TWAIN scanner, display images, browse, and print. Photo Explorer even has a handful of simple image-editing functions!

You can read more about this program at the Ulead Systems site: www.ulead.com.

Impressive scanning software

Snappy Fax 2000, from John Taylor & Associates

For Windows 95, Windows 98, Windows Me, Windows NT. Shareware. It just doesn't get any better than this! With a typical system that includes a fax-modem and printer, Snappy Fax 2000 can fax and copy documents directly from your scanner. It even includes features found on the most expensive commercial faxing software, like fax forwarding to an e-mail account! This program is an inexpensive jewel for scanner owners.

Imaging for Windows must be installed if you want to try Snappy Fax 2000.

For more information on the latest version, visit the Snappy Software site: `www.snappysoftware.com`.

ScanShare, from Stalker Software

For Mac OS. Demo version. If you have an Apple scanner on your network — or a scanner with drivers that emulate AppleScanner — you're in luck! ScanShare allows you to use that scanner from any Mac on the network: Simply select it from the Chooser. This demonstration version is fully functional for one minute per session, and it doesn't expire.

You can read more about this program at the Stalker Software site: `www.stalker.com`.

Handy utility software

GraphicConverter, from Lemke Software

For Mac OS. Shareware. Although it's best-known for importing 145 graphic formats and exporting 45 different formats, GraphicConverter takes care of a number of other image-related chores as well, including browsing, slide show creation, and basic image editing. GraphicConverter is an indispensable tool for getting your scanned images in the form you need.

For all the details, visit the Lemke Software site: `www.lemkesoft.de`.

WinZIP, from Nico Mak Computing, Inc.

For Windows 95, Windows 98, Windows Me, Windows NT. Shareware. WinZIP is a favorite with scanner owners who need to compress and archive all sorts of data so that files take up less space and are easier to manage. If you need to store a huge directory of images in Windows bitmap format, for example, you can save 50 to 75 percent of the space they would normally take up by "zipping" them. Use this great tool — you won't be sorry!

If You Have Problems (Of the CD Kind)

I tried my best to compile programs that work on most computers with the minimum system requirements. Alas, your computer may differ, and some programs may not work properly for some reason.

The two likeliest problems are that you don't have enough memory (RAM) for the programs you want to use or you have other programs running that are affecting installation or running of a program. If you get error messages like `Not enough memory` or `Setup cannot continue`, try one or more of these methods and then try using the software again:

- **Turn off any antivirus software you have on your computer.** Installers sometimes mimic virus activity and may make your computer incorrectly believe that it is being infected by a virus.
- **Close all running programs.** The more programs you're running, the less memory is available to other programs. Installers also typically update files and programs; if you keep other programs running, installation may not work properly.
- **In Windows, close the CD interface and run demos or installations directly from Windows Explorer.** The interface itself can tie up system memory or even conflict with certain kinds of interactive demos. Use Windows Explorer to browse the files on the CD and launch installers or demos.
- **Have your local computer store add more RAM to your computer.** This is, admittedly, a drastic and somewhat expensive step. However, if you have a Windows 95 PC or a Mac OS computer with a PowerPC chip, adding more memory can really help the speed of your computer and enable more programs to run at the same time.

If you still have trouble installing the items from the CD, please call the Hungry Minds Customer Service phone number: 800-762-2974 (outside the United States: 317-572-3993).

Index

• E •

• F •

• G •

• P •

• R •

• S •

• T •

Hungry Minds, Inc.
End-User License Agreement

READ THIS. You should carefully read these terms and conditions before opening the software packet(s) included with this book ("Book"). This is a license agreement ("Agreement") between you and Hungry Minds, Inc. ("HMI"). By opening the accompanying software packet(s), you acknowledge that you have read and accept the following terms and conditions. If you do not agree and do not want to be bound by such terms and conditions, promptly return the Book and the unopened software packet(s) to the place you obtained them for a full refund.

1. **License Grant.** HMI grants to you (either an individual or entity) a nonexclusive license to use one copy of the enclosed software program(s) (collectively, the "Software") solely for your own personal or business purposes on a single computer (whether a standard computer or a workstation component of a multi-user network). The Software is in use on a computer when it is loaded into temporary memory (RAM) or installed into permanent memory (hard disk, CD-ROM, or other storage device). HMI reserves all rights not expressly granted herein.

2. **Ownership.** HMI is the owner of all right, title, and interest, including copyright, in and to the compilation of the Software recorded on the disk(s) or CD-ROM ("Software Media"). Copyright to the individual programs recorded on the Software Media is owned by the author or other authorized copyright owner of each program. Ownership of the Software and all proprietary rights relating thereto remain with HMI and its licensers.

3. **Restrictions On Use and Transfer.**

   (a) You may only (i) make one copy of the Software for backup or archival purposes, or (ii) transfer the Software to a single hard disk, provided that you keep the original for backup or archival purposes. You may not (i) rent or lease the Software, (ii) copy or reproduce the Software through a LAN or other network system or through any computer subscriber system or bulletin-board system, or (iii) modify, adapt, or create derivative works based on the Software.

   (b) You may not reverse engineer, decompile, or disassemble the Software. You may transfer the Software and user documentation on a permanent basis, provided that the transferee agrees to accept the terms and conditions of this Agreement and you retain no copies. If the Software is an update or has been updated, any transfer must include the most recent update and all prior versions.

4. **Restrictions on Use of Individual Programs.** You must follow the individual requirements and restrictions detailed for each individual program in Appendix C of this Book. These limitations are also contained in the individual license agreements recorded on the Software Media. These limitations may include a requirement that after using the program for a specified period of time, the user must pay a registration fee or discontinue use. By opening the Software packet(s), you will be agreeing to abide by the licenses and restrictions for these individual programs that are detailed in Appendix C and on the Software Media. None of the material on this Software Media or listed in this Book may ever be redistributed, in original or modified form, for commercial purposes.

5. **Limited Warranty.**

   (a) HMI warrants that the Software and Software Media are free from defects in materials and workmanship under normal use for a period of sixty (60) days from the date of purchase of this Book. If HMI receives notification within the warranty period of defects in materials or workmanship, HMI will replace the defective Software Media.

   (b) **HMI AND THE AUTHOR OF THE BOOK DISCLAIM ALL OTHER WARRANTIES, EXPRESS OR IMPLIED, INCLUDING WITHOUT LIMITATION IMPLIED WARRANTIES OF MERCHANTABILITY AND FITNESS FOR A PARTICULAR PURPOSE, WITH RESPECT TO THE SOFTWARE, THE PROGRAMS, THE SOURCE CODE CONTAINED THEREIN, AND/OR THE TECHNIQUES DESCRIBED IN THIS BOOK. HMI DOES NOT WARRANT THAT THE FUNCTIONS CONTAINED IN THE SOFTWARE WILL MEET YOUR REQUIREMENTS OR THAT THE OPERATION OF THE SOFTWARE WILL BE ERROR FREE.**

   (c) This limited warranty gives you specific legal rights, and you may have other rights that vary from jurisdiction to jurisdiction.

6. **Remedies.**

   (a) HMI's entire liability and your exclusive remedy for defects in materials and workmanship shall be limited to replacement of the Software Media, which may be returned to HMI with a copy of your receipt at the following address: Software Media Fulfillment Department, Attn.: *Scanners For Dummies,* Hungry Minds, Inc., 10475 Crosspoint Blvd., Indianapolis, IN 46256, or call 1-800-762-2974. Please allow four to six weeks for delivery. This Limited Warranty is void if failure of the Software Media has resulted from accident, abuse, or misapplication. Any replacement Software Media will be warranted for the remainder of the original warranty period or thirty (30) days, whichever is longer.

   (b) In no event shall HMI or the author be liable for any damages whatsoever (including without limitation damages for loss of business profits, business interruption, loss of business information, or any other pecuniary loss) arising from the use of or inability to use the Book or the Software, even if HMI has been advised of the possibility of such damages.

   (c) Because some jurisdictions do not allow the exclusion or limitation of liability for consequential or incidental damages, the above limitation or exclusion may not apply to you.

7. **U.S. Government Restricted Rights.** Use, duplication, or disclosure of the Software for or on behalf of the United States of America, its agencies and/or instrumentalities (the "U.S. Government") is subject to restrictions as stated in paragraph (c)(1)(ii) of the Rights in Technical Data and Computer Software clause of DFARS 252.227-7013, or subparagraphs (c) (1) and (2) of the Commercial Computer Software - Restricted Rights clause at FAR 52.227-19, and in similar clauses in the NASA FAR supplement, as applicable.

8. **General.** This Agreement constitutes the entire understanding of the parties and revokes and supersedes all prior agreements, oral or written, between them and may not be modified or amended except in a writing signed by both parties hereto that specifically refers to this Agreement. This Agreement shall take precedence over any other documents that may be in conflict herewith. If any one or more provisions contained in this Agreement are held by any court or tribunal to be invalid, illegal, or otherwise unenforceable, each and every other provision shall remain in full force and effect

Installation Instructions

If you're ready to try the programs on the companion CD-ROM, follow these basic steps.

If You're Running Windows

1. Load the CD into your CD-ROM drive.
2. Click Start and choose Run.
3. Type **D:\START.EXE** in the Run dialog box. (If your CD-ROM drive uses another letter, substitute it for D: in the command.)
4. Click OK.
5. Read the license agreement, smile quietly to yourself and nod your assent, and click the Accept button.
6. Click on a program category.
7. Click on a program to read more about it (and install it if you want).

If You're Running Mac OS

1. Load the CD into your CD-ROM drive.
2. Click the License Agreement icon to — what else? — read the license agreement.
3. Click the Read Me First icon to read any last-minute information.
4. Click the CD icon to open it and display the programs.
5. Most programs are installed by dragging a program folder from the CD window and dropping it on your system's hard drive icon.
6. If the program has an icon named Install or Installer, click that icon to run the installation program.

For more information about using this CD, see Appendix C.

FOR DUMMIES BOOK REGISTRATION

Register This Book and Win!

We want to hear from you!

Visit **dummies.com** to register this book and tell us how you liked it!

- Get entered in our monthly prize giveaway.
- Give us feedback about this book — tell us what you like best, what you like least, or maybe what you'd like to ask the author and us to change!
- Let us know any other *For Dummies* topics that interest you.

Your feedback helps us determine what books to publish, tells us what coverage to add as we revise our books, and lets us know whether we're meeting your needs as a *For Dummies* reader. You're our most valuable resource, and what you have to say is important to us!

Not on the Web yet? It's easy to get started with *Dummies 101: The Internet For Windows 98* or *The Internet For Dummies* at local retailers everywhere.

Or let us know what you think by sending us a letter at the following address:

For Dummies Book Registration
Dummies Press
10475 Crosspoint Blvd.
Indianapolis, IN 46256

BESTSELLING BOOK SERIES